A Girl's Guide to
BALL GAMES

A GIRL'S GUIDE TO BALL GAMES

What Men Need to Know

SUE MOTT

MAINSTREAM PUBLISHING
EDINBURGH AND LONDON

Copyright © Sue Mott, 1996
All rights reserved
The moral right of the author has been asserted

First published in Great Britain in 1996 by
MAINSTREAM PUBLISHING COMPANY (EDINBURGH) LTD
7 Albany Street
Edinburgh EH1 3UG

ISBN 1 85158 868 X

No part of this book may be reproduced or transmitted in any form or by any means without written permission from the publisher, except by a reviewer who wishes to quote brief passages in connection with a review written for insertion in a magazine, newspaper or broadcast

A catalogue record for this book is available from the British Library

Typeset in Garamond
Printed and bound in Great Britain by Butler and Tanner Ltd, Frome

CONTENTS

Acknowledgements   7
Introduction   9

FOOTBALL
The FA Cup Final   15
In the Beginning   21
The Disciples – Shelley Webb   25
The Disciples – Elsie Revie   31
Charlie and Me   35
The Press   41
The Belles, the Belles   48
Boy-zone   54

RUGBY
(Two of) the Five Nations   63
Rugby Types   69
The Ultimate Accolade   74
Wild West Women   78
Wives, Women and Song   85
Super League   91

CRICKET
Test Match   99
Nursing a Grievance   105
Tour Operators   109

Kathy Botham	114
Space Invaders	119
My Sweet Lord's	127

GOLF
The Ryder Cup	133
Pride and Prejudice	139
Laura Davies	145
Caddies and Other Followers	150
Players	156

TENNIS
Wimbledon 1996	163
Lazy Fat Pigs	169
Mother Love	175
The Women's Movement	180
Love All	186

OTHER SPORTS
Snooker	193
Polo	199
Ocean Racing	204

A Question of Sport	213
Select Bibliography	219
Index of Names	220

ACKNOWLEDGEMENTS

Allow me to *not* say thank you to Maggie Lennon. If it hadn't been for her and one of those 'Oh, I know who'd love to write a book like that' conversations with Bill Campbell of Mainstream Publishing, I might not have missed the first week of my summer holiday trying to hit a publisher's deadline that was about to recede over the horizon. I might have drunk less than ten crates of Pils lager, as well. But then what are friends for? Thanks Mags.

Despite that ungrateful beginning, I would very much like to thank all the men and women in all the various aspects of sport who have contributed either by anecdote or interview or arrant gossip to the compilation of the story. Special gratitude must go to Clare Taylor (whose cricket team, football team and mum helped so much with the questionnaires), Shelley Webb (who not only spoke to me for hours but sent me back-up material as well), Frances Edmonds (who put me up for a night and submitted to an interview with a wretched cold), Kathy Botham (who was as straight as an arrow), my friend and neighbour Ann Wilson (who took me to hospital with her), Tommy Little and all the girls at West's Rugby Club (who didn't make me play), Ian Clayton (for letting me use the marvellous material in his rugby league book *Running for Clocks and Dessert Spoons*) and Trish Johnson (who says I can use her third Arsenal season-ticket if I'm down this year).

Also, Amy Lawrence, Olivia Blair, Lesley Gallacher, Laura Davies, Liz Kahn, Sean Bean (I just had to throw that in), Rachel Heyhoe Flint and Jon Holmes (for at least *asking* Will Carling if he'd submit to an interview).

To the sports desk and colleagues at the *Daily Telegraph*, many thanks; especially to Paul Hayward, Lewine Mair, Russell Cheyne, Gary Prior, Phil Brown and Steve Yarnell. As we're talking photographers here, special mention must go to the tennis snapper, Michael Cole, who proved he'd do anything for a pint, as usual.

As for you, Stanley Bernstein, who made the computer work, I don't think mere words can ever express the wonder and gratitude I feel.

Last, but not least, the family. Thanks to Dad for Arsenal and the golf stories. (Promise me you won't hyperventilate when you read the first sentence. It's a *joke*.) To Alison for Tommy, sanity and peace. And to Robert, for everything.

At least it's all over now.

INTRODUCTION

But women feel just as men feel; they need exercise for their faculties, and a field for their efforts as much as their brothers do ... it is thoughtless to condemn them, or laugh at them, if they seek to do more than custom has pronounced necessary for their sex.
                              Charlotte Brontë, *Jane Eyre*, 1847

The only professional footballer I have ever slept with was Zbigniew Boniek of Poland.

I say this not in the spirit of intercontinental self-congratulation but in a strenuous effort to dispel a myth: that women who love sport are merely indulging their love of men at one remove. This is not true. Women may very well adore Gary Lineker's crooked smile, Des Lynam's lazy charm, Ian Botham's impulsive heart, Stefan Edberg's blue eyes (this list is getting ominously long), but it is also biologically possible for women to love sport because of sport.

When I met Boniek and borrowed his bedroom during the 1982 World Cup in Spain, I had been lured to the event by the promise of the football (and Italy v Brazil in Barcelona, to name but one, richly fulfilled that promise) not the opportunity to fling myself at any man in studs. It was unusual to be a female football writer in those days. Perhaps it still is, but our motives are thankfully less questioned now.

In the 1990s the evidence of a long, slow revolution has never been more apparent. Women are playing sport; not merely conforming to tradition on the hockey pitch and tennis court but stomping through the mud and prejudice on football and rugby fields as well.

Women are talking sport; taking up high-profile positions in television, on radio, in newspapers – and at last we aren't being mistaken for groupies either.

Women are watching sport; how often did the cameras following Euro 96 train their lens on the painted face of a woman? Only this time the paint did not comprise the delicate stain of eyeshadow and dainty slash of lipstick, it was a ruddy great red St George's cross on a wide-eyed, whitewashed face shouting 'Gooo-on Gazza!'

And women are marrying sport; only this time the little women are less content to be left at home to mind the babies and *not* mind the stories that emanate from their husbands' hotels.

It is a brave new world – almost.

A friend of mine left her two children in the tender care of her husband one Saturday afternoon recently. She was only gone a couple of hours. When she returned the youngest boy had a horrible gash across the top of his forehead. 'Whatever happened?' she demanded of her spouse. 'He fell down the back steps,' he replied. 'But weren't you looking after him?' she said. 'Well, I couldn't watch him *and* the golf at the same time,' countered the guilty party, in a state of genuine grievance.

It would be foolish to deny the differences between men and women. Women *can* watch the children and the golf at the same time, neither very well, but at least we try. Juggling is a fact of modern life. Men, admirably straightforward, just do one thing well. They watch the golf.

But the differences between the sexes do not include one that many chauvinists insist is an indelible genetic feature of the feminine mind. Some men think women are simply congenitally incapable of understanding sport. So no matter how long we have stood on the terraces at Highbury, no matter how many runs Rachel Heyhoe Flint scored for England, no matter how many years the Doncaster Belles football team has flourished, no matter how many successful tackles a female rugby player has launched, no matter how many majors Laura Davies will win in her career, no matter how many records Steffi Graf eventually breaks, no matter how well Kathy Botham understands her action-packed husband . . . women will be deemed poor, fluff-brained specimens born to Asda not the Arsenal.

My contention is the opposite. Women can play, watch and understand sport just fine when they can break free of the constraints that their highly evolved status has conferred on them. If they can find the time and inclination between working, mothering, shopping and emoting, their appreciation of sport is second to no man's.

To prove it, I compiled a questionnaire and sent copies to as many different sports-related women's clubs and individuals as time and the cost of stamps would allow. The results were appalling (see chapter six) but I've decided to ascribe this to the wicked female sense of humour and refuse to read great significance into them.

Because every last grain of feminine instinct I possess tells me that women are ready and able to move into a much more central position in the realm of sport. They have been patronised and marginalised for decades – centuries – while men have cavorted behind the barbed wire and parapets of the great all-male sporting traditions: the rugby club bar, the footballers' dinner, the 19th hole and, above all, Lord's.

Why is it that women, so welcome with a waitress's tray in their hand or serving a pint behind the club bar, are seen as the enemy when they seek equality beyond the parameters of serving wench? Fear? Loathing? Tradition? Not wanting to discuss curtains in the tea-interval? Something like that.

Still, the good news is that most men have not reacted violently to the growing signs of female emancipation. Though some may regret we were ever given the vote, never mind the right to buy a season ticket to Stamford Bridge, there seems to be a burgeoning acceptance that a woman may one day understand the offside law.

And it would be only right and proper to point out that many of us at work in sport these days are there because of the tireless support of our dads and husbands and employers and other chaps who genuinely believe that a woman in the press box or in the scrum need not be a toxic hazard. They have our heartfelt and unqualified thanks.

As for the rest, they probably watched the televised highlights of England v New Zealand at Lord's (the women's version) and consoled themselves that things couldn't get any worse. There is news for them. Oh, yes they can.

Football

THE FA CUP FINAL

The important thing is not winning but taking part. For the essential thing in life is not so much conquering, as fighting well.
                                                                The Olympic oath

The eve of the Cup final, 1996: The Liverpool players had arrived at their hotel on the outskirts of London, buoyant, confident and under orders not to drink. Taz swished a ball about on the tennis courts, the captain had treatment for a calf injury and ten of the players had chipped in 65p each to watch one of the adult movies on the hotel's video menu. Then they tried to go to sleep.

'But we didn't get much really, because the room was really warm like a sauna,' said the captain, who shared a room, as ever, with Sammy (right-side midfield). 'And it was quite noisy because we were literally on the A41. And there was a wedding going on in the hotel. And about five coachloads of Bradford Bulls supporters were staying over for the weekend. I s'pose from that point of view, it wasn't ideal preparation.'

She hadn't bothered to wax her legs either. 'You know you're going to go out there and sweat, get untidy and look a mess, so it's a case of "what's the point?"'

Clare Taylor of England and England (the women's football *and* cricket national teams) was captaining Liverpool to their third successive FA Cup final. They had lost to the Doncaster Belles in 1994 when they were still called Knowsley and lost again 3–2 to Arsenal a year later. But this time, facing Croydon, they were favourites and the mood on the team coach down from Merseyside, all sing-songs and card schools, attested to their sense of destiny: this time they'd lift the Cup.

Meanwhile, at another time, in another world, the Liverpool wives had arrived at their hotel smack in the middle of London. Suzy Barnes, wife of Liverpool's captain, John, had considered going down on the coach with the other women of the party but had decided, in the circumstances, to fly instead.

'I knew it would be a long journey on the coach in the rush hour traffic and I knew it would be all champagne and giggling, and I wasn't really up to that being seven months pregnant, so I flew down with Jamie, my son. My friend, Nicky, picked us up and took us back to the Portman Hotel where we dropped our bags off and promptly jumped in a taxi for Harrods. We wanted to make ample use of our time down there; no messing about.

'I just bought some baby clothes and some things for the children and . . . bedlinen. Oh, the bedlinen in Harrods is fabulous. Pink. John loves them. White with pink bows on.'

It was Suzy's third Cup final with Liverpool as well, but being an old hand didn't make the sleepless night any better. 'I didn't sleep a wink. I was up all night long. I must've got up and gone to the loo about 20 times. I was absolutely shattered on Saturday. Good for nothing. It was the anticipation of it all.'

Cup final day dawned and it was a bit of a rush to be honest. The regular captain, Louie Ryde, failed a fitness test and Clare Taylor, a post office van driver in Huddersfield, became captain for the day. 'It was a bit hectic really,' she said. 'We arrived at the ground a bit late because we got stuck in traffic coming through London. We hardly had time to warm up, get off the pitch, get our kit on and straight back out for the presentations. It was diabolical really.'

The crowd, 2,500 souls, was hardly a sell-out. But Lady Millichip performed the function of royalty with distinction by greeting the players at the start. 'Look,' said Clare to her Ladyship, 'I'll try and remember their proper names but if not, I'll give you their nicknames and tell you their proper ones after.' Lady Millichip, being agreeable to the plan, was swiftly introduced to Taz, Fez, Tommo and Burkey in the Liverpool line-up.

Clare was satisfied with the turn-out of soccer's gentry. Sir Bert Millichip was there, along with the FA's Graham Kelly. 'Enough bigwigs,' she said. But it wasn't the grandeur of the audience (paying £3 a ticket) nor the setting in Millwall's new football stadium ('Actually it looks like something on an industrial estate,' she said) that she needed to inspire her performance. 'I don't think you need all the Wembley tradition. You know it's your Cup final and it doesn't matter if it's just one man and a dog watching.'

Funnily enough, although for entirely different reasons, Suzy was similarly rushed before the great occasion. 'I had to pop into London again,' she explained. 'We wanted to go to the Versace shop. Check out the handbags.

'So we went along Old Bond Street, got back to the hotel at 12, had lunch in the carvery with all the other Liverpool wives and travelled to Wembley together on the coach. Then we went up the main stairs, into the Mezzanine Bar, had a drink and took our seats. I watched about 15 minutes of the build-up on the pitch, although I did feel this year that the atmosphere hadn't actually started until the game began. I just felt: here we are. It's just like another league game really. But then the game wasn't too exciting either.'

Indeed, by far the most electric moment of the day had been the first sight of the Liverpool team in their civvies before the match. You need to summon visions of a Mr Whippy ice-cream vendor with a member of a barber-shop quartet to do justice to the gear being sported by Anfield's finest. The creamiest of cream suits, offset by blue shirt, red and white striped tie and a blue carnation in the buttonhole. Suzy laughed. 'I was waiting for the jazz band to strike up. I thought it was Peter Percival and his jazz band.'

But the match dispensed with frivolity entirely. A crowd exactly 76,507 larger than the women's Cup final watched a game with a fraction of the excitement. The best part might have been the Duchess of Kent's introduction to the teams where one could imagine Barnes saying: 'I'm Digger, this is Shaggy, that's Trigger . . .'

'John's called Digger, has been for ages, because of the old Digger Barnes character in Dallas. Nothing to do with the fact that his initials are JCB,' explained Suzy. C for Charles, apparently.

'I thought it was a desperate game. It was just long balls from one end to the other, that's what it seemed like to me. And a very disappointing end for us.' That 'end' being the moment in the 85th minute when Eric Cantona adjusted his stance and unleashed a shot through a teeming penalty area to win the match, the Cup and the double for Manchester United.

John Barnes had been noticeable throughout the game, but chiefly, it must be said, for the flash white boots on his feet. 'John was miserable after the game,' said Suzy. 'But not devastated. It had been a very flat game to watch. I wasn't devastated either.'

The same could not be said for Clare Taylor, as her horrible fate unfolded. They were favourites, this Liverpool, and yet they had failed to convert fairly solid domination into a lead at half-time. Burkey's goal, a volley into the bottom corner, had been cancelled by a strike from Hope Powell, the England international striker. 'I'd been shouting at the defence: "If in doubt, hoof it out!"' said Clare, 'but she hit the most tremendous shot. I don't think anyone could have stopped it.

'Even so at half-time, everyone was still pretty bouncy and confident. I said: "We're all over 'em. Keep battling. Keep getting to every ball first."'

Then, in the second half, the infamous corner came across. 'Burkey took it, Maria flicked it on, two of their girls on the goal line tried to clear it and it came out to me on the six-yard line. I stabbed a foot at it. As soon as it left my boot, I thought: "It's going in, this!" It hit the underside of the crossbar, bounced down over the line – clearly over the line – but it bounced back out. It was really weird.

'The ref was five yards away. I was, like, turning to celebrate and he was just there, waving play on. I think I said something like: "It effing went in!" I just stood there with me hands on me hips. I couldn't believe he hadn't given it. I mean, I know, hand on heart, I should have put it away and then there'd have been no doubt but I've watched it again on the video replay four or five times and it was clearly over the line.

'I went up to the ref at the start of extra time. I said: "We shouldn't be doing this, y'know." He said: "Why not?" I said: "If you'd had your eyes open you could see we should be winning 2–1 by now. That ball went over the line." He said: "I didn't see it. Neither did my linesman." So I said: "Cop out! Cheat!" – not nastily, just jokingly, like. Well, half jokingly. I still thought we were going to win.'

But the cruellest of all finishes was awaiting them. Penalties were needed to decide the outcome. Tommo, the Liverpool sweeper, hit the post. Jodie Handley, the youngest player at 16, missed as well and with everything resting on Fez, left-sided midfield, she blasted the ball over the top.

'I just sat there. I couldn't do anything,' said Clare. 'Tears welled up in me eyes and when I looked up I could see Fez still standing there. She hadn't moved since she'd taken her penalty. I thought: "I've got to go and make sure she's all right no matter how I'm feeling," because she's obviously thinking: "Shit, I've just lost it for 'em." I just went up and put me hand on her shoulder and said: "Hey, Fez, it's a team game y'know. Come on. Don't worry about it." And we walked with our arms round each other to the centre circle.

'It was difficult getting everyone's head back for the presentation. It was really a mixture of emotions. Laughing in disbelief, swearing and cursing and everything. How do you express how bad you feel? Most of us got round to shaking the Croydon players' hands. It was just so – so sad, really.

'All the clichés came out. "Never mind, it's not the winning, it's the taking part" and all that crap. But when they lifted that Cup if anyone had said that to me I'd have quite happily hit them. A camera crew even came up to me on the pitch for an interview. I thought: if he says, "How do you feel?" I'm going to say, "Pissed off. How d'you think I feel?" But then, when he said he was from kids' TV, I thought I'd better temper it a bit.

'Me and Taz just sat in the bath afterwards. All she kept saying all night was: "You can't feel lower than me. I feel like a snake's belly."'

This was entirely the wrong subject to raise with Suzy Barnes. 'Why is it, when someone's pregnant,' she said with severe indignation, 'that other people feel duty bound to say: "Oh, aren't you huge! Are you sure you're not having twins?" Normally, if someone came up to you out of the blue and mentioned how enormous you looked, you'd belt them round the head with your handbag. I get it like ten times a day.'

This partly explains why the captain's wife was missing from the post-match commiserations at Planet Hollywood. 'I just stayed in my room with my son and had room service. We watched telly. *Stars in their Eyes*. I didn't watch *Match of the Day*. I'd had enough football for one day.'

Being a footballer's wife, especially one expecting the couple's fourth baby, necessarily has its drawbacks . . . one being losing Cup final nights, another being a husband's reluctance to go shopping. 'If I just want John to come shopping round Tescos with me, he says: "Oh Suze, I can't be bothered with the hassle." So I say: "Put a paper bag over your head and let's go."' They've been together 14 years, ever since he moved into the house next door in Watford. 'I've been there,' said Suzy. 'I've been there and back.'

Getting back to Anfield on the Sunday morning took about six hours on the coach. 'Sick-making,' said Suzy, probably literally in her case. 'Everyone piled on to the open-topped bus when we arrived back in Liverpool. But Jamie and I didn't. We went home to find out that my daughter had been throwing up in every room and the housekeeper was rushing round changing sheets frantically. Back to reality.'

Just getting back to Liverpool was bad enough for Clare. 'I think some of the girls just tried to obliterate the whole thing by getting drunk. Half the bus was dead noisy, having a sing-song, getting drunk and being silly. In the back were the people having a quiet drink and being a bit more sombre and reflective. I was absolutely knackered. I didn't have any inclination to move, have a beer or anything. My initial reaction had been: "I'm going to give up this stupid game." But by the time we got off the bus, it was: "Right well, we're going to win it next year."

'The worst bit was having to go up and get old losers' medals again. The two I already had were on a shelf in my bedroom. The new one is still in my kitbag somewhere. I haven't even opened the box.'

IN THE BEGINNING

God's plan made a hopeful beginning,
But man spoiled his chances by sinning,
We trust that the story
Will end in God's glory
But, at present, the other side's winning.
Anon, New York Times, 1946

In the beginning, God and Eric Cantona were seen as quite separate individuals. It was only later confusion set in.

Now we live in a country where Sky Television pumps out 1,600 hours of football coverage a year and Burnley fans set fire to their manager's wife's dress in a Chinese restaurant. So we don't live in a secular society after all. At least football still provides scope for religious mania.

The origins of the sport are now lost in the mists of time but kicking a ball about has always been one of man's most unconquerable primeval urges (up there with sex and a vindaloo after lager).

It seems odd, then, that God's greatest gift to Adam was Eve. Most men in the same circumstances would have asked for a football. Instead he was given a partner. But then perhaps he asked for a *striking* partner (the Christmas-tree formation – obviously – not having been invented yet) and the Almighty misunderstood.

But Eve must have been a bitter, if distracting, disappointment once Adam's rib injury cleared up and he was able to play again. Compliments are paid to Eve's flesh and bones in the Bible but no mention is made of her strong left foot, lateral passing ability or vision off the ball. And so it continued. Women have rarely been taken seriously in football. Laundress or distraction, their role is to lurk on the periphery of the great game.

'Basically, Bill doesn't think women have any place in football,' said Grace Nicholson, wife of the former Spurs manager. 'I never saw him play for Spurs and I'm not allowed to go and see them now. I feel an outsider really, as if I was a member of the opposition.'

Neanderthal man must have kicked the odd round object about (he still does in the Wimbledon back four) but though there are hints that classical Gary Linekers existed in China, Ancient Greece and the Roman Empire, it is true to say that the British game didn't really take off until the Dark Ages, and even then, it sounds more like a poll tax riot between villages.

But by 1314 the sport had sufficient hold for Edward II, a fastidious Plantagenet, to be heartily sick of his dishevelled subjects kicking a ball about the streets. He complained about 'a great noise in the city caused by bustling over large balls'. In a sense, the old dear was right. Football was a rowdy event that rollicked through the streets paying little heed to gentlemanly conduct or even the Queensbury Rules. Men were known to die in the ruck. Of knife wounds.

Successive monarchs therefore tried to suppress the game, with fines and bans and grim disapproval. But it would keep breaking out. The rulers of Halifax were forced to fine their people one shilling for playing the game in the streets and it was prohibited in Leicester (which, but for the stricture's repeal, might have left Gary Lineker a market stall holder in Melton).

Amazingly, the Scots were the first to admit women could play footba'. Amazing because, having banned the fair sex from Burns' Night suppers for the past 200 years (not strictly honouring their hero who positively insisted on women's company on his nights out), the Scottish clansmen seemed unlikely liberationists. But, sure enough, stories have been passed down the years of football matches in the hills above Inverness between the spinsters of the parish and their married counterparts using a freshly stuffed animal bladder, presumably not unlike a haggis, as the ball. Men lined the field as interested spectators, very interested if the truth be told, for they were on the look-out for a wife. The after-match celebrations would undoubtedly have made Fiona Richmond's plunge into the Crystal Palace communal bath after their FA Cup semi-final look a little tame.

By the time we get to the 19th century and the construction of goals and pitches and rules, one thing is patently clear. Women played a minimal part. The first mention of any female in connection with the origins of football is Queen Anne, wife of King James, who once stopped off in Wiltshire to be entertained by a football match. It can't have been Swindon Town then.

In 1863 the FA was formed and the women present on the occasion of that first torrid meeting at the Freemason's Tavern, Great Queen Street in London, were probably wearing frilly pinnies and answering to the name 'Waitress!'.

The first tinkering with the offside law came a bare five years later and one can well imagine many a poor woman's sleepless night as the cogitating individual beside her muttered: 'I wonder if it should be an offence in itself to be in an offside position or whether a player shall only be penalised . . . '

All sorts of momentum was now gained. The first England–Scotland international took place at the West of Scotland Cricket Ground of all places, where it was reported that 4,000 people turned up to watch the match 'including many ladies'. There they were, in the familiar female role of helpmeet, supporter, encourager and abuse-slinger.

But only with the outbreak of World War One would women be allowed to grapple with the great game itself. The men were at the front, the women in the factories. Morale and money had to be raised. The factory women took to the fields, the football fields, to achieve both and, gradually, the public's imagination was caught and retained.

Players were the subject of transfer deals, France came on tour and the Dick Kerr Ladies, a team representing a Preston munitions factory, reigned more supremely than Arsenal or Liverpool or Manchester United in more modern times. In 1920 they won 25 of 30 matches, scoring 133 goals and conceding 15.

The apotheosis of the women's game came a year later when Dick Kerr's eleven played St Helens on Boxing Day at Goodison Park. A crowd of 53,000 roared them on, with an estimated 14,000 locked outside. The players needed a police escort to reach the dressing-rooms. Florrie Redford, Dick Kerr's prolific striker, had missed the train for Liverpool but even that failed to affect their sledgehammer domination. Alice Kell, captain and right-back, switched to centre-forward in the second half, scored a hat-trick and the Dick Kerr Ladies won 4–0. Tumult, celebration, rapture.

Followed by jealousy, sabotage and silence. The women's game was effectively dead, broken by an envious FA and by a culture that had yet to come to grips with the Equal Opportunities Commission.

But then the men made a big mistake. They started taking a few of us to matches. Poor souls: those dads or brothers or innocently experimental boyfriends who didn't realise what passions they would unleash in the breast of a susceptible female. These men were our allies, passing on their allegiance and knowledge and old programme collections, and they are owed a great debt of gratitude.

Men, in general, are not the enemy. Charlie George is one, and there is no higher recommendation than that. But there still remains a great divide. There are football boardrooms full of Tory-voting directors who once rapturously voted for a woman to be their Prime Minister and still faint at the thought of a female being invited into their inner sanctum. There are anxious parents of sedentary, couch-bound, junk-stuffing children who would rather put their daughters in care than see them play football. There are legions of football clubs who pay lipservice to the concept of family enclosures without cutting the prices or caring deeply to make the experience female-friendly.

Nevertheless, certain barricades have been breached. Readers of *Cosmopolitan,* that glossy women's magazine for all right-thinking 20-somethings at one with animal rights, the multiple orgasm and double-matte moisturising lip colour, had their liberation finally confirmed as the Millennium approached. Amongst all those traditional ads for Calvin Klein jeans and the fast way to treat vaginal thrush, they would have found one planted by the FA (emancipated wing). 'How Can I Lie Back And Think Of England When Terry Venables Hasn't Finalised The Squad?' it said; an advert for the 1996 European Championships. They followed up this inswinger with: 'I fancy the Italians because in Ravanelli and Zola you have a proven strike force working in front of a fluid 4–2–4 formation.' The furore was modest but revealing. A man phoned Talk Radio, ever the reliable barometer of public opinion, to say: 'I can't understand why the FA are wasting their money advertising to women. Women don't want to stand in the cold and watch football. They'd rather go shopping.'

No, we don't want to stand in the cold and watch football. Sophisticated creatures that we are, we would quite like to watch in comfort without the fear of some yob peeing in our pocket. And more. Women's ambitions now stretch beyond the limited horizon of getting into Frank Worthington's little black book. They want to run football clubs, report matches, play internationals, front televised highlights, and qualify as fully fledged Football League referees.

Well, we can dream. And then along comes Diego Maradona to exemplify the esteem in which football tends to hold women. He missed a Boca Juniors match, he explained, because his wife, Claudia, was having cosmetic surgery and he wanted to make sure she was getting 'great tits'.

THE DISCIPLES

SHELLEY WEBB

> *It's like finding out your mother-in-law has a twin sister.*
> Dick Lynch, American Football commentator on a player's emotion when he discovers he's dropped from the team

Neil Webb: Reading, Portsmouth, Nottingham Forest, England, Manchester United, Nottingham again, Nottingham Forest third team, Hong Kong on loan. It is the classic story of the rise and fall of a footballer thanks to two injured Achilles, age, a paunch and a degree of disillusion.

Alex Ferguson thought enough of Webb once to pay £1.5 million to bring him to Manchester United. That's when the manager found out about his Achilles heel. She was known as the wife.

'Alex thought I was a bit of rebel,' said Shelley Webb, who met the future superstar when he was a lad at Reading and she was earning more than him as a 17-year-old counter girl at Boots. 'I remind him of that when he calls me a gold digger,' she said, a dauntless, bright, giggle-prone woman who went on national television to criticise Ferguson for his behaviour.

'He wrote some comments about Neil in his book, *Six Years at United*. I thought he was totally wrong. He made things up. It sounded like Neil didn't have proper allegiance to the club and I was fuming. I thought it was really unfair of him to have a go at players when they've left the club and try and sully their reputation. It's something that managers like Sir Matt Busby and Brian Clough never had. They never had that bitter side.

'So anyway, in my programme [the BBC's Manchester-produced *Standing Room Only*] I castigated him. I just said that he was building a successful team, doing well, and he didn't need to come out with this stuff.'

Webb, Mrs, is evidently not that dolly-bird, fluff-brained appendage that myth likes to weld to a footballer's side: She Who Must Be At The Hairdresser's. She has a career in television, a first-class honours degree in English and History and a screenplay about women's football (sixth draft) on the go. But she is also a footballer's wife, which allowed her to experience the various delights of being married to a Multi-Million-Pound Transfer Man. After the cosy, family atmosphere at Forest where Brian Clough reigned in an eccentric patriarch capacity, they were suddenly swept into a new and sophisticated world at Old Trafford.

'When they're courting you, they spend time, they show you round the place, they bend over backwards. But once you've signed, you don't get any more than a "hello". That's how it goes. You're just a footballer's wife.

'At first, we were amazed by this magnificent stadium, all these pictures of Sir Matt Busby and the Busby Babes staring down from the wall. Alex Ferguson actually turned to Matt and then looked back to us and said: "Hamstrung by history, I am." It was fascinating.

'I wasn't totally seduced by it all, but I could have been. When I look back at some of the things I bought, I cringe. At United it was almost like you were on show. I always liken it to the Oscars. This big star walks down the red carpet runway and everybody says: "What's the girl on his arm wearing?" I felt that pressure really. Which is ridiculous. In fact, I used to go through agonies about it. I've never been fashion conscious. Always hopeless with my hair and make-up. It was real pressure.

'For instance... one of my dresses I only ever wore once but it's been worn by countless other people to fancy dress parties.' I wanted her to describe this specimen but, perhaps for the first time in her life, she goes all monosyllabic. 'Pink', she said. 'Frilly?' I asked. 'Yes,' she said. 'It was revolting. Oh dear.'

There was rather more to her United career, however, than a gown Frank Bruno might wear in pantomime, and it was this that brought her to the not-entirely-fond attention of the manager, Ferguson. 'When we arrived there, I said to Alex: "Have you got a crèche?" He said: "Oh no, we haven't got the room." Ha, ha. But they had a very nice players' bar, so I spoke to Bryan Robson about it and he said I could go ahead and organise a crèche in there. I'd have loved to have followed the Millwall model and had a crèche for the fans' children as well but, of course, that was never to be.

'You've got to laugh, haven't you?' she said. 'It certainly was funny at United. After Neil had left apparently Alex said to Bryan Robson: "Oh, so we don't need to have the crèche any more."'

If football is a boot camp, the Webbs have served under two of the most celebrated generals in the modern game. Clough and Ferguson. Shelley saw them up close, under pressure, and she rates one far above the other.

'Brian Clough should be rated one of the all-time greats because he did so much with so little and he did it twice, at Derby County and at Nottingham Forest. He made mediocre teams great with no money, no history, no tradition. As a manager, he should be up there with Bill Shankly and Sir Matt Busby. As a man, he's a maverick. He's one of the guys who walks a fine line between genius and madness.

'When I look at Alex Ferguson I've got nothing but praise for the way he's brought United back to their best, but, and it is a qualification, he had all the money in the world at his disposal and all that tradition. They were sleeping giants, Manchester United. I think Cloughie was a better manager, by far. He never allowed the pressure to get to him.

'I can remember John Robertson saying that just prior to their first European Cup win in 1979, Clough didn't give a team talk or anything, he just said: "I think we'll play Gary Birtles up front as a lone striker. Is that all right then?" And everyone said: "Oh. Yeah. All right, boss." No tactics or anything. He used to come into the dressing-room at ten to three and say: "Here's the ball then. Off you go then." He literally did.

'Ferguson's great failing was that the pressure did get to him and that led to him and Neil falling out.' It is an everyday story of innocent mishap and domestic farce, but one that Shelley believes cost Neil Webb his job. 'Neil was picked by Graham Taylor to play for England against Czechoslovakia in a friendly in 1992. He wanted to play. Alex Ferguson didn't want him to play. He was too consumed by the pressure of that season when Manchester United lost out to Leeds for the title, which they should never have done.

'Anyway, they were playing Wimbledon, I think, the Saturday before the England game. Neil was pulled off early, a bit bemused as to why. It was the first thing my mum mentioned when I rang her after the match to see how the children were. She was babysitting. "I saw Neil coming off. Is he injured?" she said. I said: "Oh no, he's fine." Meanwhile a guy from the press had phoned Graham Taylor to say Neil was injured. Graham Taylor rang our house, got my mum who told him, as far as she knew, Neil wasn't injured at all.

'So Taylor had a public row in the papers with Ferguson and Ferguson never forgave Neil. Ferguson decided he was finished. He played his son, Darren, instead of Neil after that in midfield. His son wasn't the calibre of player Neil was.

But the return to Nottingham Forest wasn't all bad. 'It was great to come back to Forest because, as I said to Liz Pearce, Stuart's wife, "Oh, thank God for that. I can wear jeans to matches again." Neil's career, however, was on the wane. Shelley's career, on the other hand, was gathering considerable momentum. She had been a sports columnist for the *Nottingham Evening Post* when Neil was a star in the Forest team. She graduated to the national newspapers ('Mostly the usual footballers' wives thing, but I suppose beggers can't be choosers') and then she was offered a role in *Standing Room Only*, but only because the producer was a Forest fan. 'Neil's name's been really useful,' she said, happily.

'But I remember Frances Edmonds [wife of the cricketer, Phil Edmonds] saying: "Shelley, don't you ever bloody forget you and I, we've both got first-class honours degrees. OK, so our husbands got us where we were to start with but we got us where we are now."'

At 13, Shelley had been taking down the football results on a Saturday at the *Reading Evening Post* and was dubbed Lolita by the men on the sports desk. But a real-life Lolita might have taken more note of the lads parading their talents down at Elm Park.

'Our school was very near the Reading ground, and some of the old slappers, as we used to call them, used to hang out at the club. You know, groupies. That kind of thing. I always used to look down my nose at them and say: "I'd never go out with a footballer." I thought they were terrible; thick and womanisers, the lot.' Then she married one.

The early years of married bliss were spent on the 4 a.m. northbound train from Portsmouth on a Saturday when Neil had a match in the tropics of Hartlepool. They produced two children, Luke and Josh, and then the television industry beckoned.

After *Standing Room Only* came a stint at *Live TV*, during which she reached the zenith of her career in sports journalism: she played Subbuteo on air with Charlie George. Jimmy Pursey, the lead singer of Sham 69, played too but he bit off the head of one of his players (Ralph Coates, as it happens) and was banned for ungentlemanly conduct.

'*Live TV* was an experience and it was great but I'm glad I got out when I did because I'm afraid I couldn't cope with what they're doing now. Topless darts. It's ridiculous. They're employing women for their looks, not their sporting knowledge. It's just so annoying.

'I actually rang up Sky Television once to see if anyone wanted to screen-test me. I was told they had all the girlies they needed at the moment. It makes me so cross.

'I turned up at Tottenham once to report on a match and asked where the press box was. "Cheerleaders, love?" said this bloke. "They're over there." It's a horrible feeling. You definitely feel like an alien. I remember being in the Tottenham press room (I don't know why it always seems to be Tottenham) and nobody, not one person, said one word to me. So I deliberately barged my way to the front to watch the half-time scores on television. I thought, "Eff you, everybody."'

However, in her less militant moments, she suspects most of the 'effing you' is actually done by the football establishment. 'At no club I know are any players and their family given any decent information. What would be the problem in someone compiling a file on good schools or health facilities or whatever? You don't get anything.

'When we went to Manchester United we had our dogs with us, so we chose to rent a cottage that needed renovating. Then Neil was injured. He was in plaster from his thigh to his toe. We were sitting in this flea-infested house, knowing nobody. Nobody came to see him. Oh, the Manchester United chaplain came round. This went on for six weeks. It was appalling. Really, really terrible.

'And it all stems from the fact that players are commodities. They're not human beings at all. They're disposable.'

There is definitely something of the suffragette about Shelley Webb, an unflinching fighter for human rights in a hostile environment. She is a socialist, like Alex Ferguson, once the firebrand trade union man on Clydeside. This might have brought them together, but didn't. 'The only thing that Alex Ferguson and I had in common was membership of the Labour Party,' she said.

Being partial to the flying of red flags, of course, did her no harm at Manchester United or Nottingham Forest, where these pennants flutter from the stadium ramparts every day. Being an uncowed, opinionated woman, on the other hand, was something of a cultural shock for the clubs. She can see why.

'I played for Nottingham Forest Ladies for a while and then in the reserves of a team in the East Midlands League, Division Two. I thought I might be quite good, with my dad playing for Reading . . . but I wasn't. Training was great though. I loved the camaraderie and I think that's what men have found with football. They've tried to keep it to themselves because it's such good fun. They didn't really want women traipsing into their territory.

'But I can see the day when women rise to the top in football, on the administrative side. There's been a real change in the last decade. Women are getting far more knowledgeable. In the days when Neil was still getting fan mail I noticed that it went from women just asking for a photo to discussing serious football points. There does seem to be a great comprehension.'

Are we at the cusp of a new era then? The slow and gradual arming of a corps of women with the knowledge, confidence, authority and clout to breach football's closely guarded inner sanctum and turn *The Manageress* from diverting fiction into dignified reality? 'Um, a manager's job is so demanding,' said Shelley, who has served under Clough and Ferguson, among others, and therefore seen pressure at its most unbendingly severe. 'I think she would have to be single,' she paused in deep consideration. 'And she would have to be a lesbian.' Gales of laughter. 'So she could go home to a good woman at night.

'Managers do become obsessed with the job. That's part and parcel of football. It's the army mentality: keep all the players little boys – don't give them any sense of responsibility – let them become obsessed – so they don't care about anything else.

'A woman wouldn't do that.'

THE DISCIPLES

ELSIE REVIE

I'm fairly confident that if I died tomorrow, Don would find a way to preserve me until the season was over and he had time for a nice funeral.
Dorothy Shula, wife of Miami Dolphins football coach, Don Shula

Elsie Revie, wife of the legendary Don at Leeds United, used to tell her two children: 'See that man walking past the window. That man's your father.' She laughs uproariously at the memory because that is the only option open to a woman married to a man who is married to football. At least he wasn't on his way to some scurrilous appointment with a pint or a horse or a floozy. She knew exactly where he was going. Where else would it be but his second home, his self-made empire at Elland Road?

Don Revie, fêted as one of the finest managers in British sports history and later scorned as one of the greatest traitors in football's living memory, built Leeds United with his own hands. 'He brought them up from the depths, the depths. They were nothing when he became manager, just a second division side with no history and no tradition. He built Leeds. They were his second family. We hardly ever saw him.'

How many women could say such a thing without bitter rancour and resentment for all those days unaccompanied round the shops, all those nights spent listening to one-sided conversations as Don sat on the phone with Bill Shankly of Liverpool or Jock Stein of Celtic, all those years of the children growing up with a father whose 'sons' included Billy Bremner, Norman Hunter and Eddie Gray?

'No, no, I never resented it at all. Leeds was his life. I think you have to come to terms with that very early. It wasn't as though he didn't love his son and daughter. They were the apple of his eye. It was a different sort of love he had for the team. An admiration for their skill and a concern for their welfare. You have to remember almost all his players came to the club as boys. He'd go round and visit all their landladies and make sure they were getting the right food. When one of their wives was having a baby, they'd phone Don before the doctor. We'd get phone calls at two, three, in the morning. "That's the wife just started, boss," they'd say. "All right," Don would say, "you'd better phone the doctor."

'It was a sort of obsession really. A family is terribly affected by football whether the manager is at the top or the bottom. We sent our children to boarding school when they were 12 because, don't forget, the club was the sole topic of sporting conversation in Leeds. And Duncan, our son, was getting to the stage when he was up one minute and down the next. I thought he was getting too absorbed in it and so we sent him to Repton in Derbyshire. And, of course, I'm a great believer in equality so we sent our daughter, Kim, to Queenswood in Hatfield.

'I wasn't lonely. There is nothing worse than sitting at home alone, waiting for your husband to come home and feeling all resentful. That's a big trap, a big trap. I realised I'd have to create my own interests. I was a teacher until I found I was having to dash everywhere because Don became so terribly busy at Leeds. I found I couldn't devote enough time to Don's business, so I gave up the teaching. But I'd taught 20 years. I had my golf. I'd get messages written in the dust on the piano saying, "Your diary is worse than Jack Nicklaus's!"

'But that was our life and I never resented it. Goodness me, no. Your husband has to do all those hours if he's going to be successful.'

Revie was. Leeds United went from the depths to the pinnacle of sporting achievement. He changed their strip to the intimidating all-white of Real Madrid, he invented a playing style that married the Three Graces to the Kray twins, he won the Championship twice, the Fairs Cup twice and the FA Cup once, in its centenary year, 1972 ... when I stood behind one of the goals with a red-and-white traffic cone on my head, watching Arsenal offer up one of their more abject surrenders as Sniffer Clarke scored the winning goal.

We all hated Leeds, those of us not blessed by supporting them, which was a sure sign of the Yorkshire club's pre-eminence.

Elsie won't have it that Leeds were hard. 'The only way for teams to beat Leeds in those days was to mix it. And Leeds wouldn't sit down to that, they wouldn't be intimidated. I'm shocked at the press saying Leeds were too hard. Why would Eddie Gray have had to kick anybody? I always remember Don saying if Gray hadn't been injured, he'd have been as good as Pele. Why would Billy Bremner, nine stone wet through, want to kick anyone?'

By 'eck he did though. Elsie's attitude, you suspect, is one of maternal loyalty but it would be an act of great foolishness to say so out loud. Elsie Revie hails from a passionate Scottish household in which football was the leading, often only, subject. Her father, Tommy Duncan, played for Raith Rovers and Leicester City. Her uncle, Johnny Duncan, was a Scottish international who went on to become manager of Leicester City where young Don Revie went to play. And her mother, Jenny Duncan, may have been the most fervent football lover of all.

'My mother was, if anything, keener than I was. When she was in her seventies she came to live with Don and me, and I can remember, whenever Don's team was in Europe, she'd go along to watch with the Young Supporters Club. Notice *Young* Supporters Club! They used to ring whenever the draw was made and say: "Hello, Mrs R. Is gran going?" And I'd say: "Oh yes, she'll be there." She went all over. Trains, planes, buses. Italy, Germany, behind the Iron Curtain.

'She always wore a hat, always. She never went out without a hat. And she had what she called a lucky hat for matches and Don used to say: "I've more trouble looking out for your mother's hat in the crowd to make sure she got there safely than I have with the team."

'I remember her coming back from a cup-tie in Wales once with a daffodil pinned to her hat. The bus brought her back to the door and I said to my aunt: "Look at this person coming off a bus with a daffodil stuck in her bunnet." Still, we had to count our blessings, I suppose. I said to her when she got indoors: "Well, it could've been a leek, mother, so I suppose we were lucky."'

Her background stood Elsie in good stead. She understood the necessity of living as a loyal lieutenant. 'I used to say to Don: "I'll try and die on a Monday, so you don't have to miss the match on Saturday."'

But in the event, it was her husband that died first, of motor neurone disease in 1989, the year of their ruby wedding anniversary. His death prompted a reappraisal of his character which had degenerated from sterling to scandalous in the public eye. His social crime had been to desert the English national team in favour of a job in Dubai. For this 'breach of duty' he was lashed by a thousand condemnations from within football and without. A British court of law threw out an attempt by the late Sir Harold Thompson, the then FA Chairman, to have Revie banned from the English game for ten years but 'greedy, selfish and disloyal' were among the epithets he earned in his disgrace.

'*Greedy?*' said Elsie. 'He was the most generous man in the world. He wasn't aware of money at all. He never had any in his pocket. If I went to the petrol station or the off-licence, they'd say: "The boss has been and left a bill for you." I'd say: "He thinks he's Prince Philip and I'm the equerry running round with the purse." It was a joke, it was hysterical, what the judge said about him at the trial. He lived the rest of his life under the shadow of a false impression.'

Elsie went to Dubai, rock solid in her support, not a word of dissent to be heard. 'I always said he had to do what he had to do. It made no difference to me. It was his life and his work. That was my theory from day one. I can accommodate wherever I go to the place, the people, anything. In fact, we had six glorious years in Dubai and I still have a very, very great fondness for the people. They were kindness itself and generous to the nth degree. Particularly the Maktoum brothers. We had a beautiful, beautiful villa with a pool, a housekeeper, a gardener and a cook . . . '

But a savaged reputation at home, you remind her, and she, the fiery Scot, remembers saying to her husband: 'How can you stand it? Aren't you furious about what they write about you?' He'd say: 'Waste of time to answer back. Don't forget, pet, the people who write these stories have got mortgages to pay as well. There's no point in getting upset.'

Elsie is just the formidable type – a teacher by trade and a golfer by inclination – who you imagine would make a first-rate manager herself. She knows better after nearly 70 years' experience. 'Most footballers only respect people who've been footballers themselves. It has to stem from that type of respect and I wouldn't know how a woman could get that type of respect.

'And then women aren't quite so pigeon-holed about things. I used to say to Don: "When I go out the door I'm thinking about all sorts of things. I'm thinking about the children, I'm thinking about the house, about meals, anything. When you go out that door, you're not thinking about anything but that football club." And that's the way it is. That's the way people have to be. I don't know whether a woman could do that. That's not the way our lives are. We have to be multi-faceted.'

CHARLIE AND ME

Charlie, Charlie, Charlie, Charlie,
Born is the King of High-igh-bur-y

OK, so lyricists we weren't. But sung to the tune of *Noel, Noel*, it reminded us that every day was Christmas with Charlie George in the team. When he scored that goal in the 1971 FA Cup final to seal a glorious double for the Arsenal, it was the apotheosis of hero worship for me and the lads on the North Bank, the like of which has not been witnessed since.

Dressed entirely by Millets, with a short-back-and-sides haircut and each wrist trailing limp scarves with things like 'Go Go Gunners' on them, I was hardly a prepossessing sight in my Arsenal boot boy phase. Neither was Charlie, come to that. 'Gormless,' my mum said, with his lank long hair and crooked grin. But to me, the figure in my life-sized, full-length poster staring out at my pink bedroom curtains was Adonis and Hercules rolled into one. And he had a better shot than either of them.

It was my childhood ambition to meet him. But Charlie rarely went to all those supporters' club affairs. He was a quiet lad at heart, not the flash footballer type to have 'Champagne' appended to his forename. He married his childhood sweetheart ('Susan Farge' – the name still clangs like a knell of doom in my heart), transferred to Derby and seemed forever lost to me. Until one day last May . . .

They say you should never confront your childhood idol, lest the pain of disillusion clouds all your memories of the past. But he sounded all right on the phone. 'I'll meet you outside Iceland on the Caledonian Road,' he said, and gave me specific instructions to turn left at the lights at Copenhagen Street. 'Can't miss it.'

So I'm standing on a street corner, wracked with nerves, in a very undistinguished province of North London when suddenly Charlie George, older, balder, jowlier and bespectacled – but unmistakably

Charlie George – hailed into view. We shook hands. One of his fingers was missing. 'I lost it in a lawn mower,' he said. 'Couldn't they save it?' I asked, aghast. 'Save it?' he said. 'They couldn't find it!'

We caught a taxi to Quaglino's where he ordered the lamb and I could have eaten barbed wire for all I cared. He said he didn't talk to journalists much and if he ever sees the ex-sports editor of the *Daily Mirror* again: 'I've told 'im I'll give 'im a clump.' But there was little malice in Charlie for all that. He was a North Banker himself 30 years ago. But never a yob. 'I'm a non-violent person,' he said.

Arsenal are still the centre of his existence. 'The 'ighlight of my career was being associated and playin' for Arsenal Football Club,' he said with simple pride. 'It's difficult to describe. But if you're a local lad playin' for the team you support, to turn round and see your friends be'ind the goal actually chantin' your name – well, it's an achievement in itself. Actually playin' for Arsenal meant more to me than winnin' the double. I'm an Arsenal fanatic. Always will be.'

He cared so passionately about playing for the team, he would be sick before Arsenal matches. 'I was a very nervous person. I'd be physically sick before matches, even ordinary league games and that'd just be the tension buildin' up. I was the same before that Cup final. I could feel me stomach burnin' with acid, burnin'. For some reason it only 'appened with Arsenal. When I went to Derby and Southampton, that never 'appened to me at all.'

He has watched the video of the 1971 Cup final, when Arsenal beat Liverpool 2–1 after extra-time to complete the second leg of the double, times without number. 'When I'm a bit pissed off, I put it on,' he said. 'Everyone tells me I was knackered, but if you actually watch the game, I played as well as anyone. I admit I was tired. I think it was the whole day that took it out of me, not the actual game or the occasion.'

But who's quibbling? He was the lad with the gun on his chest, standing in the right place at the right time to lash the ball with his right boot 25 yards into the Liverpool goal, and so precipitate the greatest victory in Arsenal's history. And mine. I went hoarse that afternoon at Wembley, standing behind the goal with my dad.

'George 'eaded it to me, I knocked it to Raddy and Raddy sort of knocked it back to me inside and, well, if I see the goal from 20-odd yards, then I'm afraid the ball must be struck. As soon as I 'it it I knew it was a goal. I always knew. If you watch a lot of the goals that I scored, you'll see me celebratin' before they hit the back of the net.'

He lay full length on the pitch, arms outstretched, almost crucified by the sheer joy and enormity of his achievement. Raddy (John

Radford) had to haul him eventually to his feet. 'It's the same old story,' said Charlie. ' People say why did you lay on the floor after you scored as though you was Jesus Christ? But I honestly don't know. When I scored against Manchester City in the mud, earlier on in the Cup, I laid down then as well, if you remember.' (I did. Two goals in the drenching rain at Maine Road, one of them a spine-tingling solo effort from the halfway line.) 'Even my daugh'er says: "Why did you do that, Dad?" I says: "I dunno. But it din't half kill some time off."'

☆ ☆ ☆

He was born in 1950 just off the Holloway Road in London, about a mile away from Highbury. His dad was in charge of packing at Gestetner, the duplication machine manufacturers. His mum, he thinks, was an office cleaner. 'Something along those lines. We was a working-class family, y'see. We lived in a council flat. I was the youngest of five. I say five but the eldest, my brother, died when he was six months old.

'I s'pose I was fortunate to be given a talent. God-given talent, if you like to say that, although I'm not a believer in God. Probably one of the only things I enjoyed doin' was playin' football. When I was a kid we'd play like five, six hours a day. We'd just sling a couple of coats down and play anywhere. I always played with the lads who were a couple of years older than me. I was fortunate – I had a ball. So the elder lads would knock for me. That's how I got a game.

'We 'ad a sort of stone playground. You 'ad a tree, then you 'ad swings, then you 'ad a community shed. It was about 60 yards long but then you 'ad roundabouts and Chris' knows what. And when you fell over it 'urt.' That's probably where he got his balance from.

The young George rarely graced school with his presence. 'I 'ated it. Didn't mean anything to me. It was just a means of killin' a few hours in the day. I left with no qualifications whatsoever. Well, I was asked to leave. I'd been suspended for a period of time and after a while they thought it would be better if I just left.' He suffered memory loss on the reasons for his original suspension. Then it came to him. 'I think I got suspended for not going.'

He nevertheless contrived to play football and cricket for the long-suffering Holloway County. 'The only thing I was interested in was sport. Me friends used to come round and I'd say: "Who are we playin' tomorrow and where are we playin'?" and then I'd turn up and play.' I couldn't help wondering what he got up to the rest of the time. 'Smoke, I s'pose,' he said. 'I can't give you too many clues, you know what I mean. You'll be gettin' a bestseller out of me.'

The move from schoolboy (absent) to young football apprentice was rather a shock in the circumstances. 'Even South-East counties level after school was a rude awakening, y'know. You'd got to train an' all that. It was completely different to what I'd bin doin'.'

'What, nothing, you mean?' I said, rather nastily.

'Well, that's right, yeah,' he agreed pleasantly. 'It's very difficult goin' from nothin' to somethin'.'

I didn't press the point again of his misspent school career. Charlie, I noticed, had a habit of answering questions with a coy 'possibly', like a cagey suspect under police interrogation. I tried to placate him.

'I'm just trying to get the whole picture,' I explained.

'I've just got the 'ole Bisto,' he replied calmly, as a cascade of gravy descended onto his shirt.

☆ ☆ ☆

Charlie still keeps in touch with most of his old team-mates. To mark the 25th anniversary of the double, they had a reunion at Highbury (then on to Franco's restaurant) of the first-team squad of 1971. Nabbers (Bob McNab, the full-back, whose autograph I once claimed on an old bit of flour bag in the supermarket in Finchley where I was stacking shelves at the time) came over from America, Raddy (the centre-forward) came over from Bishop Stortford and Big Ray (Kennedy, the England international) made his way from Newcastle, still battling bravely against the effects of Parkinson's Disease. They were all there, in fact, even Geoff Barnett, the reserve goalkeeper, who was always suffering brainstorms on his 18-yard line. Charlie thoroughly enjoyed himself.

'We 'ad a great team spirit. I din't actually go out with them all that much. Bein' a local lad, I used different pubs really. The Butcher's Arms or the Royal. But we all got on. Sammy Nelson [full-back] was a very funny fella. And an intellectual at the same time. I think he had O levels. And Peter Storey [midfield terminator] was a nice fella, an' all.' It is comments like this that sometimes make you wonder whether Charlie's spectacles are not of the rose-tinted variety. Peter Storey, even in my fond remembrance, was little better than a brute in the tackle (although his two goals against Stoke in the FA Cup semi-final when we were 2–0 down shall never be forgotten). 'No, he wasn't dirty,' said Charlie, with ridiculous loyalty. 'He just liked to get his tackles in.'

The same could be said for the police a few years later, as Storey was jailed for conspiring to counterfeit gold sovereigns, stealing two cars and smuggling porn videos into Britain. For swearing at a female traffic warden he was treated more leniently – a 28-day jail sentence, suspended. 'He was a good player, Peter,' Charlie was still saying.

Charlie's real mates, however, sprang from his North London childhood: the same mates who watched with awe as he scored ten goals in that 1970–71 season, half of them, memorably, in the FA Cup. He had begun the season with a double fracture at Everton and ended it a Double hero.

But the cruel law of diminishing returns applied to his life after that. He damaged his cruciate ligaments with Derby and could only manage 22 league appearances and three goals at Southampton. He permed his hair and lost a certain attraction as a Kevin Keegan look-alike.

He was loaned to Nottingham Forest, moved back to Derby and eventually drifted off to Sydney and Hong Kong before returning home when he received news that his father, Bob, was dying of cancer. 'I come back and seen me dad every day. He was in and out of hospital, then we got 'im in a hospice. That put things in perspective for me. There are things more important than football. The short time I was in the game, I loved it. Loved every minute of it. But y'know, if you lose 'eart there's no point in goin' on. Football was made possible for me by me father and once I'd lost 'im, I became a bit disillusioned and lost interest meself. It took me eight years to get over his death.'

In the meantime, his wife divorced him, he lost his pub in Hampshire and liquidated his garage business in Kings Cross. 'I s'pose you could say I was unemployed now,' he said, without a trace of self-pity. 'But there's no point moanin'. You ask my friends. They've never seen me moan.'

Twenty-five years after assisting Arsenal to the zenith of their glittering history, he helped out at the club on match days, glad-handing the sponsors. For a while he showed paying customers around the new Arsenal museum and what a heart-rending job that must have been, forever confronting your old self, fitter, richer, younger and successful.

He lived in a small flat in Highbury now, he told me, about a mile from the stadium. Back where he started then. 'I had a big 'ouse, a big mansion, with dinin' room, livin' room, utility room, you name it. I 'ad it an' I lost it,' he said, serenely. You can say this about Charlie, he contemplates with every appearance of equanimity the upheavals his life has undergone.

'I went from skin'ead to long 'air to permed 'air to no 'air now,' he remarked, a sort of metaphor for his plunging fortunes.

Perhaps he is warmed by the memory of his goals. 'I din't score many goals, but I scored winnin' goals,' he said. This was not always enough for the Arsenal manager, Bertie Mee, who was horribly apt to drop the North Bank's darling, no doubt as a reminder of who was boss. 'I din't like 'im at all,' said Charlie, predictably. 'I don't think he knew too much about football. I think he used me at times as a scapegoat when anyone had to be dropped. From a personal point of view, I felt I should have been put in the team and left in the team. It doesn't matter what anyone says, I could play football.'

It is his wretched luck that his favourite goal was scored when no-one was looking. 'It was against Real Madrid when I was at Derby... I was wearing Bruce Rioch's right boot because mine 'ad split and I remember pickin' the ball up on the box, goin' by a couple of players and knockin' it in the top corner. But the followin' day it was sort of non-existent because we got beat 5–1.

'I mean, barring sex, the best thing in the world is scoring a goal. It's probably better than sex because for that short period of time it's the... whole height of ecstasy. It is. I might be wrong, but that's what I feel.'

That made two of us then, Charlie. Because I met my childhood hero who turned out to be a lovely bloke 25 years on. And the whole height of ecstasy doesn't get any higher than that.

Footnote: It was shortly after writing a story about Charlie George in the *Telegraph* that I received the following letter. 'When Charlie was transferred to Southampton,' wrote Mike Evans from Hook, Hampshire, 'he moved into a grand, detached residence in the picturesque village of Hursley, near Winchester. His next-door neighbour was John Fairclough (now Sir John), my old boss at the IBM Laboratory just across the road.

'One Saturday afternoon John was called urgently by Charlie's wife because water was pouring from the heating pipes in George's new home. John, being a practical man, soon stemmed the breach, helped to mop up the mess and called the builder in to repair the plumbing.

'"Now I can go home and have my tea," says John.

'"Oh no, you can't!" says Charlie's wife. "You must stay till Charlie gets home."

'"But why?" says John.

'"Because unless you're here, Charlie will nut the builder!"'

THE PRESS

All newspaper and journalistic activity is an intellectual brothel from which there is no retreat.
    Leo Tolstoy (and the *News of the World* hadn't even been invented yet)

When I say I slept with Zbigniew Boniek, I mean in the literal, not the lie-back-and-think-of-solidarity sense.

It was the World Cup in Spain in 1982 and despite having no credentials, little money and an even smaller supply of sense, I had taken a coach from Victoria bus depot to Barcelona to cover the great event. I had vague commissions from the *New York Daily News*, the *Seattle Times* and the *San Francisco Chronicle* but since I was filing my copy – careful to reverse the charges – from beachside public phones the length of the Costa Brava, one can see this was hardly a sophisticated operation. I think I even posted one story to Seattle.

Anyway, I was there and dangerously enthusiastic.

By night I slept in the back of a little white Fiat that I'd hired in Tossa and by day I became a menace on the motorways, not least because the gearstick was located in the dashboard. I never really quite got to grips with this Spanish custom.

However, the man from the *News of the World* was keen to visit the Polish training camp just outside Barcelona, and since I was one of the few journalists with wheels (albeit not always pointing in the same direction at the same time), I was commandeered as chauffeur. If any British citizen who has suffered at the hands of any British tabloid could have seen that poor man's face as we screeched to a pebble-scattering halt outside the mountain retreat of the Polish national team, they would count themselves adequately revenged. He was the colour of the Italian flag.

But we had survived, as had Poland, rather brilliantly in this World Cup, with Boniek – on the brink of a transfer to Juventus – their undeniable star. This was the time of the Solidarity movement, the rise of Lech Walesa and open defiance against the domination of the Soviet Union. It was then a matter of political as well as sporting celebration when Boniek thrashed a hat-trick past the Belgians as Poland reached the semi-finals at the expense of the mighty Soviets.

Ginger-haired, freckled and inspired, he was to be the third-highest scorer of the 1982 World Cup, along with Zico of Brazil, and that was good enough for me. With the aid of a coach who spoke English, I arranged with Boniek, who did not, that I would return later that evening for an interview. The timing didn't strike me as odd for a moment. I had two words only in mind . . . 'World Exclusive'.

It was exclusive all right. Trying to find the place again on my own in the pitch dark in a vehicle of hopeless idiosyncrasy was bad enough; trying to talk to my interviewee was even worse. One of the first rules of journalism is never ask questions through a translator who has a vested interest in emasculating the replies. Boniek smiled and twinkled and rattled off great answers the length of the Vistula River, while a grim-faced Polish official said: 'no.' Or occasionally: 'yes,' for variety's sake. It was hopeless. I surrendered.

So, crushed by disappointment, I took my leave, only to be recalled and asked if I needed a bed for the night. I could have his room, Boniek said, kindly. If anyone has ever slept in the back of a Fiat for a fortnight they will fully understand that the offer of a bed of nails would have been gratefully received. I accepted graciously, a true child of the '70s; when dossing down on floors, beaches and even cupboards in a sleeping bag was perfectly and acceptably common.

It was midnight, the bed was heaven, I was asleep in seconds. Only to be awoken by the creak of a gently opening door. What followed must constitute one of the most hilarious conversations ever conducted entirely in pidgin French, our only common language, but the result was happy enough. Poland's star striker slept in one twin bed and I slept in the other.

In the morning we parted most amicably. He gave me one of his football shirts, number ten, as a memento of our slumberous night together and every security guard on duty outside felt it necessary to wink as I passed.

Women sports writers are still few in number and I have no doubt, in some quarters, are viewed suspiciously as little more than 'groupies with laptops'. This is not necessarily the view prevalent amongst the papers themselves, many of which have made huge and positive efforts to promote female writers in the '90s but it clearly remains the attitude amongst a number of the more brain-calcified jocks and their minders.

A number seem to regard women and woeful ignorance as biologically inseparable. Which is ironic, given the almost supernatural insensitivity displayed by some male practitioners of the journalistic art. Example: 'Anyone here been raped and speaks English?' a British TV reporter is alleged to have asked of groups of Belgian refugees fleeing from rebel troops in the Congo.

☆ ☆ ☆

Suzannah Dwyer is a former English teacher and the first to admit she knew nothing about football when she performed a volte-face mid-career and tried to become a sportswriter. But she was intelligent, learned quickly and was dispatched by the (now defunct) magazine, *Football Today*, to cover an England press conference when the former manager, Bobby Robson, was being horribly taunted ('In the Name of Allah, Go!') following a 1–1 draw against Saudi Arabia in 1988.

'Bobby Robson came in and I can remember thinking: "Oh god, he looks like King Lear." He looked so white and gaunt. He didn't make eye contact with anybody in the room at all. It was horrible. One or two questions were asked of him and then he said: "Have you got everything you want, young lady?" I thought: "Oh, there must be another woman in here." I really did. I didn't move a muscle. And he repeated it. I just looked up casually and he was looking at me. He said: "Have you wandered in here by mistake?" I said: "No." Anyway, he really gave me a bad time. I walked up to him afterwards, and said: "Look, I'm terribly sorry, but it's my first time here." But he wasn't very impressed, very cold and very distant. I did understand – he may have thought I was a plant. But I was very upset.

'My very next assignment for the magazine was an interview with Bobby Robson. I said: "No way!" But that's who it was, so I went down to Lancaster Gate, walked in and – I can see him now – he was drinking a cup of coffee, eating a biscuit and talking on the telephone. And he dropped the lot when I walked in.'

Ironically, Suzannah Dwyer was destined to become more famous as a story herself than as a freelance football correspondent. Her relationship with the Chelsea chairman, Ken Bates, became known to the tabloids and, typically, rather than allowing the newspapers to expose the story, Bates called a press conference and announced it himself.

'I can't begin to tell you how terrible it was. It was absolutely terrible. I still have terrible grief within me about the effect it had on my family.' She had been separated from her husband at the time, and was living with their two sons. 'It was nothing to do with them and they shouldn't have had to suffer like that. It was just gruesome.

'Ken and I were lucky to the extent that we both had a lot of friends in the newspaper industry and we were warned. But that didn't make it any easier. I felt it was incredibly brave of Ken to do what he did. He called a press conference. Oh, it was a terrible day. I remember I wore beige and I think I looked beige all the way up. I didn't want to go at all. He said I had to. The thing was the majority of the journalists there didn't know we knew that they knew, so it was the whole cat and mouse thing. And then he read that statement, which was terribly romantic and brave.'

'My wife has been for some time aware that I have been having an on-going relationship with Suzannah,' Bates announced. 'Although we have lost something, Pam and I remain good friends and companions and will continue so to be despite the matter having become public knowledge.'

'I suppose I knew when I got involved with him that we would have to face something, but I didn't know it would be so terrible.'

☆ ☆ ☆

In theory, Amy Lawrence and Olivia Blair kept one another sane. Good friends and colleagues, they both wrote for the football magazine *FourFourTwo*, where, for a while, women journalists outnumbered the men by the 1953 FA Cup final score: 4–3.

But, on closer acquaintance, you wonder whether there was much sanity to work with in the first place.

Olivia: 'I played Subbuteo for hours when I was a little girl. All on my own. My sisters always thought I was crazy. I guess that's how my knowledge of players came about, because I was always drawing up my own teams. Davie Provan, the old Celtic winger, was always a favourite of mine for some reason.'

Amy: 'It all began in the late '70s at Highbury. Arsenal against Forest. Three-nil. Brady and two from Stapleton. I was taken to that game by my best mate Jo and her dad. My family were QPR fans but even at that young age I was quite rebellious. So I got taken to Arsenal – thank God. I was six. I think more than anything the whole ambience, the atmosphere drew me in. I can't pretend I understood what was going on and for part of the time Jo and I played with some toy Wombles in my pocket. But I think the people, the colour, the noise, just blew me away at that age. From there it developed quickly into an obsession.'

Olivia: 'I used to play football with the boys at my prep school in Chichester. I was the first girl to win football colours there. I remember once mistiming a tackle and putting out the team captain for six weeks with an ankle injury.

'I was at boarding school during the 1978 World Cup in Argentina. To watch the matches I had to shin down a drainpipe at night, climb in through a window in the prefects' common room, lock the door on the inside and switch on the television – very quietly. I had a weekly subscription to *Shoot* in those days. I had about 300 copies of them under my bed in the dorm.'

Amy: 'I used to bunk off school, tell my mum I was going to the cinema or a friend's house, run down to the North Bank and pay a couple of quid to go in. Eventually I hooked up with a load of fans and we travelled the world. Well, England anyway – car, train, bus. I was about 14 or 15, I suppose. I remember my first trip to Wembley for the League Cup final in 1987. Walking through the entrance and seeing the stadium utterly red and white . . . I nearly fell over. I was really taken by that.

'When I went up to university in Sheffield to study music, it didn't stop me watching Arsenal. In the 1990–91 season I saw every game, home and away, despite living 200 miles away. I just found a way. It got silly, I must admit. Stupid. This is where obsession got stupid and interfered with me having any semblance of a grip on reality. It was a great time but it was a little bit sad.

'I was also seeing a guy who was a very, very big Wednesday fan. We lived together. It was quite wonderful for a while. And, of course, Arsenal and Wednesday were on a collision course for the two Cup finals in 1993. We were terribly excited. We thought it was some kind of cosmic coincidence.

'Arsenal won the first one. He didn't take it very well for a few hours and then he was all right. I think he thought Wednesday'd win the FA Cup and we'd both be happy. But, of course, Andy Linighan, last minute goal in the replay, thank you very much. Arsenal won two, Wednesday won nil. The following day – relationship over.'

Olivia: 'But I'm not sure women are more mature than men over football. You know, I've never felt I experienced football differently to anybody else just because I'm a girl.'

Amy: 'I've always been inspired by atmosphere. Not that I don't comprehend tactics and appreciate the nuances of the game.'

Olivia: 'When we started at *FourFourTwo*, they said we'll give it two months and we'll see how it goes. We were sitting there on that first day and the editor said: "Right, you chase Keegan and you find Venables." I thought: "Hey, what's going on? This is unreal."'

Amy: 'My head exploded.'

Olivia: 'And, touch wood, I still get a kick out of it. I mean we're not star-struck or anything. But . . .'

Amy: 'It's a buzz.'

Olivia: 'It's refreshing and I get just as much of a buzz speaking to someone, like at Stockport, as I do the big stars. I went up there to do an *On the Bench* with Danny Bergara and ended up drinking whisky in his office after the game. We're good pals now. He's one of my soft spots.'

Amy: 'One of them. We've both got millions.'

Olivia: 'Every team we go to, we come back not just with a contact, but with this emotional attachment.'

Amy: 'People in football find it a bit odd. But not as odd as I find the attitude of some player agents, though, who seem to think sometimes that we're part of the deal. Most of them are all right but there are one or two who obviously aren't used to working with women writers. They think that all females who hang around footballers are groupies, and they can't draw the line if you are a professional.

'It's as if they're saying: "I'll give you what you want" – the access to a player, the interview, or whatever – "if you give me what I want." And they don't mean financially. Unfortunately they are in a position of power because they have a hold on the player you want to speak to. They make advances and attempt to take advantage of the situation. It isn't a pleasant experience. I make it extremely clear that it's completely out of the question, but a lot of agents have inflated self-images on the backs of the people they represent and sometimes they get the hump – for want of a better word – with us for not complying with their wishes.

'On one occasion I was invited to a party by an agent, and later he tried it on. I made it clear I wasn't interested, but his pride was so dented he promptly left, took all his stars with him as some sort of symbolic gesture, and I was left on my own feeling pretty terrible. I thought: "Is that they only way they perceive women?" That's really sad. And there was I thinking I might have contributed something to the evening's conversation. How naïve! But I don't get hysterical about it. As a woman in a male domain, you're going to get involved in the odd scrape.'

Olivia: 'To be honest, I'm 30 now and I'd quite like to have a family. I'm in a dilemma because I don't really want to give up what I'm doing now. I can't imagine a better job. At the same time I can't imagine going to a football match when I'm seven months pregnant. And there's other problems. Brian, my husband, has already said that if we have a boy he's going to be a West Ham supporter. But I support Tottenham and I'd like to take my kids to White Hart Lane. We've already had an argument about it. Brian's found it quite difficult anyway, me working in football. He says footballers have got only two things on their brain and he's a bit wary about it. For a long time he didn't read the magazine.'

Amy: 'I know football will always be with me. This is brilliant. In a nutshell, I wake up every day and think: "I'm actually involved with football." It's a constant kick of adrenalin.'

THE BELLES, THE BELLES

A woman playing football is like a dog walking on its hind legs. It is not done well but you are surprised to find it done at all.
                                        Brian Glanville, football writer

Women playing football have a strange effect on men. 'Get yer tits out for the lads,' is one of them. Another is demonstrated by Brian Glanville in his often-repeated, stentorian-toned paraphrase of Samuel Johnson.

Certain men would rather their womenfolk developed a healthy interest in satanic rites instead of football, anything but trample their dainty studded size sixes all over the great people's game. 'It's a man's game,' they are fond of saying to one another, as though in search of desperate reassurance. Nothing much has changed then.

'It was the most ludicrous exhibition of the noble sport I have ever witnessed. Palpably, some of the ladies had never kicked a ball in their lives before,' trumpeted a writer in the *Western Morning News* in 1921. He must not, however, have been treated to the sight of Lily Parr in full flow, as fearsome a talent as ever ghosted past a full-back and lined up a shot from 25 yards.

It is probably unfair to besmirch her with the label the female 'Gazza' of the 1920s, but undeniably our Lily of St Helens was not the delicate little flower her name would suggest. For a start, she stood six feet tall in her stockings, had a thunderbolt shot of which Bobby Charlton would be proud, sprayed passes from midfield with the poise of Ruud Gullit and was a one-woman riot on the team bus going home.

Tommy suffered more than most. He was the bus driver for the Dick Kerr Ladies whenever out-of-town matches were involved. He would be driving along, minding his own business, when a hostelry would be glimpsed in the distance. A shout would go up. 'Tommy! Stop the bus!' Tommy would oblige and the entire team would disappear into a pub.

The words: 'Now girls, we'll not be stopping long,' were remarkable only for their complete ineffectuality.

It happened once on the way back from an away fixture at Workington that Lily was, in the words of a team-mate, 'well away'. The girls reboarded the bus without incident but about five miles down the road a thought suddenly occurred to the star player. 'Stop this bloody bus,' she shouted. 'I'm going to be sick.' She returned a chastened soul, but five miles further on, another shout went up. 'Stop this bloody bus.' 'Not again,' said the exasperated Tommy. 'You'll have to go back,' she told him. 'I've lost my bloody false teeth.'

It is recorded for posterity that the teeth were found, wrapped in paper and safely stowed in Lily's pocket. But the game of women's football was not to be so lovingly well preserved.

Seen from our modern vantage point where women footballers are represented as the 'Eddie the Eagles' of ball games – slightly freakish and funny – the popularity of the women's game in the 1920s is astonishing. When women played to a crowd of 53,000 at Goodison Park on Boxing Day 1921, the FA were sufficiently impressed to give them serious thought. Having thought, they banned them.

Football was bad for women's health, it was decreed. Although in what manner it could be worse than young ladies swiping six bells out of one another with hockey sticks was not entirely explained. The official reason for the game's dismantling was a matter of irregular expenses, a charity swindle in other words. But a good equal opportunities lawyer could have driven a coach and horses through that paltry excuse.

They was robbed, the women of the 1920s. They were denied a game they had grown to love, one that was raising huge funds for charity and drawing crowds beyond the capability of Manchester United today. They were thwarted by the old buzzards of the FA, desperate to stem this 'unsuitable' (too damn popular, more like it) tide.

Seventy years on and the game has never remotely reclaimed public favour. The greatest publicity the sport enjoyed in the climax to the 1995–96 season was the report of a brawl between the Millwall Lionesses and Arsenal Ladies in the London Football Association Cup final. Two Arsenal players were said to be knocked to the ground in the changing-rooms after the Lionesses had suffered a 2–1 defeat. 'We are trying to promote the game in the community and this is not the way to go about it,' said an FA Secretary.

Self-promotion has not been women's football's greatest strength so far. Liverpool LFC attract 20 or 30 lost souls to the touchline of Kirby

Stadium. Even the Doncaster Belles, who have dominated the modern era as surely as Real Madrid in the '50s, can only pull a maximum of 400 onlookers to the Armfield Welfare Ground, their second-hand Yorkshire home.

The Belles at least are famous, or infamous maybe, for a BBC documentary of the climax to their 1994 season. They won the championship and the FA Cup for the sixth time in their 25-year history, but all anybody seems to remember from the film, especially at the FA, was the players swigging beer, uttering four-letter words and mooning to the camera in a post-game celebration.

It was an unfortunate experience for women's football: its largest audience since 1921 and the lingering memory is one of buttocks. In the film, Kaz 'Whacker' Walker, the England striker, explained that there were times she couldn't be bothered to speak to her boyfriend, Dean, because she was so shattered from playing. Mandy 'Flo' Lowe recounted the details of drinking 15 bottles of Budweiser and being dropped for three matches because of it. 'Puked up everywhere,' she said. Joanna Broadhurst (the one with the butterfly tattoo) described a particular football friendly she had played against a police team: 'This man were marking me and every time I had my back to 'im, he kept feeling me bum. And I thought, God, what a prat.'

More Gazza-esque than grotesque, the documentary could have conveyed the feeling that the only women who play the game were northern female ruffians. 'Me 'air's a mess,' said Kaz Walker on the morn of the Women's FA Cup final, but you had the feeling she cared far less about such matters than part-time model David Ginola.

Yet, when the clouds of outrage dispersed, the main impression left behind was of a touching kinship between the players. 'It's like a family,' said Broadhurst. 'There's a lot of feeling between the players. It's not just a football team.'

That fellow-feeling in women's football has not gone entirely unnoticed by society. It remains a deeply held prejudice by those outside the game that the players, one and all, are lesbians. The leap from tough to butch is all too easily made. 'And unfortunately, or fortunately, in about 75 per cent of cases, that's true,' said Clare Taylor, who goes both ways only in the sense that she plays centre-half/sweeper for Liverpool and the England Women's Football team and opening bowler for Yorkshire and the England Women's Cricket Team.

'You can't hide away from it. I find there's a lot more hangers-on now because they know the background. Gays use it as a haven or a hiding place. They know a high proportion of the women will be gay.

It's a good – well, I was going to say breeding ground – but it's a good place to hang out if you've got tendencies that way.

'It doesn't affect me that badly. Most people know me because I've been around in football that long. They know I'm not gay; they leave me alone. I've had the odd occasions when people come up to me and I know they're chatting me up. I put them straight in the picture. I'm not nasty about it. I just explain that's not what I'm here for. Some of them are, like, stunned, because you've actually come out and said something. But most of them are all right about it.

'It's a weird situation. The fact that there are a lot of gays in football can cause problems in clubs if they fall out with each other. I've seen that in clubs I've played for before. It's happened a bit at Liverpool as well. If they fall out, they can cause aggro within the team and you can lose good players because of it. You can't hide from the fact that's what happens. It's part and parcel of the game really.

'The number of people who say to me: "Where's your boyfriend?" They're angling, waiting for me to say: "I'm gay." They're looking for a good story. But if it's not there, it's not there.

'I have had boyfriends, but it's difficult. And my situation is a lot worse, you know, with two international careers. I'm never at home or, if I am, I'm out training. Relationships will start, then end after about four or five weeks. I've only got to say: "I'm off to Millwall overnight. Catch you later," and it doesn't go down too well.

'It is, and it isn't, a shame. I'm quite happy with the lifestyle I've got at the moment. I'm very independent. I'm very selfish in a way. But hopefully, I'm not left-on-the-shelf material.'

Clare, capped for England 25 times by the time she was 30, is a post office van driver in Huddersfield. She does a permanent late shift to get Saturdays off to play hockey. She has a degree in Geography from Hull University. 'I've never used it, unless you count being a post person.' But she uses the dipped left shoulder feint she learned in the street games with the boys in Crossland Moor, West Yorkshire, where she grew up. 'There didn't seem to be any girls. If you wanted to play with anybody you had to play football. When it wasn't football, it was bikes, go-karts or tadpolin'.'

You could be forgiven for wondering whether the training of the England Women's national team is any more sophisticated than tadpoling sometimes. In answer to the question of whether British football takes the women's game seriously or not, highlights from the 1995 Women's World Cup in Sweden can be supplied.

The event was not some patronising dabble in political correctness.

FIFA took it sufficiently seriously to gather a crowd of 65,000 to their first Women's World Cup in China in 1991, although that may tell you more about the biddable Chinese than it does about the status of footballing women worldwide. Still, by 1995, a number of national teams, in Northern Europe and the USA particularly, were very sharp outfits indeed.

Norway won, a semi-professional squad, coached by Egil 'Drillo' Olsen and captained by Gro Espeseth, who may sound like a garden fertiliser but marshalled a rigid system of zonal defence to perfection. England were knocked out in the quarter-finals by Germany but the concussion had been partly self-induced.

The management, FA-appointed, were strict about not eating sausages, wearing the correct trousers and definitely not going for a drink after matches. The players were not entirely happy about this. Or team selection. Or the fact that Canada, their first match opponents, were staying in the same hotel. 'It's all right,' said an England player ominously. 'We're friendly. Till Tuesday. Then we'll kick ten shades of shit out of them.'

The herrings for breakfast were an unknown quantity and stayed that way. In one of the wiser FA moves, extra supplies of Sugar Puffs were brought in.

The only happy distraction was provided by the Nigerians when it was alleged that two of the side should have been thrown out of the tournament because they 'offered their bodies for a place'. 'We heard that story,' said Clare. 'Our reaction was to say: "If that's the thing you had to do in England, I don't think I'd get a game."'

The training of the England players had been necessarily hampered by the fact that they all had a living to earn. One worked for the DSS in Rotherham, another was a policewoman, another installed buttons on CD players at a factory in Castleford. And, naturally, the shackles of ingrained unprofessionalism were not to be lightly undone.

'I don't really think women understand football,' said Clare. 'One or two do. But, in general, I don't think they do. A lot of them play for something to do rather than taking it seriously and thinking about it. I find at Liverpool if I try to talk to them about running off the ball and creating space, they look at me as though I've got three heads. They don't think deeply enough about it. As far as they're concerned you put your boots on, get the ball and try and kick it into the back of the net. There's still a lot of that about.'

There are 50,000 players in Norway; 12,000 in the UK. The German national team is sponsored by Mercedes; the English national team has no sponsors. The Japanese women's league is professional (and this in a country with a tea ceremony) with salaries of up to £63,000. Even Italy, where the mayor of one Riviera resort gained stupendous fame for fining overweight women for wearing bikinis, has enjoyed a thriving women's game. Debbie Bampton, the England captain, actually earned money for playing for Trani for a year. Admittedly, the sugar daddy of the team was liable to refuse to pay when they lost, but the compensations were regular crowds of 3,000, a flat overlooking the Mediterranean, television coverage three times a week and idolisation by the locals. The whole town resounded to cries of 'Ciao Bampton'.

Not necessarily the two words that now ring in the streets of Croydon, where Bampton is now installed as player/manager. But regardless of the pitiful financial rewards, she is still a passionate advocate for the women's game. In that sense, she is a direct descendant of Lily Parr and her fellow munitions factory workers.

In the future, as more schools take up the sport, a surge in the scale, organisation and respectability of women's football may allow it to catch up with its hype as one of the fastest growing sports in Britain (not difficult from virtual scratch). Until then, the glory days remain locked in that brief era in the '20s when Lily was the queen of the dressing-room banter. She walked in on pre-match preparations once to be confronted by the familiar sight of elastic stockings, bandages and strappings and her team-mates dressing for the fray. 'Well, I don't know about Dick Kerr Ladies football team,' she said. 'It looks like a bloody trip to Lourdes to me!'

BOY-ZONE

Why haven't women got labels on their foreheads saying, 'Danger: Government Health Warning: women can seriously damage your brain, genitals, current account, confidence, razor blades and good standing among your friends'?
                              Jeffrey Bernard, *Spectator*, 1984

There is a classic snippet of BBC footage in which a female reporter, clad in an ill-advised pink cardigan, picks her dainty way across the jostling terraces at the Dell to complain about the treatment of women in football. Her hectoring tone, however, is spectacularly undermined by a bemused, shaven-headed yob who cannot for the life of him understand why some bint is lurching past him talking to herself. He follows her, his whey face wrinkled in mystification. Finally he spots the faraway camera and just as she delivers some profundity as the punchline, he breaks into a stupendous leer.

He is preserved for posterity now in the BBC archives in Manchester. I never did find out who he was, but he remains an indelible memory. Not least because the bint was me.

It was 1989 and we were working on a short film for the investigative sports series *On the Line*. My job was to expose football's disgracefully misogynous attitude to women in a ten-minute item called 'Boys in the Boardroom'. This was about as difficult as finding a footballer at the bookies. Ron Atkinson helped us off to a flying start. 'Women in football?' he said. 'I think women should be in the kitchen, in the discotheque, should be in the boutique. I don't think they should be in football.' He, no doubt, felt his stance was utterly vindicated when a highly placed woman in the football hierarchy once said to him by way of casual conversation: 'I see your son's playing today.' Dalian Atkinson was indeed playing. But he is not Ron Atkinson's son, as might be guessed from the fact that he's black.

This helps to explain why the boys in (and out of) the boardroom were of one mind on the subject of women. 'It's a man's game, innit?' said a Liverpool fan polled outside Anfield on the subject of female fans. 'I mean, women go in the Kop, like, but they shouldn't be in there.'

'The boardroom is the sanctum of the male directors,' said Bert McGee, then chairman of Sheffield Wednesday, at which club in those days women were invited to partake of their tea and buns in another room, a thick brick wall away from the gentlemen. 'Terribly Victorian, aren't we?' he said, with a shameless grin. He was not alone. At that time, two-thirds of the top-flight clubs banned women from the hallowed boardroom, including those that had every right, as football directors, to be there. One woman described her feelings of frustration and humiliation when she had been physically barred from entering the Tranmere boardroom by the then chairman of the club. 'The Tranmere boardroom!' I gasped in sympathy. I mean, it's not exactly Raymond's Revue Bar, is it?

In the caring '90s, you wonder what the FA, having preached and pontificated about the urgent need to attract women to football, have done about this continuing and alarming discrimination. Sort of nothing, is the answer. 'There's nothing specific in the FA rules that talks about discrimination,' said Mark Sudbury, the FA's public affairs officer. 'We've taken on board women's football, we're tackling racism but with regard to what individual clubs do, our influence is fairly limited. As long as the clubs are operating within the rules of football, the clubs have a fairly free hand. But the FA certainly does not support any all-male attitude. We now have female members on the FA Council.' How many, I wondered. 'Well, only one at the moment,' he conceded. 'Out of 92.'

However, it is true that Graham Kelly, the FA's chief executive, boycotted a Professional Footballers' Association dinner in 1996 because it was an all-male affair, which could be construed as a giant step for womankind. But ask the FA how much unofficial pressure they can put on the guilty clubs to open their masonic boardrooms and the answer is hardly encouraging. 'The relationship between the national governing body and the individual club varies,' said Sudbury.

'You mean it depends how much of an old bugger the chairman is?' I said.

'Absolutely correct,' said Sudbury.

No change there then. Back on the telly, I was cinematically outraged. Thoroughly warming to my theme of wronged womanhood, I delivered a few impassioned lines on the subject of fellow football journalists. 'There are those,' I observed, 'who regard women in the press box as a rather nasty perversion of nature. I think they'd rather we were at home weeping over the afternoon movie or peeling the spuds.'

Since I was married to a football writer who had only ever seen me weep over Arsenal videos and had certainly never witnessed a potato in my hand, this was an outrageous exaggeration. It was a grain of truth dressed up in more layers than Danny La Rue. But, in some ways, it was a prescient little film. The former Assistant Chief Constable of the Merseyside Police was seen to say that since women were known to be more tranquil and more responsible than men, the male bastion of football would learn to embrace them as a civilising influence. (It remains an incidental irony that the speaker was Alison Halford, soon to sue the Merseyside Police, yet another male bastion, for sex discrimination.)

Football has indeed recognised the wisdom of her words. Women have been wooed by all-seater stadia, loo paper in the ladies, wholesome beans in the restaurant and the cheekbones of David Ginola. And it has worked, to a degree.

When Gazza cried in the semi-finals of the 1990 World Cup, on the brink of defeat by Germany, it only served to clinch the devotion of the maternal army. The whole pattern of football fellowship was changing and had he ridden the triumphal open-topped bus from the airport wearing a set of plastic boobs he could not have heralded the new dawn more appropriately.

Some men still don't like it. It seems to cause the same disquiet in the male psyche as did female ordination in the Anglican church. 'The response has been one of deep, neurotic, emotional revulsion,' said one female commentator on the subject of women priests. The same could be said for football.

'You can't come in here. There's men going about with their bits out,' admonished Andy King, the Mansfield manager, as I stood in a corridor, awaiting a word with the reserve striker. Bits or no bits, I reminded him, it was discriminatory to throw me out while my fellow journalists (bit-resistant men) were allowed to stay. He threw me out anyway.

This is usually the case. Practice dawdles so far behind the law that it resembles Matt Le Tissier on a bad day for Southampton. I was painfully reminded of as much by my doctor once. 'Is this you?' he said, brandishing a Scottish daily newspaper during the highly undignified circumstance of a six-week check-up following the birth of my son. 'Is what me?' I gasped. 'This!' he said, proceeding to regale me with a hilarious item about a female sports journalist who had rung Rangers Football Club to find out if any crèche facilities existed so that she could breastfeed her infant at half-time. 'Yes, it's me,' I grudgingly confessed, bitterly wishing I'd had the sense to live out my life as a surrogate man, never admitting to the ownership of children at all. But the doc seemed delighted. A notorious woman on his couch.

To some men, of course, all women are notorious. 'Oh yes, Sir Alf Ramsay, did speak to me once. To poke me in the chest when he found out I was going to the Mexico World Cup with Geoff,' said Judith Hurst, the wife of the England centre-forward who scored a hat-trick in the 1966 World Cup final. 'We were in some country, I forget where, just prior to the World Cup in Mexico in 1970. I was staying in another hotel as the wives always did and I had a dreadful, dreadful cold. Geoff was going to give me a lift back to my room when Sir Alf suddenly appeared. "Is it OK if I give Judith a ride back to her hotel?" Geoff asked him and Sir Alf poked me with his finger. He said the team was going to Mexico to "bring the pot back", as he put it, and he didn't want any interference. I said: "I understand. There's no way you'll see me or hear from me."'

But just in case, the authorities took the precaution in those days of barring women from almost everything, including the celebration banquet the night in 1966 when England had won the World Cup. 'I was waiting outside the dining-room at the Royal Garden hotel with a group of other wives when someone told us that Bobby Moore had just been presented with the Cup,' said Judith. 'I remember Tina Moore, his wife, turning to me and saying: "Perhaps I'll read about it in the papers tomorrow."'

All you can say in the male defence is that those were the days before *Woman's Hour* had discovered PMT, when men just thought women were bitchy and illogical. To be honest, some of the women thought so too. 'You're going to get bitchiness from women in any profession,' said Judith. 'I remember when Geoff wasn't picked for the first team at Stoke. The manager, Tony Waddington, said: "Judith, don't be upset with me because I haven't picked him." I said: "Oh, for God's sake, that's one thing you will never hear from me. I haven't the right to say anything." But, obviously, he'd had it from other women, other wives. All I can say is there must have been a lot of weak men out there.

'The Stoke wives – they were a bit . . . they didn't get my sense of humour, I don't think. Perhaps they had a bit of a chip on their shoulders about us being southerners. The bitchiness showed, now and again, and I'd do things to wind them up even more. I remember once,

I had a ring on, which, when I think about it now, was very ostentatious, but it's a long time ago. It was a cold day and someone said: "Obviously you can't get gloves on over that ring!" So the next week I wore Geoff's great big gloves and made a point of showing her I needed gloves four times my size to cover my ring.'

But, you suspect, it is not women's bitchiness that most offends the boys in the boardroom, rather the woeful, they believe congenital, ignorance of women on matters football.

Pamela Sharp, a 41-year-old student at the University of East Anglia, gained national notice in 1995 by applying to the FA for the England management job. 'I do know there are eleven players in a team,' she said, offering her credentials. Her blueprint for success included taking the team training in warm-weather climates, insisting they looked good and smelt nice on all occasions, gaining sponsorship from Givenchy, Boss and Armani and replacing the kit with 'something skimpy in lycra'.

It is this kind of feminine frivolity that can get women a bad name in football and cause the man's man types to feel the need to express their love for a team only in a high-testosterone environment. Women are saps. They can ruin a whole match, even a 3–3 thriller, with an inappoite remark about the Persil whiteness of the opposition's shorts.

This is certainly true of the crustier misogynists, brought up in an age when women rarely wore trousers and could cook food more exotic than a Safeways frozen lasagne; it is a surprise to find it true of a young, cinematic sex god who has steamed in various states of lascivious undress with Melanie Griffiths, Joely Richardson, Theresa Russell, Amanda Donohoe, Liz Hurley and Emily Lloyd. Most men in such circumstances might appreciate women's finer points. Sean Bean does in a way, he just doesn't particularly want them at football.

'It's genuine love,' said the ardent Sheffield United supporter who has been Romeo, the baddie in a Bond movie and Lady Chatterley's bit of rough in his time. He was also in the process of separating from his wife. She cited Sheffield United as the other party involved.

A tattoo, '100% blade', adorns his left arm. 'It's sometimes 'ard to understand for some people that it's a genuine love affair. It causes . . . all sorts.' He enacted the scene.

Her: 'You love them more than you love me.'

Him: 'Course I don't.'

Her: 'Why don't you have a tattoo of me on yer arm then?'

When Saturday comes he likes to find himself in a Ford transit van on the way to Bramall Lane, meeting mates, having a few pints, going to the ground, pouring Bovril on his pie ('nice and juicy'), having a few pints after and maybe staying overnight to watch a pub game Sunday morning. 'It's always a laugh, like. Great to watch. Everybody's still a bit pissed and then you go to the pub.'

The luvvie profession has mellowed him slightly. 'I realised I was quite good at acting and from then on I thought no matter what anybody says I'm going to go for it. I were very confident about it. I mean, the lads called me a fairy and all that, but that's understandable. I'd have probably done the same myself if the tables were turned.'

As part of the ultimate test of his loyalty to the Blades, he was once asked what he would give up first: football or sex. The FA will be proud to learn he hesitated. 'I think you'd have to keep sex,' he said. 'Bloody hell. I'd rather have a shag than watch a nil-nil draw in February in front of about 9,000 people.'

Even so: 'Football's a man's game. It's like, you wanna be with yer mates, don't you? Put it this way, I wouldn't like to be on a Kop-full of women.' He paused. 'Wait a minute,' he said. 'I don't know though . . .'

Rugby

(TWO OF) THE FIVE NATIONS

It is never difficult to distinguish between a Scotsman with a grievance and a ray of sunshine.
P.G. Wodehouse, 1935

Murrayfield, 2 March, 1996. 'O Flower of Scotland'; O who would dare tamper with those majestic words that make grown men weep and even the Scottish hooker clench tightly his jaw before the match begins. But does it really say:

And stood against him
Proud Edward's Army
And sent him homeward
Tae think again?

About 97 per cent of the conscious humanity encountered the day Scotland played England for the Grand Slam were definitely of the impression the words were: 'Tae *drink* again.'

They had a proper grievance, of course. They had lost. To the enemy. Even so, the drowning of sorrows began before a ball was kicked. In the queue for the train to Edinburgh in Glasgow hardly anything could be heard save the din of bottles chinking in their Safeway's carriers disguise. On the train itself, packed to the gunnels, people spoke fondly of the efforts of the transport police to maintain a 'dry train' in the face of insurmountable odds and empties.

In Ryries, a purveyor of fine ales, 20 steps from Haymarket Station, Evelyn MacLean was on Southern Comfort. It was barely noon but, as she said, if she had to act as landlady to six fellas in her living-room (the usual quota from Aberdeen who miss the last train home) she needed to keep her strength up. Her mate, 'Sad', on pints, was parading his new haircut: completely bald save for a few strategic thistles and a punk's quiff on top. (He had Christmas trees carved specially for Yuletide and dragons for the Welsh match. 'It's seasonal,' he said.)

In the Murrayfield carpark, the boots of Bentleys and Range Rovers were agape revealing great swathes of smoked salmon and rivers of champagne. 'We've got 35 relatives here today and many hangers-on. My sister-in-law and I do the food,' said Marjorie Waddell, daughter-in-law of Herbert Waddell, once captain of Scotland and the British Lions. 'Bacon and egg rolls and soup.' These were the essentials. Special drinks? one inquired. 'Anything,' she said firmly.

The 113th Auld Enemy clash (Scotland 9 England 18) would be toasted all morning and mourned all night; a night when bonhomie would spill over into amorous adventures or retching over hedges but never – hardly ever – into the sort of strong-armed violence that all had witnessed on the pitch.

This is rugby's great appeal to women. One of them, anyway. 'I once snogged 13 men after a match in Ireland,' said Fiona, a nurse. 'Eleven,' corrected her four friends simultaneously.

Rugby is a game of two halves, those halves sometimes being somebody's leg. This by no means precludes female support. Women are quite capable of applauding violence, provided the rules of the game are being adhered to correctly. 'It's fast, it's physical, it's passionate,' said Fiona, that nurse again, whose ward rounds must be a sight to behold.

But given women's predisposition to enjoy the sport, and their role model Princess Anne in the stand, it was curious how many had been persuaded to stay at home by their menfolk on this particular occasion. Fears for their safety? Not exactly. Scotland were poised on the brink of a Grand Slam and every tartan-blooded bloke worth his caber wanted, indeed yearned, to be there.

'My wife wanted to come,' said Michael, a solicitor. 'She actually nearly had a ticket.' These bogus words could have been snatched from the mouths of hundreds of middle-aged men clutching a crystal goblet full of Bollinger in one hand and that other passport to happiness (a ticket) in the other. One had been damn fool enough to phone home. 'Her language was really quite dreadful,' he said, shaken.

'D'you know,' said a banker from Kent. 'When my wife does come I enjoy it more.'

His Glaswegian friend, in the insurance line, looked frankly scandalised. 'That's a typical English remark,' he said.

'No, I definitely enjoy it more,' insisted the banker. 'Because I don't lose any brownie points for going to a game when she can't come.'

'I'm glad I live in a liberated country,' said the insurer. 'We suppress women up here.'

'That doesn't happen in Kent. It's the other way round.'

'Look, the wife knew I was coming here today. It was pre-planned. She understands.'

'Ah but,' said the banker, knowingly. 'You'll pay later. In ways you may not even realise at the time.'

☆ ☆ ☆

Sad was going to pay later, in ways he probably knew all too well. But that did not deter him from attacking the day with gusto. 'I was born in Glasgow, live in Kirkcaldy, work in Rosyth and drink in Edinburgh,' he explained. His wife apparently understood the situation. 'When January comes she battens down the hatches. She knows that I'm unavailable for functions until the rugby season's over in March.'

This, it turned out, included bringing her home from maternity hospital following the birth of his son. Irresponsibly, his wife had given birth the very day before Scotland–Wales, thereby placing her husband in an impossible position. He was utterly torn between Gavin Hastings and 'Baby Sad'. ('We couldn't decide on a name'.) In the end, he threw himself on the mercy of the nurses. 'I was having kittens. I begged the hospital to keep her in one more day.' Fortunately, the medical staff, trained to recognise emergencies, obliged and Sad went to the match.

There have been many great moments at Murrayfield in Sad's life, but one he remembered with particular glee was the time he and five or six friends gatecrashed the women's loo and sang with a lusty fervour (in paraphrase of a famous Scottish song): 'Will ye go, lassies, go, and we'll all go together . . .'

Going together, in another sense, has not always suited the players' wives. The nerve-twanging tension and the fervid patriotism, expressed on the field in brute collision or swivel-hipped bursts of virtuosity, have to find another outlet in the stands. For Suzie Ackford, watching husband Paul play lock for England in the 1990 clash that won the Grand Slam for Scotland, the memory is not entirely a happy one.

'It was a really bad experience,' she said. 'I found it so disappointing: the people and their behaviour. So much so, I would find it hard to go back. The political side had come into the sport more and more. The hatred of the English was evident, and at the time it was a very deep-seated hatred of Thatcher. Devolution had become more part and parcel of their life. The hatred seemed to be far more intense than it ever was and they seemed to bring it into the competitive arena of rugby.

'I felt very uncomfortable throughout the match surrounded by

Scots. It was very intimidating. And afterwards – the gloating! We had to be with the Scottish wives and, God, they gloated. But I suppose I take my hat off to them. Maybe if I'd been in their shoes, I'd have gloated.

'I seem to remember, at the post-match dinner, I walked out. They started singing 'Flower of Scotland' and I did walk out. The comments and the sniggering, it was horrible. Penny Moore and I were both very upset.'

Curiously, this extension of the on-field conflict seemed not to apply to the Scottish fans who made a great point of not punching an Englishman when they saw one. 'It's one of the things I like best about rugby,' said Evelyn, who, being disabled, was able to apply direct to Murrayfield for a ticket. Sad pushed her to the stadium in her wheelchair in return for a pint. 'The camaraderie. Everybody mixes. There's more banter. Nae animosity. I wouldnae go to football.'

Since this would involve watching either Hearts or Hibernian (Edinburgh's finest but neither worldbeaters at the time), it was an entirely justifiable decision, but the spectacle at Murrayfield on this particular day was no less gruelling an experience. Dean Richards, a 6ft 4in, 17st 8lb police officer with the Leicestershire constabulary, arrested every move Scotland could muster with his threatening bulk. Around this Hercules, England played with such defensive zest that Rory Underwood, the record-breaking winger, was a loiterer without intent until 11 minutes from the end. Paul Grayson, the insurance broker/fly half, kicked every England point on the board.

In the crowd, Romayne Wainwright, wife of the Scottish captain, sat with her parents, her brother, his wife, Rob's sisters, his parents and a few cousins, two of whom had threatened to streak if Scotland won. 'I don't know if they were more relieved than disappointed at the end,' said Romayne.

Wainwright was unable to play a blinder on the day. Midway through the first half his head was in collision with a fist thrown by Jason Leonard (although the England tight head prop escaped a ban later when video footage of the incident proved inconclusive) and later admitted suffering concussion although he played on at the time.

'At times like that I get very cross with the person that did it,' said Romayne. 'Very, very, very cross with the person that did it. Other than that I just worry. I didn't have a clue what happened this time. I didn't see it. But I realised something had happened. You could tell he couldn't really see.

'Things like this do tend to happen in Calcutta Cup matches. Two years ago he broke his cheekbone and this time it was the clashing between wrist and head – or however you politely put it. They have to be the worst moments. Watching Rob play rugby, it's one of those things that's very, very hard to explain. I've always found it very difficult. It's painful, absolutely.

'Few Scots will enjoy sitting at a Calcutta Cup match. There's a fair amount of aggro in the crowd. A lot of quite partisan people come up for that particular match. You can tell them by the fairly moronic bi-syllabic chants: 'Dean-o, Dean-o!' I thought Scotland might win. I knew we would play the better rugby, but whether that would be enough . . .'

It was not. The England victory represented the triumph of pragmatic caution over precarious creativity. Did this rob the attending women of their satisfaction? Not necessarily. 'We're just driving round the car-park looking for talent,' confessed Ann, a chartered surveyor in a Range Rover. 'Three of us haven't got tickets.'

She was not at all worried by this omission. 'It was so offensive the last time we went to a game – Scotland v France – that we left at half-time. We arrived a little after it started. Ros (from Auchterarder, who works for a middle-eastern gentleman) was shouting daft things like: "Why don't they all have a ball" and "Come on France!" A few women round about us laughed but the men said: "Oh, I hate it when women get tickets and they don't know anything about it." We were having a good time and enjoying ourselves but they weren't having any of it. They were aggressive and swearing. It was quite offensive actually.'

The indissoluble silliness of women's remarks at ball games has ever been irksome to men, who are, of course, waging a kind of war in their own minds. However, it was difficult to be entirely sympathetic to the cause of male high-minded seriousness when the next two men to walk through the gates were wearing full tartan regalia except in the sporran region. Two Sooty hot water bottles hung in place of the more traditional attire.

It would also be fair to say that not all the males clustered there doubted womankind's ability to comprehend the glorious game of rugby. Roddy Dunlop, for one, had once refereed a match in which Kim Littlejohn, the captain of the Scotland women's rugby team, had played. 'Kim went into a tackle so hard, the girl she hit started crying. As a referee it was quite awkward. Kim caught her right under the breast and she was lying there at my feet. I thought: "What the hell do I do? Rub it better?"'

This neatly explains the problem of women at rugby. It's so male. 'It's a men's thing,' said Marjorie Waddell, whose husband had been reserve for Scotland on their wedding day. 'So he was either going to marry me or play.'

So, what was the conclusion from a day out at Murrayfield? That women are tolerated at these great events, but not necessarily encouraged. But there is a footnote: the post-match festivities would be lost without us.

'D'youknowwhoyouremindmeof,' slurred a bewildered-looking bloke in an England shirt (not Will Carling) on his way back from the bar in Ryries. I said I didn't know who I reminded him of and braced myself for the revelation. 'Stephanie out of *Baywatch*,' he pronounced. Now I was not entirely sure who or what Stephanie out of *Baywatch* might be, but one had to suspect that a very small swimming costume and very large silicone implants came into the equation somewhere. In which case, it struck me that his alcohol consumption must have been somewhere near heroic that night. Delusions like that don't come cheap.

RUGBY TYPES

The justification for rugby is getting lashed in decent cities.
                    Paul Ackford, former England lock, 1996

Rugby is a sport that invites men to sellotape their ears to their head and run amok in strict formation. But that is only a dictionary definition. As with all sports, it is the unfettered spirit that counts, especially when served by a barmaid of no mean attribute.

This, of course, implies that rugby union is played by violent alcoholics, somewhat oversized for their age. This is a wicked lie. Some of them, like scrum halfs, are quite small. Indeed, there is a pleasing logic and democracy about a sport that can cater so well for such dramatically variant shapes and sizes. It is to a prop forward's advantage, for instance, to be shaped like a brick-built coal bunker and share an IQ with a lump of nutty slack. A back, on the other hand can be as cerebral as you like, brighter, lighter, faster, trickier. Swamp Thing meets Tinkerbell.

If one supposed for a moment that female support of rugby union owed anything to the gamut run between no-necked hulks and dainty-footed whizz-kids, it might help to explain the sport's burgeoning popularity and television deals. This may not be remotely true given womankind's traditional high-mindedness. On the other hand, Will Carling's legs did become a major female preoccupation for a while. It would perhaps be foolish to deny that the structure of the player as well as the structure of the game has enormous appeal to those of the female persuasion. In that case, for the uninitiated, a short guide may be in order, all the better to spot talent when you see it.

Hooker – The snarling pit bull terrier of the team whose job it is to hook the ball back through the scrum and intimidate the bone marrow out of every rival back just by being there, glaring and unmuzzled. Built on the squat side, he may be taller lying down, which he often is.

Brian Moore was a hooker. He once challenged a new-found friend to a drinking contest. 'I'll drink this one,' he said, brandishing a bottle of red wine. 'And you drink that one.' Moore did. The friend didn't, sinking to the floor with a third remaining in the bottle. Moore tried to drag him back to consciousness to finish the offending dregs. 'Leave him alone, you animal,' said the distraught wife of the coma victim. 'Haven't you done enough?' That is a hooker.

Props – There are loose-head and tight-head props, which sounds vaguely like a prediction of their physical state after a succession of scrums. These gentlemen are usually conspicuous by their very long arms and almost total lack of neck, which may have been lost on some far-flung field in a previous match.

They are not all insensitive brutes, however. Sean Lynch, the Irish forward, had such a deep-rooted terror of spiders that the day a kind friend and team-mate threw a rubber insect at him on the bus going to a match, he leapt so high in the air in terror his head went through the baggage rack.

Locks – Otherwise known as second row forwards, they are the tall guys of the team, frequently off-duty policemen. I met a Scotsman at Murrayfield who had a theory about this. 'England have a machine that stretches 6ft 5in men until they're 6ft 11in and then they put them in the police force,' he said, whisky in hand. 'They tell them to bash the minorities from Monday morning to Friday night and on Saturdays they bash the Celts.'

Number 8 and the Flankers – It is said that brain is now intruding on the brawn, and a trusting nature would seem to be the key asset in this position. Any man willing to shove his head up near the backside of his team-mates in the scrum must have a great deal of faith in their personal habits. But we should not be surprised. The scrum is the physical incarnation of male bonding.

The half-backs – The intelligentsia of the rugby team. The fly-half thinks he is in charge. The scrum-half knows he is in charge. The latter is the easier of the two to spot on the field, by virtue of his pocket size. His job is to retrieve the ball from the scrum and pass it to the fly-half (or stand off) who, like the quarterback in American Football, is regarded as the senior playmaker. This is a sexy position. 'When we won the league championship, all the married guys on the club had to thank their wives for putting up with the the stress and strain all season,' said Joe Namath, New York Jets quarterback. 'I had to thank all the single broads in New York.'

Wingers – The speed merchants. Rory Underwood, an RAF jet pilot, was the archetype for England. Then Jonah Lomu of the All Blacks was invented. At that point all comparisons between wingers and whippets became redundant. Now and forever the most apt zoological metaphor would be a charging rhinoceros.

Centres – The sworn enemy of the flankers, these are the cerebral functionaries of the back line. Once again the words 'in theory' require insertion. For although Will Carling, who made his name at centre for England (and in a Chelsea gym, to be fair), passed A levels in English, Geography and Economics, he was rarely accused of being a dry academic.

Full-back – In theory, the goalkeeper, protected from the mêlée by his withdrawn position. In fact, the man most likely to be trampled. How does one qualify for the post? 'The reason I played full-back was because I wore glasses and couldn't see,' said a former schoolboy prodigy. 'If you can't see what's steaming towards you, you can't be afraid.' But you can learn. He's in banking now.

☆ ☆ ☆

Of such characters the wonderful game is comprised. But as any discussion with a rugby aficionado will prove, the main attraction of the sport is not the tactics but The Tour. Going away, *en masse* and insensible, is what it's all about. In quaint bygone days, when women knew their place (and it wasn't in the second row), the men had the frivolity of the tour to themselves. No more. Women have learned to join in.

'We were playing drinking games on the ferry coming back from the Ireland–Scotland game in 1995,' said Ann, better known as Ann-and-tonic in her capacity as a staunch supporter of the Scots away. 'I had to drink Baileys with vodka and tonic. And it curdled. There was Bovril in it as well I think. I wasn't sick, exactly, afterwards, but I did have to go out for some fresh air. Those were the days,' she said almost wistfully, 'when I didn't need to get my stomach pumped afterwards.'

Women are gaining respect. In the clubhouse at Edinburgh Wanderers a plaque stands over the bar. 'It took God six days to make the earth, then he rested,' it says. 'Then he made man and rested again. Finally he made woman. Since then no bugger ever rested.'

This is sheer old-fashioned posturing. The fact is that when certain male players from the club were obliged to share a bus with a women's team on tour, the men were by no means the sorrier of the two. 'Everyone got a wee bit drunk,' said a male witness. 'One of the girls had committed the heinous tour crime of swapping her team shirt with a young Welshman on the disco dance floor the night before, so she was ordered to strip off to her bra and pants and hop up and down the bus, singing "I'm a goblin". She did this, and it turned into a bit of an orgy. All the girls started stripping off to the tune of 'Singing in the Rain' ... and,' he said, glancing round nervously, 'I don't think I want to say any more actually.'

Whether rugby women are as bad, or indeed worse, for drink as their male counterparts is one of those points which will never be resolved. In masculine minds, there is no contest: 'If the girls get as drunk as the men, it doesn't work,' said a man on a train bound for Murrayfield. 'They let themselves down a bit. I think we've got a higher standard of drunkenness.'

The women don't see it as a contest either. 'I think we're fairly horrific,' said Clare, Ireland supporter and nurse. 'But men are worse because they get so trashed they don't make any sense. We never sink quite to the same depths when we're pissed.'

Either way those depths and depravations are an inexpungible part of rugby's innocent attraction and there are many ways a drink-fuelled rugby sort can enjoy him/herself while away from the domestic rein.

Furniture Removal – On the 1974 British Lions tour to South Africa, the great Willie John McBride had graduated from one of the lads to elder statesman of the team. He looked on, but rarely joined in. On one particular night, the manager of the team hotel was becoming rather concerned for the safety of his fixtures and fittings in the hands of 30 hairy, hulking and, by now, rather boisterous players. 'I have to tell you,' said the hotel manager anxiously, 'that I shall be forced to call the local police if this carries on.' McBride looked at the manager and puffed gently on his pipe. 'Tell me this,' he said finally. 'Will there be many policemen?'

Exaggerated Behaviour – Moss Keane, the monster lock from Kerry, gained 41 caps for Ireland and one ardent admirer from Australia the day he engaged her in idle conversation. 'Scuse me, are you the Moss?' enquired a petite, blonde Aussie girl of the second rower. He agreed to the charge. 'You know,' she said, 'you are one hell of big man.' He assented again. With her eyes barely reaching his belt buckle, she further enquired: 'Are you all in proportion?' He was forced to admit he was not. The light died in her eyes, only to be rekindled when he said: 'If I was in proportion I'd be 9ft 10in.'

Pure Escapism – Concern was voiced by a gentleman of the cloth at an emergency AGM of the Limerick Bohemians when 72 players went on a weekend tour of Amsterdam for a sevens tournament (at which they were knocked out in the first round), one mere week after they had failed to drum up a second XV to play Carrick-on-Shannon 15 miles down the road. 'Well,' said a member of the Amsterdam party, 'to the best of my knowledge, father, there are no whores in Carrick-on-Shannon.'

☆ ☆ ☆

And finally, never let it be said that the supporters of rugby are any poorer for ideas of enjoying themselves. The infamous 'Sad' of Kirkcaldy, one of Scottish rugby's most dedicated followers, told me in tones of hushed reverence about his brush with the England supporter of his dreams.

He was queueing outside a kebab shop in Chatham as part of the festivities surrounding England v Scotland 1995. They noticed a BMW, containing a smartly dressed young Englishwoman, pull up at traffic lights beside the shop. It was an invitation too glaring to resist. Sad and his pals decided to stage a spontaneous anti-Sassenach protest. Lifting eight kilts in unison, they mooned the occupant of the car but they had seriously misjudged their prey. In a flash (as it were), the woman was out of her car and round to the pavement where she ripped down her leggings and mooned them back. She had a red English rose tattooed to her left buttock.

'Never,' said Sad, 'have I been upstaged by a woman! What could we do? We just bowed at her feet and chanted: "We are not worthy."'

THE ULTIMATE ACCOLADE

Congratulations, Marilyn. But why marry one ball player when you could have had the whole team?
Mae West, on the news that Marilyn Monroe was marrying Joe DiMaggio of the New York Yankees

The blonde and the ball-player is an integral part of Western culture: Billy Wright and a Beverley Sister, Gazza and Shazza, Marilyn Monroe and Joe DiMaggio. Mae West, famously, had her doubts about such unions but they remain an enduring feature of ball-game lore.

Never, however, did they reach the zenith of 1995, when a modern-day knight in shining armour (the captain of the England rugby union team) was rumoured to be seeing a modern-day princess (Diana, Princess of Wales). The relationship of Will Carling and Princess Di was a social phenomenon waiting to happen. As royalty descended notch by notch in national esteem and grandeur, so sportsmen had been mounting (as it were) step by step in public regard and celebrity. There was always a chance they would meet in the middle. And they did. In a gym in Chelsea.

The trysts, if they could be called such, are long past, and both parties remained studiously silent. All we know is that Diana (House of Windsor) prompted Julia (house in Putney) to ask Carling for a divorce. The degree and intensity of the relationship is no longer an issue. What remains a source of legitimate sporting speculation is what did a princess see in a player?

Carling was not, of course, your sozzle-brained, vegetable-eared, bawdy-singing oaf of rugger-bugger legend. He was officer-class, originally destined for Sandhurst, whose shy and sensitive side had been revealed in the poems 'Love' and 'Mutual Evolution' that he wrote for his public school magazine. Plus he had modelled, oiled-up and semi-naked, for a glossy magazine. A princess abreast of the news may have noticed such details.

The news of their liaison, whatever its nature, fed the scandal sheets for weeks. But few mentioned the sheer predictability of it all. If the Princess was in search of a prince worthy of the name, she could look no further than rugby. Indeed, where else in the realm of sport could her eye have possibly alighted?

Whilst the captaincy of the England football team had fallen to the miraculous Gary Lineker, others before and since have suffered a more turbulent history. Few are destined for Sandhurst. One in living memory has been jailed for drunk driving and was also implicated in a pizza parlour skirmish when a fire extinguisher was, accidentally or otherwise, let off. Some, quite a lot actually, drop their aitches.

The England cricket team, though clad in swathes of white (when not in their pyjamas), presented an altogether more satisfactory class of swain, but one or two captains in recent history may have strayed a little too far from the path of righteousness. The former England cricket captain and the barmaid springs to mind. The former England cricket captain and Miss Barbados. The former England cricket captain and the Tiger Moth. Then, of course, the reigning England cricket captain at this time had a Mancunian accent.

There remained only a few ball games to choose from. Hockey? Too obscure. Rugby league? Too northern. Polo? Major Hewitt. Charles, for that matter.

Rugby union was the natural choice. On the cusp of professionalism, it still radiated a Corinthian charm, its practitioners imbued with a spirit of vigour and duty with no great sponsor's logo daubed across their shirts. This, however, makes it sound as though Brian Moore, the pit-bull hooker of the era, would have been a suitable companion for a princess.

In fact, only the captain would do. It must be significant that in their reported telephone chats, her pet name for him was 'Captain'. While no princess worthy of the name would ever admit as much to herself, it would not have been the same thing at all to fraternise with a tight-head prop.

And there was one other attraction, surely. Carling's sweet face only slightly inclining towards pudge, his cleft chin and his spectacular armoury of brawn had always been alluring to women. Huge fascination centred around reports that his legs were so muscular he couldn't cross them.

He remarked on this himself. 'There were married women, enclosing pictures and saying: "Please call this number when my husband is out, then come round." I used to open all my mail, but I was so shocked at some of the explicit things I read, I now ask that the letters are opened before they get to me. I'm not a great flirt. I can't handle women coming on.'

Once the captain and the Princess had discovered mutual interests, on the bench press or wherever at the Harbour Gym, their friendship must have flowed from empathy.

Both were somewhat separated from their peers by circumstance. Both had been elevated in rank from their starting point in life and discovered that, as nature dictates, the rarified air of altitude makes it rather hard to breathe at times.

'There was now this line between me and the players,' said Carling. 'Not them and us. But me and them. Whatever they might say, they expected me to set the standards, to behave in a certain way, and that was a terrible realisation for me at that age. I couldn't be one of the boys anymore.'

It did not help, in either situation, that the Establishment – the House of Windsor in one case and the Rugby Football Union in the other – appeared less than enamoured by the conduct of their most famous and glamorous, and as they would see it, wayward charges. Princess Diana appeared on BBC1's *Panorama* to vent her spleen on the royals, precipitating talk of a divorce. Carling called the RFU a bunch of 'old farts' during a television interview, precipitating his swift and metaphorical beheading. He was swiftly reinstated by public outrage. But the Princess and the ball player were united in rebellion, if nothing else.

Carling had often been the *bête noire* of the House of Twickenham. They perceived in him a vulgar thirst for money. He ran his own business and advertised Quorn (a food product that the Old Farts might have confused with a hunting term). He talked wistfully of professionalism. He had an agent. He was a dangerously modern prodigy.

Just so the Princess. The clothes, while far frumpier than rock-pop PR Julia Carling's, were still several cuts more curvacious than the straight-and-stumpy modes favoured by the Queen. Cleavage and blatant photogenic awareness were apparent. She had also, of course, been having an affair with a Major who played polo. She was an even more dangerous modern prodigy.

So they met and prospered in mutual understanding. Carling was no stranger to royalty. The Princess Royal had been Scotland's patron for years, singing 'Flower of Scotland' with almost treasonable gusto. Edward had been called upon to declare the 1991 Rugby World Cup open, the Queen had attended the final at Twickenham and Carling might even have said, 'Pass the salt, your Majesty', when invited to lunch at Buckingham Palace. 'I've sat down with the Queen and six guests. It's quite scary. I've met Prince Charles as well. I feel very privileged. That's all come from rugby.'

The meeting with Prince Charles almost certainly predated the assignations with Princess Diana and so was unlikely to include a conversation of the 'Was that my wife I saw you with last night?' variety. Its mention merely stresses the aristocratic circles in which our finest sports celebrities are now required to mix. Collision was inevitable and indicative of a new world order where sportsmen now rank with royals.

We will never know exactly what she saw in him. Fellow-feeling and a sympathetic (well-sculpted) shoulder, perhaps. He had the right number of names (William David Charles Carling), the right birthplace (Wiltshire), the right background (father Bill was a lieutenant-colonel in the Air Corps) and the right education (Sedbergh). He was of the right stuff. Ahem.

We will never know exactly what he saw in her, although blondes were always his thing. Julia, his wife at the time, noticed this. 'Will doesn't like it when I say his friends are all the same, the rugby stereotype. It's like the blonde he has to have on his arm, the ultimate prop.'

Perhaps Carling just went for the ultimate blonde.

WILD WEST WOMEN

Serious sport has nothing to do with fair play. It is bound up with hatred, jealousy, boastfulness, disregard of all rules and sadistic pleasure in witnessing violence: in other words it is war minus the shooting.

George Orwell, *The Sporting Spirit*, 1945

When Tommy Little talks about his work, it's enough to make the strongest stomachs heave. Blood-caked faces, contorted limbs, fractured bones, broken noses, blackened eyes. He is a dramatic story teller. You can almost hear the howls of agony and the splintering of bone as he speaks. Is he a war photographer? people often ask him. Not exactly, he replies. 'I coach the West of Scotland women's rugby team.'

For reasons that society has yet to fully come to terms with, women are taking up rugby with a vengeance. At least 18 of them turn up faithfully two nights a week to train at West's ground just outside Milngavie, north of Glasgow. It is frequently raining, invariably freezing, and sometimes sleeting for variety's sake. The squelch of mud and the thwack of bodies accompanies the cries of the coaches. Nicknames are tossed around like cabers at the Highland Games.

'Anyone seen Sicky yet?' says Tommy. Sicky? 'Yeah, Sicky Vicky, the scrum-half. Seven stone when she's wet through. Allergic to dairy foods. We covered her entire car with cheese slices once. She couldn't go near it.' As we speak, Vicky Ellis arrives. 'Hiya, Sick,' says a teammate. Already out there on the training pitch are Squidgy (she looks like Princess Di), Plod (a policewoman, obviously), Armpit, The Islander and Roger Rabbit (perhaps best not to inquire). The four male coaches encourage and abuse in equal parts.

'She runs better than Ann,' says Andy 'Coops' Cooper, the senior coach, of a new and generously porportioned recruit. 'Mind you,' he adds, 'Ann's got a broken toe.' Ian Busby, 'Buzz', is another senior coach and Colin Wallace is also helping out tonight, receiving coaching in return from the wing forward on how to get on *Blind Date*. He has his audition next month.

The girls are a classic case of all-sorts: students, secretaries, physiotherapists, nurses and a couple of farmers among them. Tommy is sure one of them has a cattle farm because didn't Shona say only the other week: 'I cannae play, Tommy, a coow's stood on me foot.'

It becomes evident why recruitment becomes an obsession. Tommy has devoted months to trying to persuade the sweetest-natured children's nanny of his acquaintance to become a player. 'But Tommy,' she said reasonably, 'why would I want to do that when you're always talking about those terrible injuries?'

'It's all right,' he said. 'You can be a back.'

Coops is, if anything, worse. He has been known to accost strange women in Safeway's. 'I was at the check-out on one occasion with the wife when I suddenly saw this hand reaching out for the "Next Customer" sign. I thought: "Bloody hell, that's a decent-sized hand." So I turned round to take in this very powerfully built woman. Well-proportioned, but a strongly built woman all the same. I said: "Have you ever thought about playing rugby?" Well, my wife disowned me and the woman turned me down flat. But I still see her. I always manoeuvre my trolley to be near her and have a chat. She's still turning me down, but you never know.' Perennial hope is a fundamental necessity to those associated with women's rugby. It is not easy to subvert the laws of man-made nature by insisting on the rightness of women knocking seven bells out of each other and being proud to be called a hooker.

At West's, even four years after the foundation of the women's club (and 130 years since the formation of the men's club), there are voices of dissension emanating from the unisex club bar. 'Well, some of the older members were a bit surprised and shocked that women should want to play rugby,' said Alasdair Burnet, the club president. 'Some still are. I felt it was a bit much for women, myself. It's a male sport. They'll call me a male chauvinist but they're not built physically to play rugby. There's lots of other games that women can play but it just seems that women just want to do everything men do. To prove some sort of point. Hockey's okay. Even football. But rugby's different. It's like boxing. It's ludicrous. The next thing women will want to do is box.'

Frank Hogarth, a long-time member and past president of the club, was in possession of a theory that women could damage their reproductive potential by playing rugby. 'They leave their fertility on the field,' he said ominously.

The women's team and their coaches have become reasonably inured to the objections. 'The coffin-dodgers just don't accept it,' said Tommy. 'They say: "Women shouldn't be allowed to play football. They should be at home looking after the kids." I've had those sort of things said to me on numerous occasions. Questions have been asked about the players' sexuality as well. Why did they want to play a male game? Did they want to be men? Obviously in female sport, you get a lot of people who are gay. We've got some gay players here, but we don't bother. If they can play rugby that's all we're interested in. But some people at the club say: "Tommy, Tommy, is this you out with your dykes!" It takes me all my time to keep quiet.'

Objections are not confined to sexuality and aesthetics. 'One thing that upsets me is the way they actually behave,' said Heather Burnet, wife of the president, soberly. 'They can get very drunk in here.' This takes some thinking about. You feel it pertinent to mention that the odd rugby-playing male has been known to take a pernod and lime, or somesuch, following an England–Scotland international from time to time. 'Drunk men and drunk women are different,' insisted Mrs Burnet. 'Drunk women just appall me. It is something I just abhor. And they really do go over the limit. Sometimes we come to dine in the restaurant and they're over in the corner, and it's just an unacceptable side, I think.'

It will evidently take a while before the sense of invasion by foreign bodies is supressed in most of those rugby clubs that have been persuaded to take on a women's section. Meanwhile, a number of traditionalists probably avert their eyes when they walk by the noticeboard proclaiming the women's forthcoming attractions. A placard on the subject of the 'West Girls Ski Sunday': was prominently pinned to the board on this occasion, with an eye-catching sub-text. 'NB', it said. 'To those requiring equipment (ooerrr!!!) I need to know your height and weight but since some people would not want their weight on the noticeboard (Tommy, Thelma . . . etc) you can whisper it to me when you pay your deposit.' There was also a reminder that the forwards' training would include 'rucking, mauling, scrummaging and lineout' – a fitting description, it would transpire, of their recent tour to Dublin.

There is little point in denying that women's rugby is peopled by those who tend to enjoy a Guinness at half-time. Do not take my word for it, ask the utility player. 'We travelled on the boat on Thursday night. Drank most of the time. Had about two hours sleep. We had a rule that you weren't allowed to drink non-alcoholic drinks after 9.30

in the morning. Then we had a game at three. We were absolutely rotten.

'We were told if we were going to be sick, we had to come off the pitch and people were coming off at half-time and drinking Guinness. We won 23–0. And then of course we celebrated well into the night.

'One girl just decided she would take photos of as many men's genitals as she could, if she could persuade them to lift up their kilts. I think she got about 16 in one night. We wondered if we pinned them up on a board whether they'd actually pick out their own. We thought they'd just plump for the largest and say that was theirs and categorically deny that the smallest was anything to do with any of them. We didn't put it to the test, I hasten to add.'

Since the speaker is Penny Latin, a highly articulate, well-educated producer-reporter for the BBC, it is evident that women's rugby is no more the province of dangerous oafs than is the male code. Dangerous yes, but not oafs.

'I didn't really drink a lot before I played rugby. I sort of despised it. I had a boyfriend who played a lot of football and they'd go out and get roaring drunk and I'd look down my nose at it in horror. I hated him for it. I couldn't see the fun in it. But when you're in a team, it's such a different thing. No-one needs to get drunk to have a laugh but we do have an outrageous time. It's like there's no limits. The boundaries of what's allowed and what's not allowed disappear. You set your own rules about what's decent. We say: "What goes on on tour, stays on tour."'

It would be easy, from the tenor of the conversation, to hobble away with the impression that women's rugby is the antidote to Alcoholics Anonymous, an Alcoholics United if ever there was one. It is not the physical challenge of drinking ten pints a night, however, that attracts the devotees, it is the physical challenge of the sport. Staying alive, and things like that.

'One of the best days of my life was the day I played a full 80 minutes – and lived,' said Gail Gyi, the team comedienne and sometime winger.

'The aggression and the power and the stamina is something that suits me physically. I'm quite an aggressive person and I can put that into the game,' said Penny.

'I love running full tilt into somebody I've never met before. Oh, it's great. The passion of it, the aggression of it. I've been in a game where a girl got bitten,' said Shiona McLeod, the 5ft 3in, 9 stone stand-off.

But if the unfettered robustness of it all is an attraction, so is the rare freedom to look and behave like *Just William* while a coach on the sidelines is shouting: 'Go on, Nae Tits, move yerself!' 'I think what I love most about the sport is that all kinds and shapes of people are acceptable,' said Ann Savage, a research scientist designing instruments for clinical diagnosis and the prop with a broken foot. 'I've always been a frustrated athlete. A lot of stout, fat people are.

'I tried rowing but I was too short and too heavy. I tried football but I couldn't turn quickly enough, couldn't run quickly enough and couldn't kick the ball. Then I tried rugby and I took to it.

'Some of the men I work with are in their 50s and 60s. I think they like women to do girlie things and wear high heels. A few have expressed disapproval, but their opinion in the end doesn't matter. My husband is very supportive and very encouraging and I don't think my parents were completely surprised. They'd have been far more shocked if I'd taken up figure skating.'

Apart from grit, determination and thighs of steel, there is not a great deal the average rugby player has in common with Jayne Torville. Tight-head props tend not to augment their smiles with lipstick or hand-sew sequins on to their jersey. When you're under a pile of ten bodies, with your face imprinted in the mud and several studs embedded in your bottom, smudge-proof mascara is the least of your worries.

'You don't care what you look like when you play rugby,' said Penny. 'You don't care that you're covered in mud. Sometimes you come in and you're black from head to toe and it doesn't matter. It's a very liberating experience for a woman.

'I've got rid of a lot of concerns about my body and appearance since I started playing. I used to have a problem with it. There were times when I didn't want to get dressed because I couldn't bear the way I looked. Definitely, I had a real problem with it. But here, everyone is treated equally, no matter what size and shape you are. If you're big you've got a valuable role to play that someone skinny couldn't.

'We're an unusual group of women. We're not competitive with each other about how we look. Society, women's magazines, they don't say that. It's all "skinny, skinny, skinny. Beautiful, beautiful, beautiful." Rugby is the opposite. The women are very close. There isn't any bitching. It doesn't seem to exist.'

There is, however, Gail. Gail not only exists, she is a force of nature. In her own estimation she is a winger, the female answer to Jonah Lomu. 'Gail,' said Tommy, wearily, 'the only thing you've got in common with Jonah Lomu is your colour.' On this particular day, Gail was not training. She had broken her ankle in three places during a game at

Dalkeith and was enjoying a period of recuperation, largely in the bar.

Gail and rugby collided by accident. 'I went to a softball game on Glasgow Green,' she said in her strong 'arrogate accent, augmented by Cockney after 12 years in London. 'But it was too organised and regimented for me. Then they wanted me to play in a red tracksuit and that was the last straw. But while I was there I met Kirsty and Ann-Marie, two girls who play 'ere, and they said: "Ooh, you look like you could play rugby. Come and watch." And the next thing you know, you've got boots and you're playin'.

'I'm playin' it really to get fit but it's a lot more physical than I'd imagined. Look at these,' she said displaying a set of fingernails of which Cruella De Vil could be proud. 'I used to have real long nails. All like this but they cut them off in rugby. The referee comes along and cuts them because if they're too long they could scratch somebody's eye out. There's no underwire bras allowed either because girls can stick 'em in you.

'Well, I wear underwire bras and I said to the ref the other day: "How are you going to check? Just you try it and I'll have you for assault, mate." He was laughing. He was good fun actually.'

Men, those with an interest in survival anyway, know to be nothing but good fun around Gail. She has rarely encountered anyone with the gall and rashness to criticise her hobby. 'I think men are fascinated more than anything. They look at you twice and you can see 'em thinking: "Well, she doesn't look butch," because it's still got this butchiness associated with it, rugby. And then when they get over that and decide you're not, their fascinated and want to know all about it.'

This even applies to Derek, the boyfriend, who once became more closely associated with women's rugby than was entirely good for him. 'It were against Edinburgh Accies when I played me first ever 80 minutes. Usually I'm only on for about 40 minutes or whatever, but this time we were dead short and they said: "You've got to go on." We were totally the underdogs and we won.

'Well, Derek, who'd never seen me play before, got the shock of his life. I had mud all over me, gumshield in, ears taped back, scratches and bruises, shin pads on, nails filthy, hair like the Wild Woman of Borneo. I looked like hell. Derek had to be the linesman because the real one hadn't turned up and I pushed him out of the way once. I just didn't see him. "Do I know you?" he said, when 'e'd struggled back to 'is feet. I thought it would put 'im off me but he was quite thrilled really.'

But for the time being, the thrill was all young Colin's, the assistant coach. Gail, in her celebrated role as a former participant of *Blind Date*, ITV's social phenomenon fronted by Cilla Black where men choose women for dates and vice versa, was coaching him for his audition.

'Did you get chosen when you were on?' everyone wanted to know.

'No, 'e chose number two, din't 'e? But they only went to Dubai. I said: "Dubai! I work for a travel agent. I could get there for ten pound."'

WIVES, WOMEN AND SONG

Marriage is not a word but a sentence.

Anon

Cyril put me right. Lulled into thinking that rugby had outgrown its boy-zone tendencies and matured into an appreciation of women as individuals, partners and soulmates – Cyril put me right. In a hostelry known simply as The Duck, nestling alongside a verdant village green, my man, every inch the former prop (but only if the team was very short that day), cleared his throat and launched into a rendition of one of his favourite rugby songs.

'Oh, how I love her baldy head,' he sang to the tune of the old French song 'Allouette'. 'How I love her baldy head. Baldy head. Baldy head. Oh, allouette . . . '

We progressed. Oh, how he loved her furrowed brow, her squinty eyes, her broken nose, her double chin, her swinging . . . and so it went on into ever-deepening vulgarity until he came to a rapt and final appreciation of her knobbly knees and webbed toes, with crashing communal choruses from all around him.

This was his rugby club's hymn to womankind, the same rugby club that went on tour to Leicester and had to stop at Lesmahagow, barely an hour out of Glasgow, to let the lads off to relieve themselves. There was a barley field alongside the coach and the next thing Cyril saw was one of his team-mates stark naked running through the field being chased by another member of the team.

That was *not* the same tour as the one when a player woke up to find himself in bed with the one-armed bandit from the hotel lobby. That was Mull. Also the scene of a memorable conversation. 'Do you fancy a shag?' said one of Cyril's mates to a young woman with whom he was dancing. 'Maybe later,' she said, gazing into his squinty eyes. 'But no' wi' you, pal.'

In the circumstances, the conjoining of rugby players and women for any length of time above ten minutes looks unlikely. But, if you think that, you are wrong. Despite all evidence and protestation to the contrary, a surprising number of male rugby players are having truck with the female of the species these days, even going so far as to marry them.

Rugby wives: one can only imagine how the very words must strike terror into the soul of Will Carling. After barely a year of marriage, the British public had an image of the England captain's chunky, dimple-kneed frame being torn apart between the manicured clutches of ex-friend Diana and ex-wife Julia. Once again, a sportsman's wife had come to occupy that position in life: My Least Favourite Opponent. But that ain't necessarily so.

Suzie Ackford runs three businesses, makes millions and is married to the former England lock, Paul Ackford. Laurie Redmond is a hooker and a mistress. But she has heard all the jokes before. In fact, she is a PE mistress who played hooker for Whitehall Rugby Football Club, which she founded, and is married to the former England international, Nigel Redmond. Neither strikes you as the type to have air between the earrings. Certain gentlemen in rugby, however, beg to differ.

'I can remember once arriving in the Twickenham carpark during the World Cup in 1991, myself and a colleague and Sharon Dooley [Wade's wife],' said Ackford (Mrs). 'We drove in and as per usual the majority of the people around us were men and they were appalled that we had tickets. They thought it was a complete waste. And yet we love the game, we understand the game, we feel we've actually given a lot to the game in the support we've given to our respective other halfs. But these men were very, very angry. "What the hell do you think you're doing here?" they said, 20-stone porkers from your local rugby club, all under the influence of alcohol.

'That's the one thing that repels me about rugby: the assumption that women are not really part of it. It's like some of the comments made by Will Carling in his biography. I was a little hurt by them.'

The comments in question contained Carling's philosophy on dealing with players' wives, quoted in his authorised biography. 'Wives can never be involved in team matters, but a few question selection. It's human nature: they want their man to be successful . . . Suzie Ackford, Sara Andrew and Karen Hill like to talk about matches with me. The safest thing is to agree with them . . . I'm pleased that they enjoy rugby, but discussing selection decisions with them is the last thing that I want,' said Carling.

'I'm hurt in that he sometimes sought out our opinion,' Suzie Ackford responded. 'I don't think he would ever admit that though.

Views are too entrenched in rugby. The fact that Will has to say he never listened to women's comments is a fairly good example. There's a general bonhomie about women coming to rugby. But there is no real belief that women understand it. And that view is held in the stands, in the carpark, across the board.'

Ditto Redmond (Mrs). 'I have had some dreadful experiences,' she said. 'At one point I was involved in the committee of the Women's Rugby Football Union and we were looking to host an international at one of the rugby clubs in the south-west. I approached a couple of the committee gentlemen at Bath where we had a good connection because Nigel played there. They said: "I've never heard of women's rugby." I said, fair enough, and spent ages talking them through it and our hopes to host a full international event, England v Wales. He said: "Well, I suppose we could possibly give you a ten-minute slot on the pitch before one of our home matches." I just looked at him and said: "I'm terribly sorry, but have you any idea how patronising you are?" We had it at Richmond in the end.'

To augment the classic slights, neither woman received her husband back from international rugby in the same condition she lent him. Ackford: 'He's had broken fingers, stitches in his face and he's got cauliflower ears.' Redmond: 'He's had both elbows operated on twice, knee operations, ankle operations and he's got very thin hair on top – well, he's bald to all intents and purposes – and his scalp looks like a map of the world with all the scars on it.'

But, when all is said and done-in, both women still harbour a love of the game undimmed by contemplation of their husbands' physical imperfections. 'It's a wonderful game,' said Redmond. 'There's nothing else like it, both as a spectator and a player. It involves so many skills as well as channelling physical aggression which I think all of us possess. Women can get as much pleasure out of it as men.'

'People tended not to want to sit near me because I did shout rather a lot when Paul played,' said Ackford. 'I certainly saw things that gave me heart palpitations but he never had a serious injury, thank goodness. He was knocked out once though.

'It was England v Argentina and there was a schoolboy playing for the Argentinians, I think he was a prop at the time, by the name of Mendez. What happened was this boy thought somebody had infringed on his personal space (he had his balls squeezed actually), so he turned round and hit the closest thing which happened to be Paul.'

Video footage of the event clearly shows the swinging fist, the jarring contact and the buckled knees of the 6ft 6in police inspector who was subsequently carried, prone, off the pitch. 'Paul was out like a light, completely unconscious. He became known as "Glass Jaw" after that. But I was nearly on the pitch with my umbrella, whacking this young man. "How dare you . . . ?"

'You do get rather caught up in it. There are quite a lot of occasions where Paul's come off shaking hands at the end and I won't speak to an individual because they tried to gouge his eyes out or punch him or whatever. I do tend to take it personally which is ridiculous. Purely emotional. Illogical.

'And I answered back, especially when I was with my mother-in-law, if people shouted abuse from the stands. I would turn round and say: "Excuse me, this is Paul Ackford's mother. Would you not say such things?" Usually they were very embarrassed. Rugby supporters tend to be very chivalrous, especially towards mothers. I think if I said: "I'm his wife," they'd just jeer at you and continue.'

Rugby-going foulmouths uttered words against the Underwoods at their peril. The mother of Rory and Tony Underwood became a celebrity in her own right, going so far as to star in a pizza commercial with Jonah Lomu, all thanks to the decibels and dervish impression she gave in support of her boys. Annie Underwood's legend almost threatened to surpass that of her sons' who were the first pair of brothers to play in an England team since the Wheatleys, Arthur and Harold, in 1938.

She has been one of life's irrepressible enthusiasts, moulded not in the environs of Twickenham but in the tiny village of Kuala Pilah, nestling in a valley in the Malayan jungle. Annie was the eldest of eight children who lived with their parents in a two-bedroomed house equipped with a very wide bed in the children's room so that all eight siblings could be accommodated side by side. Her father worked as a government clerk and her mother died when she was only 12, leaving Annie to become the surrogate mother to the brood. Her brothers and sisters called her 'Big Sister' with proper deference.

Her life was changed irrevocably. In her youth she had been a tomboy and was dressed as a boy by her father to whom she was a favourite, but the cooking, baking, washing and ironing restrained some of her more vigorous impulses and the nuns at her convent school did their best to expunge the rest of her less feminine exploits. She met the Englishman, James Ashley Underwood, when she started work as his shorthand typist in the Far East branch of Harrison Lister Engineering. 'No hanky panky,' she insists. They married and began the production line of little Underwoods, four altogether, two of whom would play on either wing for the England rugby team.

Rory, named in the wild west tradition after the actor Rory Calhoun, was the first to break into international rugby. 'Rory was even tough when he was a baby,' said Annie 'He was breast-fed by me for 11 months. It must be mother's milk that made him so tough. Trouble is, he drained me so much, I didn't have any left for the others.'

With or without mother's milk, the children enjoyed an idyllic childhood of glorious sunshine, endless sport and Sunday afternoon picnics in the jungle. 'I'd bring a small stove and fry bacon and eggs while the boys swam in the river. The smell of the cooking would bring out the butterflies. It was a lovely, lovely childhood.'

By the time Tony was eight, however, the family was obliged to move to England. It was a new world in every sense for Annie Underwood. It was cold, it rained and she met rugby. The boys were enrolled at a public school in the north-east that insisted on their pupils playing rugby and their mother became a fixture on the touchline. Schoolboy matches, colt matches, county matches: she was there. 'That was natural because I do shout,' she said. 'I ran up and down the touchline shouting: "Come on, darling!" Once a woman stopped and said to me: "Don't call rugby players darling!" And I said: "I call them whatever I like. That's my son."'

Ash Underwood died when Tony was only 13. 'It didn't seem to affect me so much at the time,' he said. 'It was later in life I found out how much I missed him. But my mother did and does fulfil a dual function. She brought us up by herself and she was the disciplinarian. She was strict and we were basically stifled to a point that was embarrassing. My mother couldn't accept the informality with which the sexes mixed over here. She wanted us to concentrate on studies and sport and forget about women. In Malaysia, girls are expected to be virgins when they marry. I gave my mother a lot of grief in my teens.'

Annie has always been unrepentant. 'I always believe when you go to school – no hanky-panky. Of course, I have mellowed as I get older. As long as they are happy, I am happy.'

'Now I am older, I can see that the protectiveness was her way of showing love,' said Tony. 'I feel I can never repay her. Rory feels the same. Our mother's happiness is really at the forefront of whatever we do.'

As evidence, he offers the story of his withdrawal, injured, from the field against South Africa in 1992. As he was being carried through the tunnel a television camera zoomed in on his prostrate form and clearly captured the word 'Shit!' on his lips. 'The first thing I thought of was my mother's reaction. The next time I saw her I was very sheepish, but to my surprise she was quite understanding. "Don't worry," she said, "but I'm glad you didn't use the F word."

SUPER LEAGUE

On the chest of a barmaid in Sale
Were tattooed the prices of ale
And on her behind
For the sake of the blind
Was the same information in Braille.

                                                                                      Anon

The oop-north phenomenon of rugby league has seemed quintessentially male down the century. Women have been the honorary jock-straps of the sport – they can do no more than offer their support. The barmaid in Sale would have been required to pull the pints for the players as opposed to pulling on the shorts to play herself.

Then the Super League happened. Flash names (Bradford Bulls, London Broncos, Sheffield Eagles), a summer schedule, a female president of the rugby league. Women were busting out all over. About time, a rich seam of passionate involvement with the game had been tapped.

Deep in the annals of recorded time it transpires that women were playing the game themselves. 'We first tried to start a rugby team just after the Great War, when there was a pit strike on. We organised a game up at the Rovers' fields but it ended with men complaining so we had to play soccer instead. Then in 1921, when there was another strike, we decided it was rugby or nothing, ignored what the men had to say about it and went ahead,' said Mrs Alice Brear of the women of Featherstone who formed their own rugby league touring team. 'It was Mrs Williams who set it off, a big woman who lived in Mashams Square. There were lasses from all over though. I played a prop forward and a woman from Pontefract was the goal kicker. She could kick as well as any man and she'd only one eye.'

In 1996, they reckon about 550 women, one-eyed or otherwise, play organised rugby league. The problems haven't changed much: menfolk scathing, women reluctant and babysitters required for the bairns. But nothing an iron will and desperation cannot overcome.

'At 22 I had two small children, two broken marriages and was utterly dependent on social security. We lived on thirty pound a week,' said Jackie Sheldon of the Wakefield Panthers, the only woman in Britain to hold rugby league's highest coaching qualification. 'I come from Featherstone and a big family where most of the men played rugby league. My three brothers played, my three cousins played. One of them played professional with Featherstone and Bradford Northern. My great grandma was a tremendous Featherstone supporter. She used to watch all their games on the television, so my Mum told me.

'When Featherstone won the Cup I was only small and I can remember the whole town going down to Wembley to watch. We'd been in school all week making banners and decorations for the match. But playing the game was something I'd never dreamed of. I was always quite a big person and although I liked running about and being active, I was embarrassed about my size and shape. I played netball, but I was embarrassed about my legs.

'I left school at 16 when I married. We had Leanne but it didn't work out. I got married again but my second husband walked out when I was seven months pregnant. We were living with his father at the time. We had just been given a council house because I was pregnant, but we hadn't moved in yet. We were still living down Weldon Road just behind Castleford rugby league ground with his father. But my husband decided he wanted me out of the house. He had found somebody else, I think. He hired a van and moved me and Leanne, my daughter, that night. There were carpets in the house but not much else.

'When I had the baby he came back. We had a reconciliation but he buggered off when Craig was two months old. I think it was for the best, now. At that point I was very dependent but I'm so fortunate to have got out of it, to be honest. I hung on to the wrong sort of people. Now I've got a lot more sense. I'm a lot more independent now and sport's helped me a lot. Of course it has.

'But for a while, when the second marriage ended, I was really down in the dumps. I had nothing. He'd been unemployed and after the first couple of years Leanne's father, my first husband, had stopped paying for her as well. I went to the social workers and said: "I just can't cope." And they said: "Look, come to the community centre and meet other women just like you." So I went and they were running very basic introductions to sport aimed at getting women, the unemployed and the disabled into some kind of activity.

'I went round and had a go. I'd lost weight by now, down from 14 stone to about nine. I had a go, liked it. I took an exercise to music course which would let me teach keep-fit to other women. It was partly funded by the education department but I needed to raise money myself. The women, the one-parent families and their kids, helped. They did sponsored walks, swims, anything to help and they raised £200 for me.

'In the end, the Warwick Panthers women's rugby team was formed by accident. They just emerged from a taster session run by the local authority to introduce women to a variety of sports. Redhill women's team was another one. We've been playing six years now and won the Cup five consecutive years and the National Division title five consecutive years as well. In the whole history of the club, we've only been beaten once. By Redhill, in the league. By two points. I don't want to take anything away from them, but we played terrible that day.

'My best moments are when I come off the pitch and think: I did really well today. I played for Yorkshire once and got the player of the match award. I think that shocked a few people because I think there were a lot of better players than me but it was my workrate in that particular game.

'I've played all over. I've played hooker, I've played centre, I'm a real utility player. But my main position is second row. I feel I play a better game in there. You don't get a right lot of injuries. I've never been hit in the scrum. The only main thing I've broken is my wrist during the first Cup final I ever played. I had to be taken to hospital and potted up. But I don't like talking about injuries. It's not about that, rugby.

'It's just great fun to get out there. It's a relief to go training on a Friday night. Just forget about work, forget about home. I can leave everything behind and do what I want for that hour.

'On a match day I get up, have me breakfast, get the kids ready, run round, throw all me stuff in me bag, get me boots, get me gumshield and toddle off. There's not a lot of time before matches. Craig, my son, comes with me. My daughter, Leanne, used to come with me but she's old enough now to go and see a friend. But Craig – he's 11 – comes regular. He actually runs on with the water and the sponges. He comes on the pitch at half-time as well. He comes to stand next to me while we're having a team talk at half-time. He's a good supporter. He always tells me if I've done something wrong.

'After the match, we all socialize quite well. We go down the Travellers pub in Featherstone, just along the road from the High School where we play our matches. It's run by Tommy Smales, the old Great Britain rugby league player who played for Halifax and Bradford

Northern. He's good to us. We meet the supporters. We get quite a lot. Mums and dads of the girls' team come down. We don't get big crowds. About 50 or 60 on some days if we're playing in a Cup semi-final. Other days we might just get two or three. The *Wakefield Express* and the *Pontefract and Castleford Express* carry our reports regularly. We write them and send them in. The *Yorkshire Post* has mentioned us as well, not as much as we'd like though.

'Because it's such a male-dominated sport, it's this thing that you shouldn't be playing it. No-one comes out and says it, but it's underneath everything. It's unfeminine, they think, therefore you're unfeminine. And there's a lot of married women with families playing it, so it's not true it's a sport for lesbians. Not only gay people play rugby.

'I don't think you can change it. It's society in general and it will always be like that. There is nothing you can say or do to change it. Girls will always be put off by the image of rugby, by the tackling, by the fact it's a contact sport. But we have to just live with it. It doesn't mean women will stop playing. It will attract the sort of women who get over barriers: married, gay or whatever, the sort of women who don't give a bugger what other people think.'

They're straight-talkers who administer rugby league as well. Kathryn Hetherington, a founder and director of Sheffield Eagles and president of the rugby league, left no-one in any doubt about that when she became the first woman rugby league council member 12 years ago.

'I was seven months pregnant at the time and I was BIG. One or two of the men were a bit shell-shocked. Well, you could have rolled me down the street. Me daughter turned out to be nine-and-a-half pounds when she were born and I was carrying a lot of water.

'At the time one bloke, Bob Ashby from Featherstone Rovers, threw a tantrum and walked out. He said if that's the way things were going, he was going 'ome. You know, I can have some sympathy with the bloke, because he saw it as an all-male world and women had no place in it. But I'm good friends with Bob now. It didn't last long. He can laugh about it now.

'I was born into a rugby league family. I've four brothers. Three played professionally and the eldest, Gary Cooper, was 14 years older than me so by the time I was six he was playing. He used to take me places, point things out to me. It was like an education. He was a full-back. One of the 1962 Great Britain tour of Australia. It was a big thing in Featherstone.

'Then I married a rugby player, Gary Hetherington, and we eventually formed the Sheffield Eagles 12 years ago. As a player, Gary was mainly a hooker, but he could play in a lot of positions. That was his problem really. It worked against him. What club did he play for? Have you got an hour? Wakefield, York, Leeds, Huddersfield. He had one game for Wigan. About ten clubs altogether.

'Well, I've always been street-smart. You learn to dodge and weave. Before I left school – well, when I should have been at school – I used to work the markets with my brother. I've been in all aspects of selling, actually. Wholesaling, retailing, double-glazing. I was quite successful at that. I was the first woman to join the so-called quality club for selling so much.

'So then we decided to set up the Eagles. Gary had played for all those clubs but he was never happy politically. He never felt the set-up was right. He decided he might like to start up his own. But it was very, very difficult because the first week our backers went bust. Cable television. People don't realise the amount of hard work and heartache that's gone into this. If we hadn't had our background, I don't think we could have done it.

'Originally, Gary was going to be our representative on the council but they said you can't be, you're still a player. I think they wished they'd said, "Yes, come along!" when they realised I was the alternative. I wasn't that bothered about being on it, to be honest, until I realised they didn't want me. I can see why. I was a woman, I was married to Gary who was looked at as a bit of a "red under the bed" at the time and me brother was also considered a bit of a firebrand in 'is day. He was an intelligent bloke playing at a time when intelligence was looked upon with grave suspicion.

'Some were very supportive, I must admit. David Oxley, Reg Parker, who was chairman at the time. They realised the implications of me being knocked back from the council. But some didn't want me and they said so. One bloke in particular was against it because of my brother. He'd played with him and he wasn't any good was this fella. And me brother had continually told him so. Really tactful me brother, and I'm tarred with a bit of the same brush, actually.

'But now I'm president, I've been trying to heal a big rift between the Amateur and Professional game. It's not easy as you can imagine. It seems to be men's deep psychological need to dominate one another. I think women are more able to use their common sense. They're not ego-oriented.

'I don't call my working relationship with my husband "side-by-side". We're adjacent. He's got his way and I've got mine and they're not the same. I couldn't work with him day-in, day-out. I'd knife 'im.'

The smooth, sweet path of women in sport was ever thus. Even Mrs Williams and the Featherstone Ladies rugby team had their problems – like what to wear on the pitch. Their kit, pictured in old sepia photographs preserved for posterity, seemed to consist of striped jersey, bath hats and wide-rimmed skirts that modestly covered the prop forwards' knees.

'Well, you should have seen us,' said Alice. 'We had to use the Rovers' kit and boots and then walk down to the ground. We had a woman referee – and scores of men came to watch. I think the men enjoyed it after a while, although they made fun of us a bit and we didn't like bending down in front of them to scrum off.

'We played all over during that strike; Sharlston, Castleford, Ponte. They'd take up a collection for us, going round with a bucket, put on hot soup and buns for the strikers and dish out raffle tickets.

'It was a good thing while it lasted but it had its drawbacks. I used to have to leave the young 'uns with a woman down the street and she fed them up till I came back – but you can't carry on like that. The other thing was, having to walk home in your muck and fill the tin bath for a wash.

'We did it all again during the 1926 strike but there wasn't much call for women's rugby after that.'

Cricket

TEST MATCH

Ten out of eleven women care very little for cricket for cricket's sake, and though from the goodness of their hearts they insist on coming to the grounds ... it would be kinder to all concerned, and less like cruelty to animals, to leave them quietly at home.
D.L.A. Jephson

Lord's, day one of the England Test against India: the gatemen are famous at Lord's. They once refused to let Mike Brearley (captain of England at the time) through the Grace Gates although he was driving a car with the words 'Mike Brearley' written in bold letters along the side. But I must have struck lucky. Mine let me in.

'Are you sure you're you?' said my man sternly, examining my pass.

'Well, I was when I got up this morning,' I replied, 'but it was a bit early. I could be wrong.'

'Don't talk to me about early mornings. I was up at 5 a.m. The Mrs ...' He began to say, then obviously thought better of it. Hastily, he changed tack. 'I used to work for London Underground, so I'm used to getting up.'

I should have quit while I was ahead. 'Can you tell me where to go for the press box?' I asked.

'To hell and back,' he replied.

Still, there was nothing remotely sexist about this exchange. He was giving me a hard time because I was an animate object trying to gain admittance to Lord's, not because I was female. But only a dozen steps needed to be taken to find an act of chauvinism in progress.

Marie Bidwell, cricket lover and vice-president of an American bank, was laying out vast tracts of salad in a corner of the Members' lawn (Members of the MCC, that is, the justly famed Marylebone Cricket Club), putting the final touch to a splendid alfresco luncheon soon to be served to a number of her clients. She wore a floral dress, a blue beret and the serene expression of one who sees a picnic disposed about them and has already drunk a glass of champagne for starters.

'My husband's an MCC member and we're just doing a bit of entertaining,' she explained. 'I love cricket, love it, and I've got a ticket but, as it happens, my husband said he wanted a lot of baguettes. He doesn't realise it takes me an hour to put the butter on them. He thought they just – you know – arrive.'

'So the men have gone to watch the cricket and I'm here doing to the food. I don't mind. I enjoy doing picnics. Most British women do.'

I left her to the arrangement of grapes and mounted the stairs to the press box (the jaws of hell) just in front of Graham Gooch, another former England captain, who, true to tradition, was struggling to get past a steward. 'I don't think you're allowed up there,' the official was saying, but Gooch strolled boldly past him. If only he'd shown such devil-may-care against West Indian bowling.

We arrived in time to see the truly affecting moment when Dickie Bird, the famously eccentric umpire, came out to officiate in his 66th and final Test. It was a tumultuous and tearful farewell. The all-male contents of the Pavilion stood and applauded as he made his way down the steps, the teams formed a guard of honour as he stepped on to the pitch, all four corners of the ground rose to give him a standing ovation. He waved to left and right, soaked his hanky with tears and then gave Atherton out, lbw, fifth ball.

I knew who'd be watching this with mounting apprehension. 'All that extra washing, Sue!' she'd be saying. Marjorie Wyatt is Dickie Bird's sister and has looked after his washing (and everything else) for nigh-on 40 years. 'I've always done 'is washing, even when mother was living,' said Marjorie. 'Me mother used to say, "You do it better than me," and I've always done it. But it didn't seem as *mooch* then, in those days – you know – when 'e weren't on the Test panel. But now – oh dear. I get quite a lot of those overalls they wear, you know. I mean, they're quite 'eavy. Hard work, Sue. We'd be a good advert, wouldn't we, for soap powder?'

They'd be quite a good advert for familial bonding as well, she living on one side of Barnsley where they were both born and raised, he on the other side in a 17th-century cottage that Marjorie comes in when she can and 'does'.

'This is it, Sue, y'see. You can't work week to week with me broother. Even month to month actually. I've seen me go six weeks and then 'e's rung me up and picked me up and he's had these two *enormous* bags of washing. You're not just talking about these umpire's smocks and shirts, it's these thick socks they wear and, on the odd occasion, these white 'ats. Well, I'm not very successful with the 'ats.

'I iron everything as well. It's a bit embarrassing because of the creases, you know. The ironing leaves crease marks. But 'e says, it will be all right, they'll drop out, they're clean. I did notice though a few weeks ago, 'e was unpacking the washing and 'e was looking at all the shirt collars. I thought, "Yeah, you're looking for that black line, aren't you?" because they can be really black, can't they, white collars? So I scrub them.

'Oh no, 'e never complains, but he checks that they're white.'

Somehow you can tell that the Birds were brought up in a well-regulated household where their father was a miner and their mother a housewife. 'Women didn't do much else in those days. Mother was Pentecostal and father was Church of England and all three of us [including sister Sylvia] went to Sunday School.

'But growing up, the 'ouse'old were just domineered by sport. My sister and I were fed up of it all because me father doted on me broother, I think he was the favourite. They were football mad. Football and cricket. My memory is of the front room being cluttered up with cricket bags. Well, you know what size a cricket bag is. And stumps. And bats. On Saturday afternoons the television was *on* and it was *sport* and if you wanted to watch anything else it was *im*possible. You might as well not be in the room if sport was on. It caused some arguments.

'So as you got older and wanted to bring boys back 'ome, it was virtually impossible. Therefore, Sue, I'm not interested in cricket or football. I've never been to a cricket match in my life.'

In the end, however, Majorie did meet Mr Wyatt, a stone mason. They met at a dance in the local church hall. She was married at 24 and is still doing Dickie's washing.

'I clean the cottage too. It depends when 'e's home. It could be once a fortnight. It could be once a month. It depends when 'e's home, Sue, y'know. 'E's quite a tidy man. Not untidy at all, y'know. But 'e natters. Oh, 'e natters. And I think to myself, 'e makes these big important decisions on the cricket field and yet it's "Oh, Marge, the tap's drippin'. I can't stop the tap drippin'." I say, "Well, I'll do it. I'll see what's the matter." Then 'e'll say, "Look at the dust all over since the last time you were 'ere." Y'know. That sort of thing.

'But 'e washes his own cups up. 'E does hate making his own bed, though. 'E always says, "Tuck it all in *well*" – are you with me, Sue? – and then 'e can just slip the sheets back and sort-of slide in. Oh, 'e doesn't like makin' beds, it gets to 'im. Makin' beds and frying fish.

'I call 'im Dennis. I don't know how Dickie came about. The family name 'as always been Dennis. We went to a celebration last week in our 'ome town. There was a Lord and Lady either side of me, like, and I'm chattin' on. Dennis this and Dennis that. Finally the lady, she looked at me and said: "By the way, dear, who's Dennis?" I didn't realise, y'know.

'I do think 'e's forfeited such a lot for cricket. But I don't think 'e'd have been at the top like 'e is if 'e'd been married and 'ad a family to raise. 'E's given everything ... 'e's given his life to cricket. And now 'e's got to this age, I think 'e longs to have a little child, y'know. Especially a boy. I mean, 'e would have been over the moon. So I think 'e 'as given up a lot, a lot for cricket. But 'e doesn't regret it because 'e loves what 'e's doing.

'Anyway, I'll carry on with 'is washing, whatever 'appens. We've got this system going. We're not a family that shows a lot of feeling but I'll carry on as long as I can. There's only me and 'im now.'

☆ ☆ ☆

The lunch interval at Lord's, you swiftly realise, is an institution no less solid and venerable than the Bank of England. Hampers are agape, tartan rugs strewn, Camembert breathing and bottles uncorked (especially bottles uncorked).

'It was your worst nightmare,' Michael Heycock could be heard to say over a glass of red wine. He was a Japanese restaurant proprietor – the Nippon Tuck in Canary Wharf – but more to the point, he was an MCC member who had witnessed the horror of *women* being admitted into the Pavilion at Lord's for the first time the week before in honour of the women's England v New Zealand Test match. Apparently, MCC members have no objection to women being allowed on the pitch. But the sight of females in the pavilion had left them reeling in shock.

'It was your worst nightmare,' Heycock repeated his allegation. 'I was there with a friend who brought his wife and she was sitting there and all the men were on their best behaviour. Suddenly I noticed she was saying to my friend: "You've got your MCC tie on, darling, and you've got the MCC hatband on, don't you think that's a bit too much?"' His hand trembled at the memory, threatening to slosh wine over his immaculate cuffs and cufflinks.

'Then she said: "And, by the way, I think those colours are awful. Why don't you change them?" And there was this fridge-like cold going round the room with everyone thinking, "Oh, this is it!" It was a horror.

'Then she was saying: "Well, I've got to get back because we've got to decorate the bathroom. And I'm not sure whether it should be pink or grey." And all the guys are sitting there thinking, "This is what it could be like every day. You can't have women in the Long Room. We don't want it to be like Ascot where it all gets very frilly and silly."'

By now he had recovered his poise and no longer was his red-and-yellow MCC tie (the friend's wife was right; the colours *are* awful) imperilled by Beaujolais spillages. He even went so far as to say that he would vote for women being allowed to become members. 'Yes,' he said, 'because there's a 25-year waiting list and before the first woman is in, I'll be dead.'

I spied Marie Bidwell again, serving the buttered baguettes. 'Do you want to speak to my husband?' she asked and kindly brought him over. I wondered if he could explain himself. 'It's simply the way she wants it,' he said, slightly bemused. 'We have a wonderful understanding. I'm a cricket fanatic and she's very keen and we've put on these little parties together for about ten years. It's wonderful. I do my bit behind the scenes. She's done more than me, but she always does. We have a partnership. She's very happy.'

And to be fair, the women, all about me on the Member's lawn (including Eleanor Oldroyd, the doyenne of Radio Five's sports broadcasting) *did* seem incredibly happy and certainly not embittered by their necessary status as mere 'guests' and 'spouses'.

'No, NO!' said Yvonne Mills, quite forcibly. 'I don't think women should be allowed to become members of the MCC. The men have been members for a long, long, long time and I don't think we females should interfere.'

This only served to confirm what Herbert Hanna, a former company director, now retired, already knew. 'Women don't want to join.' I pointed out that Rachel Heyhoe Flint did. 'She is a lady professional cricketer,' he replied. 'Lady professionals might want to join. But they shouldn't. Shouldn't be allowed in. It's a nice, pleasant club that men like to belong to and men have belonged to it for a great number of years. You will always get a belligerent fringe. But women will never be allowed in the MCC.'

His wife concurred. 'I don't like cricket,' she said. 'I come because I like being with my husband. I like seeing him enjoy himself. But I don't like cricket.'

Mrs Frances Biddle said she was Scottish, but she hoped the quintessentially English traditions of Lord's would never change. Her husband, the ex-Mayor of Salisbury and a member of the MCC for 'a hundred years', she said, had been obliged to stay at home this time.

'He's 87,' she explained. 'It's the first day he's missed in all these years. He's very well but he's just getting a little bit slow and it's a long day. But he came down to see us off in his nice MCC tie, his navy blue shirt and his lovely trousers. I've come as his emissary.'

In fact, there were a number of emissaries on duty. Round, quite a long way round, at the Full Toss Bar a group of actuaries were drinking pints, utterly heedless of England's fight back from the painful position of 107 for five. They all appeared to be involved in corporate entertainment, although it was true, they admitted, that they were mostly entertaining each other.

Their position on the women question was varied. 'My wife reckons the most awful day of her life was watching the Gillette Cup final,' said Tony Mason. On the other hand, Patrick Byrne owed his attendance at the match to the sudden unavailability of his boss – a woman. 'She's pregnant and she had to go into hospital with a blood clot,' he explained. One of his party was scandalised. 'That's no reason to miss a cricket match,' he said. 'If she was a man, she'd be here.'

Lord's is simply redolent of men. The little splodges of begonias in baskets fool no-one. Men in red and yellow ties, men in unwise shorts, men on mobile phones, a boy being escorted out by a policeman and two drunken men to the rear singing: 'Let 'im go, let 'im go, let 'im go!' in a reworking of the notorious football song. There had even been men in the ladies loo. 'I had to put a notice on the door,' a woman explained to me, 'that said: "This sign means ladies *not* laddies." I found them in there yesterday and I didn't like to barge in, in case they hadn't adjusted their dress.' Typical woman. Ever thoughtful.

As the gloaming fell over London, causing Dickie Bird to fuss endless fuss with his lightmeter, David Gower, another former England captain, emerged to lean nonchalantly against the press room wall. I wondered, since he is reputedly brilliant at the cryptic questions posed by crossword puzzles, if he could tell me why more women don't come to cricket.

'They do,' he countered. 'We used to spend a lot of time on the balcony scanning the crowd for women. There was always some there. Scattered about.'

He'd been made, fairly recently, an honorary member of the MCC. Had he, I wondered, upon receipt of his tie, exercised his vast intellectual faculties to consider the plight of women still condemned to a twilight world of semi-existence by the all-male denizens of Lord's? Had he, in short, thought of returning the tie and refusing the membership as a mark of solidarity with the oppressed?

'No,' he said.

NURSING A GRIEVANCE

I only wish some of the players' trousers fitted better.
  The Duke of Edinburgh, when asked if he had
  any complaints about modern cricket in 1987

We should be obliged to the Duke. He is only saying what countless women have said before: that cricket is no more than a strange social ritual, involving the ruination of a pair of white trousers, a big tea and the most arcane and bizarre set of rules that man has ever devised.

Pauline, the Glaswegian auxiliary nurse in the long-term geriatric ward of Hairmyres Hospital, looked utterly flummoxed. 'Well, there's stumps at one end,' she said, pondering her description of the game of cricket. 'Someone throws the ball and they stand in a big circle, don't they? People get out. And I think that's about all I know.'

Here was a woman thoroughly *au fait* with megakariocytopoenia, mesenteric adenitis and Dupuytren's contracture, and she'd never heard of deep square leg. She thought white flannels were ridiculous in the circumstances, whether they fitted the players or not. 'Because, you see, they rub that ball and all their troosers get mucked up. That would drive me mad, that. And it's not as if they're playing at night where they need to be seen or anythin'.'

The trouble with cricket to those not gently and thoroughly indoctrinated on the playing fields of Eton or wherever, is that learning all the rules and the lore and the language (where 'ducks' and 'maidens' and 'backward short legs' roam mystifyingly free) is well nigh impossible to the latecomer. You might as well ask Phil Tufnell to explain what homonymous hemianopia might be as ask the uninitiated the meaning of a 'googly'. The nurses at Hairmyres in East Kilbride were a classic case in point. They wanted to help; indeed, a lifetime's vocation was devoted to comforting those in need but no matter how great their willingness, nor how inspired their guesswork, the mysteries of cricket remained stubbornly closed.

It made you wonder whether the rules of cricket had been specifically devised by the male of the species to keep women at bay, rather like the Lord's Pavilion. For instance, the tea towel description of cricket, sold with mischievous relish in summer seaside resorts, is almost poetic in its obfuscation. 'One team goes into bat, the other team stays out in the field,' it says. 'Two batsmen from the team that is in go out to bat. The rest of the team that is in stay out in the pavilion until one of their team is out . . .' and so on until even the descendants of W.G. Grace wonder what manner of game we are describing. This is a deliberate ploy by the tea towel manufacturers; its purpose – to amuse. The deliberate ploy perpetrated by the MCC, the Marylebone Cricket Club, otherwise known as the font of all chauvinism, has an entirely different purpose. To foster the sport, nurture the rules, and, one suspects, make precious little effort to attract the fond attention of women and visiting Americans.

What has happened to a batsman when he's 'got his eye in'? I asked Ann, Beth and Janette in the Nurses' Administration block. 'Has he got a black eye?' Janette wondered. 'Is it something to do with Roman numerals?' Beth wanted to know. 'Is it "eye" as in "eye",' said Janette, 'or "I" as in "I"?' In the end, I explained it meant the batsman could see straight. 'For goodness sake, why don't they say so?' said Ann. She went to a cricket match once. Her cousin was playing. 'It was the most boring God-awful afternoon I've ever had in my life,' she said. 'Bar none.'

Beth had once watched Rolls Royce v the Fire Brigade in East Kilbride, but even she had to admit: 'I've got two sons and I love all the sports on the telly, but I don't understand cricket at all.' Janette concurred. 'I love watching sport but when I see my husband watching cricket I say: "You know, Jim, that is one game I just do not understand." In the snooker, the commentators keep genning you up, so even if you were an absolute beginner, you would know what they're talking about. In cricket they don't.'

Ann thought being 'out for a duck' involved going up to the local pub for lunch, and so the intriguing conversation continued.

A leg break: 'Nothing to do with our Accident and Emergency Unit.' Beth at least knew that. 'A ball that comes low,' pronounced Janette. 'Hits the leg, no, those things . . . the pads. Or goes above them.'

A bouncer: 'A man who evicts people off the pitch,' Ann thought. 'With a leg break or an arm break, if necessary,' elaborated Beth.

Dead balls: 'Is that something like Brewer's Droop?' said Beth.

Backward Short Leg: 'Someone standing behind the wicket,' hazarded Janette. 'Kneeling down,' said Beth. 'That's a dangerous place to stand,' said Janette. 'Our Jill got hit with a cricket bat on a Sunday School outing. At the very first swing of the bat – she was standing behind him – and the bat hit her in the eye. What a black eye she had. Oh, she had some keeker!' (And speaking of unusual terminology, it should be explained to Sassenachs unfamiliar with the Glaswegian vernacular that a 'keeker' is a black eye of monumental proportions.)

Upon the image of cricket, they were united. 'It's a closed shop,' said Ann, 'where women put up, cook up and shut up.' 'It's upmarket, public school and for the likes of John Major, isn't it?' said Janette. 'It's a class thing in England,' said Beth. 'It all goes back to the days of the Raj, which is why they wear white. It's the military thing. Being in uniform and wearing white in hot countries to reflect the heat.' 'I think they always look very smart,' said Janette.

'Until they start rubbing their balls,' said Ann.

'Which balls are you talking about?' Janette enquired.

'Well, that's where they rub them isn't it,' said Ann, proving quite knowledgeable after all.

'I always think: "How are they going to get that out of their trousers?"' said Beth, at which point any semblance of order was utterly destroyed. For posterity, Beth wished it to be known that she was talking about the red stains from the ball polish.

Most sportsmen know that backward short leg is not a position where you field kneeling down. It is something that boys learn, seemingly by osmosis; even the ones who hate cricket, all sports in fact, and prevail on their mums to write notes. Girls, on the other hand, are almost wilfully under-exposed to the great sports. How else can you account for the unanimity of the opinions on the ward?

'Borin',' said Jacqueline, a clinical audit nurse whose own mother and father met at a cricket match. 'It's just a fancy game o' rounders.' She was, however, the only women in the entire hospital who seemed to know that a cricket team comprised 11 players. She was also familiar with the tea interval. 'That's when they all sit about and eat cucumber sandwiches. The cricketers' wives are in competition to make the best cakes. I saw a programme about it once. To be a cricketer's wife, you've got to be a good scone maker.'

Margaret, her colleague on the day wards (for tests and small surgical procedures), fully understood the reasons behind cricket's failure to embrace the female (except in the literal – barmaid – sense). 'It's just tradition. Like the church. Until recently no woman was allowed to become a priest either. I must say I think it's quite bizarre that the church has managed to change and when it comes to sport – nothing.'

They did understand the concept of 'sledging', the proffering of foul abuse at a member of the opposition in order to render him apoplectic and useless. Not only did Jacqueline understand it, she used it quite frequently as a tactic when playing ten-pin bowling with her husband. Perhaps men have under-estimated women all this time.

No-one guessed correctly what a googly might be, although several made anatomically incorrect stabs at an answer, and as for the length of a cricket pitch, guesses ranged from 15 feet to 100 yards. If the latter were true, one can only imagine how Mike Gatting would have invented a new way to be out. 'P & BBW' – 'prostrate and breathless before wicket'.

TOUR OPERATORS

Up, breakfast, stretch, practise, play, bathe, bar, steak, bed. Same company, day in, day out.
                                            Ian Botham on touring, 1986

Ten years later Botham might have amended his description: 'Up, read *Noddy*, mash rusks, stretch, practise, buy Pampers, play, bathe the children, bar (curtailed), bedtime story, steak, bed, up at midnight, up at 3 a.m., up at 5 a.m., up . . .' As came forcibly to the notice of the England management, women and children (not to mention nannies, mothers, fathers and second cousins once removed) are now firmly part of that vastly elongated venture known as the cricket tour.

Ray Illingworth, the former England captain whose wife Shirley had been present with him for nearly a month of the tour to South Africa 1995–96, caused a furore at the end of a deeply unsuccessful series by appearing to blame the nuisance created by wives and families. 'I don't care what anyone says, it is difficult when family and friends are on tour. There have been a lot of distractions and the team have not been as focused as they were during the first part of the tour.'

But there was an answer to that. 'Well, I think he's a dithering bloody old twit,' said Lindsay Lamb, wife of the former England and Northants cricketer, Allan. 'To say that wives should be banned for three or four months from seeing their husbands is outrageous. It's totally outdated. Allan's a bloody sight less likely to get up to no good if he's with his wife than if he picks up some old tart in a bar. He's been sleeping with me for 17 years, so he's going to be a sight less active than with anybody else.

'How can you expect a marriage to last if your husband's away for that long?'

This is a very good question that has exercised the mind of many a cricketing wife since man first invented the steamship to carry away husbands, and their bats and balls, to Australia.

To those unacquainted with the phenomenon, it should be explained that the Test Series cricket tour – three and a half months in some far-flung country with its sun out – provides man with his most cunning double-whammy: maximum opportunity to misbehave and minimum chance of the wife finding out. Until, that is, the tabloids.

But even before Botham and the Miss Barbados allegations, there were signs that things were far from well in the imperfect peace of paradise. By 1975, the male idyll of women-free touring had been wretchedly shattered. 'Our hotels were turned into kindergartens,' said Bob Taylor, the former England wicket-keeper, on the presence of wives and children on England's tour of Australia. 'Wives and families must never tour again with players,' declared Keith Miller, the former Australian all-rounder in the *Daily Express* the same year. 'There is little team spirit and even less fight. Women and children come first for those players who have families. To hell with the pride of England seems to be their motto.'

To this day, two distinct sides remain at loggerheads. On one side, wives point out it would be helpful on the connubial bliss front if they met their own husbands occasionally. On the other side, the England management believe England cricketers are on tour to play cricket.

The only flaw in the management's cogent argument is that our mental picture of the touring cricketer is not necessarily one of him flaying a fast ball to the boundary. More likely, he is seen prone on a sunlounger with an ever-deepening tan, lager in one hand, a Havana-sized joint in the other, and a raft-load of nubile nymphettes at his feet impatient to become the subject of the next day's *Sun*'s lurid headline.

This is undoubtedly unfair; a wild, reckless and irresponsible over-statement founded on gossip, malice and, er, solid fact. 'There were a ring of guys, not mentioning any names, who had a competition in the West Indies to see how much you had to pay a girl to get her into bed,' said cricket's most famous female eyewitness, Frances Edmonds. 'One gin and tonic, two gin and tonics . . . Sometimes, it wasn't even that. She bought *him* one.'

Frances Edmonds is a famous chronicler of England cricket tours. Her two books on the subject, *Cricket XXXX Cricket* and *Another Bloody Tour*, were both bestsellers, propelling her into a realm of sporting fame slightly bemusing to someone with a double first from Cambridge in modern languages. She is, she insists, just as interested in European politics, art and 16th-century French literature as she is in slow left-arm bowling. If not more so.

Nevertheless, as the woman who wrote: 'Some of the guys, it is true, would do well to be more vaccinated than others, and judging from some of the dubious late-night ethnic "Room Service" wandering round on our corridor, prophylactic penicillin might not be counter-indicated either . . .', she deserves to be regarded as no less than an oracle on the subject of cricketers on tour.

'I have been in bars,' she said, 'when an England cricket team arrives and it is basically full of women trying to get off with cricketers. *And it doesn't matter which one.* Women are prepared to go to bed with any one of them just because they think it's a big deal. I find it kind of sad that as a woman you feel you have to sleep with an important man to make you feel good.

'My friend was the editor of *Options* magazine when she sent a female reporter down to a hotel in The Strand where the Australians all stayed when they came here on tour. This reporter said – and my friend believed her – that she slept with the entire Australian cricket team. She went through the lot of them, or rather, they went through her.'

The fact that Frances has been sleeping with a cricketer for the past 20 years adds in no small measure to the authenticity of her stories. She married Phil Edmonds, of Middlesex and England, after meeting him at Cambridge and soon gave up throwing crockery at him when it became clear his line and length were better.

Rarely, in the days that Phil toured with England, did she wile away the lonely days at home pondering what he might be getting up to. She had gainful employment as an interpreter. 'He'd go away to Pakistan and I'd be rollicking round Rome, Paris, London and New York. Letting him worry about me was not a bad way to be.

'I believe in relationships you've got to have balance. If one's completely got the upper hand whether it be financially or whatever, you're in trouble.'

Just what sort of trouble, Lindsay Lamb can explain. 'If you're an attractive sportsman there's always going to be some old slapper who's going to chuck herself at you. I suppose we, the wives, push it to the back of our minds . . . But there are limits. If I ever caught Allan at it, let me tell you, he'd think a piece of corrugated cardboard under Waterloo Bridge was Buckingham Palace. I'd clean him out. I'd take him right to bits. I'd take the works. Seriously. I think he knows where he stands.'

These women are the foundation of a solid innings, just as surely as any Geoffrey Boycott batting manual. 'Women? They're the driving force. They're behind their men,' said Mrs Lamby, as she is respectfully known in the trade. 'They keep the home together, keep the kids happy, keep the businesses going. If you take Lamby going away on tour for three or four months, I've got to do everything from changing lightbulbs to changing tyres to coping with any crisis thrown at you.

'When the men are at the top they can't be bothered quite honestly. Everybody wants to know them. Everyone thinks they're brilliant. But let them get dropped, or have their egos a bit dented, and they cling to you. All of a sudden they need you. Allan, touch wood, hasn't had many difficult times but when he does he leans on me more. Occasionally, it will annoy me. Because when he's down he needs me so badly and when he's on top of things I'm just, sort of, there. It's important for me to keep building him up because he's our bread and butter, but, believe me, I don't dance to his tune.'

You begin to see the scale of the England management's domestic problems. Mischievously nicknamed the 'Knitting Circle', players' wives have evolved beyond the 'stitch one, purl one' brigade. They have proved themselves to be sentient beings, with opinions; dangerous, subversive opinions in some cases.

Frances, for instance, has said a few choice words on the subject of the average cricketing male's intellectual capacity in her time. Things like: 'Some of the England team are not exactly Mensa material and others often appear totally vacant.' This trait has not always endeared her to the characters involved but no-one need doubt the impeccability of her research.

'I over-reacted when I called them stupid and ignorant,' she concedes. 'They're not stupid, actually. That was my defence. Basically, a woman to some of these guys is someone you bonk or someone that stays home to look after the kids. If you don't fall into either of these categories, you're a problem. There's no room in their heads for women who are something else. My gut reaction to that was to call them idiots.'

She does, however, have a degree of sympathy for both sides – male and female – in the modern predicament in which cricket has found itself: the wife and children on tour. 'I understand why Illingworth got a bit cheesed off in South Africa. There's the wife and the three kids and the nanny – now that is a problem. You don't want the guys to be up all night with teething kids a few hours before a Test match. But while Illingworth would probably adduce that argument, how many broken marriages do you want out of cricket?

'Someone suggested to me that banning wives from the recent World Cup in Pakistan was a way of imposing a "No Sex" rule on the players. I said: "It's not No Sex – it's No Wives." Men and managers don't mind bonking the odd barmaid because there's no commitment, no squealing kids and no wife nagging in the background. A barmaid is a bonk, a wife is a serious deflection. So we're already on different tracks here.

What they think is OK, isn't what you as a wife think is OK.'

Mrs Gatting undoubtedly did not think it OK when her husband, then the England captain, was rendered a victim of a barmaid's revelations. Mrs I.T. Botham was far from OK when her husband, on tour in Barbados, was featured in a *News of the World* headline: 'I Laid Out Coke . . . Beauty Queen's Night of Passion With Botham'. There is no knowing what the England management's reaction would have been to these alleged events had not the beady eyes (and chequebooks) of the tabloids been trained upon the scene.

So what does a wife do? 'A lot of women are in complete denial,' said Frances. But Susie Emburey, married to John (ex-Middlesex and England), isn't one of them. 'There's going to be temptations. You've got stewardesses, groupies, and men are pretty stupid. Look at them, they're ruled by their willies.

'But, do you know what? I've been married to John a long time and if I ever found out about anything I'd be really pissed off. Obviously there are times when I've had my doubts, but there are other times when I think: "I really don't want to know." I try to forget about it. I feel if you start worrying about these things, you'd be a nervous wreck.'

Cricket has yet to come to terms with the women who regard their husband as a husband as opposed to a deep square leg. The sport doesn't know what to do with them, other than blame the familial kerfuffle when England lose yet another series. Quite likely certain players were indeed distracted by the boisterous contents of cots in their room, but equally likely England were going to get cuffed anyway. The failure of male bonding cannot always be laid at the hotel room door of the women.

'It's a big myth that all the men bond together anyway,' said Frances, privy to the workings of two separate tours: winning in Australia and losing in the West Indies. 'If you're winning everybody's in a good mood, on the plane, in the bus, wherever. If you're losing the bitching and the backstabbing amongst the men is worse than anything the women could produce. It's all predicated on winning and losing. The spirit when we were winning was amazing and when we were getting hammered it was appalling.'

It would seem to suggest that squalling infants and nappy rash is not then the sole reason England have struggled to play winning cricket. But try telling that to the England selectors. Many still believe the rot set in 20 years ago when Alec Bedser, then Chairman of Selectors and confirmed bachelor, caught sight of his fast bowler entering the portals of the tour hotel. 'My God,' said Bedser, 'he's got a teddy bear under his arm.'

KATHY BOTHAM

The first part of our marriage was very happy. But then, on the way back from the ceremony...
                              Henny Youngman, American humourist

Kathy and Ian Botham have been married 20 years. Yes, she has heard all the jokes. 'That's not a marriage, that's a sentence' and other sundry witticisms from people who would prefer to be manacled to a radiator for 20 years rather than conjoined in holy matrimony to one I.T. Botham.

But, as ever, appearances can be deceptive. 'He's a very, very loyal person. He's always fun to be with. He was quite good looking. He still is quite good looking. And he's very generous. Probably too generous at times,' said Kathy, running through her husband's good points in the front drawing-room of their glorious North Yorkshire home. The place has a Jane Austeny feel. A picturesque village green is on display through the Georgian windows and tasteful ornaments are set on the shelves just-so, like the field placings of a careful captain. Over at deep square leg, on the opposite wall, an oil painting of Botham in full batting flow catches the eye. My God, she must love him.

'Actually,' she said, 'I found it the other day looking a bit sorry for itself, so I stuck it up. Just for the time being... until I can find a nice mirror.'

Kathy Botham is categorically not the 'little woman' of tabloid legend. She is neat, immaculate and possesses a very definite force field. The first words I heard her say were: 'Shut up, Shiraz!' as she brought a large and obstreperous dog to instant order. Ian chose the name, incidentally.

'I think in the early days, Ian was definitely the top dog in our relationship, because he's a very strong-willed person, very determined. In the past he's been arrogant. Top sportsmen are not particularly easy to live with. Ian was terribly selfish in the early days. He admits it now.

He said he was an absolute sod to be with. And he was.

'It wasn't easy. But then your confidence grows. I suppose all the events that happened made me more determined. When the press wrote about me as "the little wife left behind" that probably helped me because I thought: "To hell with that. I'm not that type of person. I'll show them I'm not." I think it's pretty equal now.'

'All the events' is some euphemism. Kathy has been attached all this time to a man (once compared by his former agent to Biggles, the VC, El Alamein and a tank commander) who regards brushes with authority as compulsory. Botham Takes Drugs (admitted). Botham and Miss Barbados (denied). Botham Goes To Hollywood (but he wouldn't take acting lessons). Botham In Fight With Ian Chappell (admitted, but not the beer glass in face part).

'He's no saint. He's been an idiot at times. But he's nowhere near as bad as he was made out to be. The trouble was, even in the periods of calmness, I was always thinking: something's going to happen. I'm a worrier. He was always saying, "For goodness' sake relax," and I was thinking, "No, there's somebody out there brewing something else this very minute." And when we went out, we couldn't relax as a couple in public. You know, you'd be in a restaurant with friends and some idiot would come over and be rude to Ian. People did that. And, obviously, you'd think, how's he going to react? It was just a nightmare.

'It affected the children. I think it affected Sarah more than Liam and Becky. Looking back, it changed Sarah's personality for quite a while. She became withdrawn and lost the confidence that she had. I suppose that's understandable when you see your father's name plastered across the newspapers and your Daddy's picture supposedly with other women. You can protect them from so much but kids aren't daft. We always had to reassure her that when Daddy went away it wasn't going to be the last time she ever saw him. You know how little ones' minds work.

'Liam was different. I can always remember shortly after we'd moved in here – I can't remember which particular disaster it was, but I'd just had a phone call from Ian. I always used to scream and shout over the phone because he'd ring up and say: 'Look, Kath, guess what . . . ' I was ranting and raving and I heard this clink, clink, clink and Liam was staggering up the stairs with a gin and tonic. 'Here you are Mummy,' he said. 'Don't worry.' He must have been about eight or nine then.'

Kathy married Ian shortly before her 21st birthday. 'It's amazing we didn't get more pressure from our parents not to go ahead. Virtually within a few weeks of meeting, we'd decided we wanted to spend the rest of our lives together. I know it sounds very romantic but that's how it happened.' She gratefully abandoned her business studies course at a polytechnic in Coventry and worked for her father instead, repping in the percussion instrument trade. It was an omen. The clash of cymbals has followed her everywhere since.

'I think I've been honest enough to say that if it weren't for the children, I might have packed my bags and gone because at times it did get too much. But then you've got to ask yourself, if I do that, what am I going to do? I'd given up my college career and I was one of those people who'd got O levels and A levels but had no idea what she wanted to do with her life. I was going to apply to be an air stewardess I think, but I met Ian in the meantime.

'The stories? Things always seemed to happen miles and miles away. You think, is there an ounce of truth in this? I'm not naïve enough to think everybody's perfect. I mean, marriages don't last long nowadays. But the "Other Women" stories were so far-fetched. As far as I'm concerned anyway. I was always quite happy with the explanations I was given. The prime example was the 1986 West Indies tour, that Miss Barbados thing. I mean, my father was over there when it was all supposed to be happening. Ian spent most of his time with my father, rescuing him from the rum bar and playing dominoes with the locals.

'And other wives were over there at the time. Susie Emburey was there with John. Ian was playing nanny to their children. She rang me up to say it was so unbelievable. That was nice. I flew over. They all said "Botham's Wife Flies In To Save Marriage," but I was going anyway. The only good thing about it was I got upgraded from economy to business class on the flight. All these media people were on the plane, you see. It was amazing. Margaret Thatcher wasn't front page news that day, we were.'

The recent publicity over Botham's bid to become a Test Selector must have been like old times. But Kathy knows better. 'Hmm. I have got nothing to say about that,' she said. She did, however, speak out in January 1996 on behalf of the scapegoat English cricket wives who were being blamed for the poor showing of their menfolk in South Africa. 'I think for anybody specifically to blame wives and families is very unfair. One or two of the wives rang me afterwards to say thank you for putting our views across. They can't speak out because it would make things difficult for their husbands. But someone's got to stand up for them. I mean, in the past there has been the occasional wife that hasn't been good for team spirit. I suppose some wives could say: "Oh, I don't want you to go out tonight, I want you to have dinner with me." I never said that to Ian. He would come and have his cup of tea, have a shower and then he'd go. Sometimes he'd come back in half an hour, sometimes he'd go for a couple of hours. But it's our future. If you start to interfere, you're putting added pressure on them. Aggravation from the wife doesn't help.

'But it's awful for the wives left at home. I used to get terribly, terribly upset before each tour. For weeks on end I could hardly bring myself to be civil towards him. I used to put him through hell because I was so emotionally drained by the fact he was going.'

She was not helped by the world's assumption that by staying at home she was conforming to the stereotype of a Mrs Mop either. 'It's not just me staying at home doing the housework and cooking the meals. There's far more to my life than that. Ironically, though, what's given me the most satisfaction is bringing up the children and the fact that, wherever we go, people say what fantastic children they are, how impeccable their manners are and, generally, how well they've been brought up.

'Of course, people say, "They're Ian Botham's children, it's easy for them." It's not easy for them. It's *not* easy for Liam now in his sport. He's always going to be compared to Ian. He's had those kind of articles written about him already – "I hope he's not going to be a thug like his father," and that sort of thing.

'But I think whatever happens, Liam will be able to handle it. He's had enough experience from a very young age and both Hampshire [where he plays cricket] and West Hartlepool [where he plays rugby] are very conscious of that. But he's very much like Ian, anyway: a bit arrogant, a bit selfish, very single-minded. He's not as fiery-tempered as Ian, but then Ian wasn't like that in the early days. I think it's because of all the stuff that's been flung at him over the years.

'Ian always said it was very important to him to have his wife and family with him. I always remember Bob Willis saying to me – because Ian and Bob are good mates – that out of all the players he ever toured with, Ian was the most homesick. Ask any of the lads that toured with him. They never saw him with other women. He was the one having a few pints in the bar with the lads. Ian never went nightclubbing, maybe occasionally, but on the whole he prefers male company. Probably, at times, he's ill at ease with females.'

This hardly sounds like the Botham of legend, bestriding the Alps in the footsteps of Hannibal or brazenly beating the Australians single-handedly but Kathy is clearly acquainted with all the more mellow sides of his character. 'He's very thoughtful,' she said. 'Little things. Like he goes off to the Far East quite a lot and I always get my Singapore orchids back. He remembers perfume and he's only ever once forgotten my birthday, which isn't bad really for a man.'

He did not forget this year. 'My husband bought me an Aston Martin for my 40th birthday. It's only brought out in nice weather.' I'd seen it. Sleek and blue and kept under a cover in one of the outhouses at the end of the drive. In return, she sent him to Russia for his 40th. 'Chechnya?' I hazarded. 'No,' she said. It was a fishing trip on one of the great Russian rivers. 'Log camp. Flying in by helicopter. He's thrilled to bits.'

And so one of the sporting world's most publicly dissected partnerships is happy to report its continuing vigour. 'I've definitely got stronger and probably a bit harder personality-wise.' After all the stories, all the phone calls and all the headlines, Kathy Botham could say that her husband, OBE and oil painting, had never once been unfaithful to their marriage. Did she really believe that? 'Yeah, I do,' she said. 'Yes, I do.'

SPACE INVADERS

A friend told me that one night, when she and her husband were making love, she suddenly noticed something sticking in his ear. When she asked him what it was, he replied: 'Be quiet! I'm listening to the cricket.'

Vicky Rantzen, *The Observer*, 1978

Rachel Heyhoe Flint must have been a shock to the male system. How many cricket-obsessed worlds must have been turned upside-down by the discovery of a woman with such vast and irrepressible talent at the game. At first they declined to believe it. 'Girls don't play cricket,' said a police constable witheringly, when she tried to share the blame with her brother and his mates for endangering all pedestrian life by playing cricket in the street. But in the end she became the single most valuable role-model women's cricket has ever produced.

Though stripped of the England captaincy, in controversial circumstances nearly two decades ago, Heyhoe Flint remains synonymous with women's cricket. Her very name is suggestive of a jolly comic-book heroine who thwacks balls to the boundary and runs foul of starchy schoolmarms jealous of her vivacious temperament and vivid talents. She is the sportswoman's answer to Roy of the Rovers.

She was the first woman ever to step on to the hallowed Lord's turf in a playing capacity. 'Hallelujah!' she admits she wanted to shout as the Grace Gates opened to admit her.

She scored 30 centuries during a career remarkable for its cavalier exuberance, she played in goal for the England hockey team and was awarded the MBE in 1972. During her reign as England cricket captain, she did not lose a Test and her team beat New Zealand for the first time in a decade. She scored a century in her first Test as captain and a century in her last Test as captain – out, symbolically, on the last ball of the match.

That first Test was played at Scarborough in 1966, a momentous year for English sport (the Jockey Club, facing a court case, finally gave way and allowed women to hold a trainer's licence). 'Women's cricket received very little attention then,' said Heyhoe Flint. 'Len Hutton said it was a bit like watching a man knit. That is what used to gripe me so much. I played in that first Test as captain with about three and a half people watching. I scored a century and rushed out very immodestly the next morning to buy all the Sunday papers to read about myself. But I couldn't find anything except a little lower case result at the bottom of the bowls column of the *Sunday Telegraph*. Perhaps they thought we were still bowling underarm. It was that lack of coverage that made me determined to trying and promote the sport.'

She did the job so thoroughly that by 1976 there was a body of opinion, stiffly held and dressed in tweed skirts, that Heyhoe Flint was rather full of herself. She had, after all, been nicknamed 'Lizzie' as a child after the precocious Violet Elizabeth Bott of *Just William* fame. Her brother used to sort her out by holding the vacuum cleaner over her head so that her plaits were sucked up the machine. The women who ran cricket had no such recourse and so they summarily sacked her instead. The timing, like a Gower swish outside the off stump, could have been better.

Just prior to the machinations that would see Heyhoe Flint the victim of the chop, she scored one of the greatest Test-saving innings in the annals of women's cricket. When Michael Atherton performed a similar feat, scoring 185 not out against the South Africans in the winter of 1995, he was hailed as a man on the brink of immortality. When Heyhoe Flint scored 179 against Australia at the Oval to save the Test and the series, the conversation of two old darlings on the women's committee was overheard by a journalist. 'You would think she's the only player we've got,' said one, as the heroine of the hour came in to receive acclaim, a kiss from her husband and a glass of beer. 'Wouldn't you just,' said her companion.

Nevertheless, the innings itself is not in any way diminished by comparisons with Atherton. She was facing the fiercist of bowling – Raelee Thompson and Sharon Tredrea were the Australian pace twins, known inevitably as 'Thompson and Lillee' – and the most mountainous of tasks. Dismissed for 134 in their first innings, England had failed to quell the exuberant visitors who made 379, captained by a turncoat Scot, Jan Lumsden. 'The beggar!' said Heyhoe Flint, who went in to bat with 48 for one on the scoreboard, knowing she must stay there until dusk the following day.

She did, but the tension was so unbearable that the Yorkshire all-rounder June Stephenson had found an old brush in the locker-room and was obsessively sweeping every nook and cranny to distract her from the play. 'In the end, it was so clean, the girls were throwing down sweet papers and fag ends, just to give her something to do.'

On the field, Jan Allen batted for almost 50 minutes, scored nought and burst into tears when she was out. Mrs Mop in the locker-room had scored nine in 40 minutes and Megan Lear, a tender 21, fashioned a partnership with her captain worth 104. But the real heroine, denying her natural bent for swashbuckling, was Heyhoe Flint who even contrived to rid the fray of the dangerous Thompson. 'I flashed outside the off stump, Raelee went for a catch at first slip, broke two of her fingers and retired.'

Had Heyhoe Flint scored eight more runs during her eight and a half hours at bat, she would have broken the women's world record held since 1937 by a player rejoicing in the name – inaptly for a star of the summer game – of Betty Snowball.

Afterwards the innings was declared by her hero, Colin Cowdray, as a masterpiece. He wrote with fulsome praise in *The Cricketer* magazine: 'Rachel Heyhoe Flint's technique and concentration, adopting a role foreign to her temperament, had the look of Sir Leonard Hutton or Geoffrey Boycott at their best.'

Did Boycott ever mention this accolade, I wondered, when in the company of the all-conquering Heyhoe? 'No,' she said. 'He mostly recounted – with many four letter words surrounding it – the couple of times Dennis Amiss had run him out.'

☆ ☆ ☆

There is a certain waitress in the Chatterbox Coffee Shop in Whitstable who has never been known to get the change wrong. No matter what the complications of teacakes and doughnuts, she is there, resplendent in the confidence that her sums will come right in the end. She is Wendy Wimbush, waitress and ground-breaker, the BBC's first female cricket scorer. She works in the coffee shop in her off-season, just as she delivers a morning paper round on her bike. 'There's no money in it, but it's quite good exercise,' she said matter-of-factly, and you can only wonder at a life that combines the mundane with the exotic quite so effortlessly.

For when not shoving copies of the *Daily Telegraph* through Whitstable letterboxes, Wimbush tours the great cricket grounds of the world. She has spent 15 of our winters in the Australian sunshine, visited New Zealand three times, the Caribbean twice. Until 1991 she was the BBC's number one cricket scorer and so great was her eminence that many people think she does the job still.

She is meticulously orderly. She works with a towel on her lap so that pens cannot roll off her desk and stain her skirt. 'Which happened to me once,' she explained in a tone stern enough to denote it would never happen again. She cannot remember any calamitous mistake she might have made. She cannot even recall a minor one. 'My great virtue is that I never panic. That's vital. If you write they ran two and you find out later they actually ran three, you can adjust it. I use little sticky strips that typists use because I don't like crossings out.'

Wendy Wimbush is, almost inevitably, a vicar's daughter who grew up with three brothers and a passion for trainspotting. 'I'd stand there for hour after hour at Whitstable station writing down the numbers and names of the trains. I loved steamtrains. But I think it was because I lived in a vicarage with all those brothers – and my father had an accident and was in a wheelchair – that I used to go out sometimes just to get away from it all.'

At 14 she was called upon by her father to act as scorer for the St Peter's Church cricket team, comprising mainly choirboys. The same could not be said for the many England teams for whom she has scored since but her working methods have largely stayed the same. Her vital powers of concentration remain undimmed.

'What I think makes me a bit unusual is that I can work and concentrate in a room packed with people all jabbering away at once until deadlines beckon and panic sets into their brain. In the morning, it's absolute chaos but they expect me to concentrate. Just occasionally, I get very exasperated and tell 'em to shut up. I've got a bell which I sometimes ring. Especially at the Oval, because it's terribly bad acoustically. The boys' attention seems to wander so they start fooling about, making paper aeroplanes and you feel a bit like an old granny telling them off.'

Wimbush was working in a large bank in Pall Mall when she was plucked off the benches at Canterbury cricket ground one day to work for Jim Swanton, the famed and respected former *Daily Telegraph* cricket writer.

'Amanuensis was the word he used to use for me, which is the Greek for handmaiden I later discovered,' she said, characteristically deadpan.

Wimbush was nobody's handmaiden, certainly not in the intimate sense. 'Just think about it,' she said. 'In 1974 when I started work with Jim Swanton I was still fairly young, unattached. I could have had a whale of a time. There were plenty of men about, all the players and whatnot. You could have been a real good time girl. But I thought, "I'm not going to do that because I want to be taken seriously." I heard the men one day talking about somebody else – they were organising a sweepstake on whose room she'd be seen coming out of next and I thought, "They're never, ever going to do that to me."

'In the beginning it was fairly tough because, you know, you were quite poor and you could have done with a few good dinners. But, you see, you'd only have to sit and talk to someone for people to put two and two together. So I kept myself very much to myself to begin with. After a while people realised, as I was working with Jim, that I was there to be serious. Not only that, they found out I did a good job.

'After Jim retired, I carried on working in the press box for other people and they all used to pitch in. They'd send an envelope round – I wasn't supposed to see – to pay me. It was just word of mouth. I'd type all the letters for the Australian cricket team, Brian Johnston, John Arlott. People would get an extra lunch box and say: "Here you are. Have that for your tea." They were ever so good to me. I think it's because they realised I did a good job and they'd be up a gumtree without me. Then they made me a member of the Cricket Writers' Club and I've been treasurer for the last ten years. I'm sure they only had me because I can add up.

'I think if I hadn't come to this, I'd have been a bookkeeper or something like that. There's something lovely about adding four or five different numbers and they all come to the same number. I remember once doing a long column of figures at the bank and it came to a million. It was so exciting, all these numbers coming to such a big round figure.'

Cricket is also famous for its big round figures: Mike Gatting, Allan Lamb, Beefy Botham (it's curious how many of them are named after Sunday lunch). Wimbush has a deep and abiding appreciation of their talents. 'My favourite player of all time is Viv Richards. Oh yes. He had skill, audacity, power, stroke play,' she said of the former West Indian captain, a prodigious batsman and useful medium pace bowler, who once told Frances Edmonds that if she ever came back to Antigua, she'd find herself buried in concrete blocks at the bottom of the harbour. (This might have had something to do with page 147 in her book *Another Bloody Tour* in which she says of him: 'To the casual observer his demeanour appears to be demonically arrogant in victory and truculently petulant at the slightest hint of adversity.')

Nevertheless, for his on-field exploits he makes the Wimbush Hall of Fame as does Bishen Bedi, the Indian slow bowler ('I used to love watching him'), Ian Botham ('little short of astonishing when you think what on-field deeds he crammed into ten years'), England captain, Michael Atherton ('He has great will-power. I approve of will-power'), the Australian pace bowler, Dennis Lillee ('a tremendous favourite of mine'), and former Aussie captain, Greg Chappell ('that wonderful tall, upright driving'). 'But the sheer audacity of Viv was breathtaking,' she concluded.

Her admiration for the unbridled aggressors of world cricket is in stark contrast to her contemplative hobbies that include gardening and cross stitch embroidery, 'which my friends say I only do because it involves a lot of counting,' she said.

Hers is an extraordinary life. A globe-trotter who has never owned a car, a waitress who has worked in the white heat of live television broadcasting, a woman excited by a row of numbers adding up to a million and a century by Vivien Richards. And she is entirely satisfied with her lot. 'I've never missed in the slightest having children. I don't know, for one thing, if any man could cope with a wife who was one week here, two weeks there. I can't think he'd be pleased to sit still while his wife toddled off somewhere. I certainly have never met one who seems to think that would be OK.

'There was someone is Australia I was fond of, but he didn't want to get married. He's an identical twin and I think he would have married his twin brother, if he could. Yet I can lob up to 50 places in Australia, four or five in New Zealand, four or five in the Caribbean and people will give me a good welcome. Even a few in India. I can't say my social life's ever suffered.

'I hope I'll never want to stop scoring. I can't think of a better way to spend a summer's day. You see, you never know what might happen.'

☆ ☆ ☆

Warwickshire retained the County Championship in 1995 and no-one looked much further than Dermot Reeve as the principal reason why. An all-right batsman and odd-job bowler, he nevertheless marshalled his forces with guile and effect from beneath a Dylanish floppy hat that any self-respecting hippy would have discarded in the 1970s. He styled a winning team from a happy team and, if the price was to tolerate his mild eccentricities, Warwickshire were only too happy to pay.

The Bard of Birmingham, he composes his own songs, does impressions (a better Imran Khan than Imran Khan) and has introduced 'team smile breaks' to the normal routine of Warwickshire cricket practice. Where on earth, you wonder, does he get it all from? And then you speak to Monica Reeve, his mum, and understand.

'I meet lots of interesting people on my travels,' she said in a rare moment of repose. 'Like in New Zealand I met a man from Accrington who was called Stanley. I think he said he'd been born the year Accrington Stanley won the Cup and so his parents named him after the football team. He was fluent in seven languages. You should talk to him. He's a very interesting character.'

Monica Reeve is a rover. She has lived in Hong Kong, explored the Yangtze River in China, travelled throughout India, regularly tripped through the Antipodes and, above all, followed her youngest of four sons through his triumphant career as a professional cricketer.

'My next-door neighbour said to me last year that she didn't know why I had a house. I could just as easily pitch a tent in her garden,' she said amid characteristic gales of husky laughter.

Her nomadic career began, as these things so often do, with a father who took her to cricket. 'I was born and brought up in Lancashire and my father would take me to Lancashire League games when I was quite small. I saw Walcott, Worrell and Weekes. I've seen Richards and Warne and Garner. After a while, I'd go by myself. Oh, I'd be about 11 or 12, I suppose. It was safe in those days and I was quite gregarious. I used to look and see where a good game was on – Accrington, maybe, or Oswaldtwistle or Church or Burnley – and go along on the bus.'

Fifty-odd years later the venues had changed somewhat. It was Bloemfontein or Johannesburg or Calcutta or Jaipur. It was whilst in India in 1992 that Mrs Reeve, previously only famous as being Dermot's Mum, became something of a *cause célèbre* in her own right. The official England scorer, Clem Driver, had become ill during the tour of the sub-continent and an emergency replacement was required.

The England management looked no further than Ma Reeve, who had been scoring at King George V School in Kowloon before a number of the England team were born. 'I'd gone out there because Dermot was in the squad but I was travelling around on my own. Of course, when I started to score I had to join the official touring party.

'Well, when I turned up at Calcutta, they said: "You'll have to join us and stop going off on your own." So I turned up at the hotel with my rucksack and the manager said: "Where's your luggage?" I said: "That's it." Of course, he laughed and said: "We can't really have the official scorer with a rucksack. You'll have to get yourself a suitcase." So when we got to Madras I went and bought a suitcase in the market, and all I did was stick the rucksack inside it.'

You wonder whether *Wisden*, the bible of world cricket, has an asterisk by the scores of that 1992-93 tour: '*The first official lady scorer at England level in the history of cricket. (Rucksack in her suitcase.)' Probably not.

Dermot is supremely proud of his mother. 'She never misses a day's play,' he enthused. 'I've never known anyone so knowledgeable about the game. Male or female.'

Her exploits are all the more remarkable when you consider that the year Warwickshire won the Championship, and the NatWest Trophy come to that, Monica turned 63. 'I've got grey hair and wrinkles and osteo-arthritis that's not getting any better. I don't know how long I can keep going round the world but I certainly don't intend to give up yet.

'And it's not eccentric at all.' She bridled at the very idea. 'There's an awful lot of people travelling around. I just like sport, watching sport, all kinds of sport. I regret I was never given the opportunity to play. I think I'd have been quite good at it.'

MY SWEET LORD'S

They bring him out of the loft, take the dust sheet off, give him a pink gin and sit him there . . . He sits there at Lord's saying: 'That's Botham, look at his hair, they tell me he's had some of that cannabis stuff.'

Ian Botham, 1986

You would think that members of the Lord's Committee had been hatched from eggs or in some way pollenated into existence. Their contact with, and reverence for, the female sex seems so remote they can scarcely have sprung from women. Mothers are out of the question in their case, never mind sisters, wives, daughters and female wicket-keepers.

For over 200 years the MCC, Marylebone Cricket Club, has declared a No Women policy. No women members, no women in the Pavilion on match days and no women guests allowed. They have hesitated to append the notice 'No Dogs or Women' above the hallowed portals, as some men's clubs are wont to do, but the sentiment is there nonetheless.

A poll of MCC members was taken in 1988. The subject: Should women be allowed into the Pavilion as guests? It was absolutely and overwhelmingly trounced. Three years later another motion was put to members: that women be allowed to join the 20-year waiting list. The radical suggestion was defeated by 2,000 votes. Ten thousand members failed to vote at all. 'I think they're all dead actually,' said Rachel Heyhoe Flint, the woman whose application for membership had precipitated the action.

Male chauvinist piggery, under siege from feminism, realism and ready-meals from Safeway's, has retreated so far at the end of the 20th century, but it will retreat no further than the Grace Gates at Lord's. For some strange reason, the mere sight of a person in a skirt – unless it be some cross-dressing member of the committee – puts fear and foreboding into the heart of the stoutest cricket buffer. And, funnily enough, they're proud of it.

Chris Rea, former British Lion and Scottish rugby international, came to Lord's to interview for the job of PR and Marketing Manager of the MCC the very week after Will Carling's infamous remark about rugby being run by 57 'old farts'. 'It was a wonderful gathering and really quite daunting,' said Rea, who has faced the might of an All Black prop forward with barely a wince in his time. 'I was confronted by the MCC Treasurer and the MCC President, who was Sir Oliver Popplewell at the time. He looked at me and said, "Well, you won't find 57 old farts here. There are 18,000 of us."'

The honourable Sir Oliver, judge of the High Court of Justice, Queen's Bench Division, was being whimsical on behalf of his fellow members. But not that whimsical, as Heyhoe Flint discovered during her part-jocular, part-serious endeavour to allow women access to that mystic realm of unalloyed masculinity, the membership of the MCC.

'The only reason I did that was (a) a bit of fun and (b) it's the greatest cricket club in the world and yet when you look around on match days there are thousands of women sitting in the crowd but none of them in the Pavilion. Why shouldn't women be admitted?

'People got confused in thinking I instantly wanted to be an MCC member. I didn't. It was really as much for all the hundreds and thousands of women who are interested in cricket. I was trying to get the constitution changed on their behalf so that in future any women who wished to join the Club could do so and take their place in the queue.'

She wrote off to the MCC for an application form in the name of R. Flint. Suitably misled, the form came back to her, whereupon she prevailed on Jack Hayward, the Chairman of Wolves, Dennis Amiss, the former England Test batsman, Brian Johnston, the BBC cricket commentator and Tim Rice, surely the only MCC committee member ever to win an Oscar, to act as her sponsors. 'Not bad names really,' she said.

The vote – but not all – was lost. 'I had silly comments like: "Utterly impossible, there aren't enough lavatories,"' to the younger category who were all for it. Two and a half thousand members voted for it, which isn't bad, including my husband because I ticked his form in the appropriate box and sent it back.

'Yes, I will try again. I'm not one to alienate people, chain myself to railings or go on hunger strike. You've got to do it in the right way so that people say, "She's not such a bad old stick really." And if I did ever become a member I would love to become involved on the PR and marketing committee because I feel there is a contribution that could be made.

Alison Fisher: woman's answer to Stephen Hendry (without the spots)
(© Stephen Lock)

Laura Davies: 'I'd like to look like Elle McPherson but I don't' (© Gary Prior)

Mary Joe Fernandez: strong arm, dainty sweat (© Michael Cole)

Anna Kournikova: 'very cute but almost freakish in how spoiled she was' (© Michael Cole)

Chanda Rubin models the 'Babe's Bloomers' (© Michael Cole)

Gail Gyl: 'I looked like hell. The Wild Woman of Borneo' (© Tom Kidd)

Women's rugby: 'They leave their fertility on the field,' said a former (male) rugby club president (© Russell Cheyne)

Women's football: 'A woman playing football is like a dog walking on its hind legs': Brian Glanville, (male) football correspondent (© Philip Brown)

Charlie George: as was (circa 1971)
and as is (left). Either way . . .
'The King of Highbury'
left (© Gary Prior)
below (© George Herringshaw)

The Featherstone Ladies rugby team: 'The goal-kicker could kick as well as any man and she'd only one eye' (photo courtesy of Ian Clayton)

Allan and Lindsay Lamb: 'I'd clean him out. I'd take him right to bits' (© Phil Coburn)

Kathy Botham: 'If it weren't for the children I might have packed my bags and gone' (© Steve Yarnell)

'I often feel they appoint so much from within that they can't widen vision sufficiently to see the way to change. Look at the cock-ups: the soil in the pocket incident, the ball tampering affair, the tour itineraries that absolutely knacker everybody because they go on and on. It's all so crazy, I just feel I could make some contribution to the game.'

Very likely their lordships and gin-swillers abhor the very idea of women encroaching on the running of the game but there is little evidence of trouble-shooting efficiency in many of their own day-to-day deals. An example: 'Who was that man I've been talking to?' said an England selector to the England bowler, Bob Willis. Willis looked at the man in amazement. He had been talking to the England spin bowler, Phil Edmonds. Another example: 'Good morning, Roy, good morning, Peter,' said Alec Bedser, chairman of the England selectors genially one morning . . . to Ray East and John Lever during Test trials in 1973.

On the other hand, they can rally magnificently to a crisis. Tim Rice tells the story of a member who peacefully passed away in his seat during a match at Lord's. His remains were fortunately discovered early in the morning and so, to spare fellow members any discomposure, two members of staff were deputed to sit on either side of him in a propping capacity until the end of the day's play when he could be unobtrusively removed.

One wonders whether he was escorted, for the last time, through the Long Room. Probably so, there being no ban on the deceased, merely the distressingly female members of the human race.

It might interest those, however, who insist women are plotting no less than a storming of the bastion with battering ram and missives from the Equal Opportunities Commission, that this is not actually the case. 'I don't want to sit in there. It's a pretty awful place,' said Susie Emburey, of the famous old room with its bats and balls in glass cases, W.G. Grace glowering down from the wall and a portrait of Graham Gooch that makes him look like Desperate Dan.

'I don't see the big deal. There's linoleum on the floor with stud marks all over it. It ain't any Mecca. Believe me, you're not missing a thing,' she said, one of a privileged band of women who have gained entrance to cricket's sacred temple thanks to the employment of her husband as a slow arm spinner. 'I suppose I should feel privileged but it doesn't mean that much to me. I'd rather sit up the Nursery End anyway and get a suntan.' Mrs Emburey is an Australian by birth.

'The men that run cricket? Both [I.T. Botham] was absolutely right about them. They know nothing about cricket. They're all "Yes-men". They're all ex-public schoolboys who sit round a table and not one of them is prepared to stand up and say, "I don't agree with this!" They're wallys. I'm sorry but they are.

'John has been with Middlesex for 25 years, he played in the Bicentenary Test and *he's* not a member of the MCC. He's on a waiting list. Lord's has been his ground for the last 25 years and he's still on a waiting list, number 999. He's got to wait for 998 people to die before he can become a member. It's pathetic. Bloody old fogeys,' she said with Antipodean passion reminiscent of Dennis Lillee.

Even the quintessentially English Wendy Wimbush, the vicar's daughter turned BBC cricket scorer, has fallen foul of a member in the Pavilion. 'It was funny. One day last summer I was coming up the stairs of the Pavilion (I'm allowed to be there to get to the radio booth on the roof) when I was spotted by a member. "Woman in the Pavilion!" he shouted, raising the alarm. So I showed him my pass. "Oh, Wendy Wimbush," he said. "How nice. I've admired you for so long. What a pleasure." And I thought, "What a prat! You daft old buffer!" because a few minutes ago he was making all this to-do. But I didn't say anything.'

'I suppose,' said Frances Edmonds, being characteristically generous, 'men just feel threatened. They want to get away from women. Find a place of solace. Even now I go to dinner parties – not my mates, I hasten to add – where they say, "Right, the men will now pass the port and you women can bugger off into the sitting-room." You know: only men can understand the serious issues of life like sport and politics and you can go into the drawing-room with the ladies, drink coffee and talk about Pampers.'

If only it were that simple. The trouble is, to many a man's consternation, women want to talk about sport and politics too. But for all the last bastions of the old buffer like the Valley of the Peace Cricket Club outside Christchurch in New Zealand, which bans all women be she wife, fiancée, mistress or even barmaid, there are small signs, accompanied by a good deal of creaking, that things are changing.

'I know that the MCC is still perceived as a very old, élitist, sexist club where the members do little else than fall asleep,' said Chris Rea, the man responsible for enhancing the image of the MCC. 'But that's not true now. It's a less and less accurate picture. We're trying to come out and into the 20th century.' He paused. 'Admittedly, it's almost the 21st century now. But change is a slow process.'

Golf

THE RYDER CUP

I couldn't breathe. I couldn't swallow. The sphincter factor was high.
                                    Hale Irwin on the Ryder Cup, 1991

The Ryder Cup is a blood sport. A brutal and mesmeric exercise in loneliness, aggression and relentless pressure. 'It's ruthless stuff,' said Mark Calcavecchia, who halved his singles match with Colin Montgomerie in 1991 having been four up with four to play. Devastated, he fled the course. His wife, Sheryl, had to bring him back. David Love was even more succinct in 1993. 'I almost threw up on myself,' he said.

It was, therefore, a chalice not untouched by poison that Bernard Gallacher inherited when he assumed captaincy of the European Ryder Cup team for the excursion to Kiawah Island in 1991, otherwise entitled the War on the Shore – The Commotion on the Ocean. The searing experience was summed up by his wife, Lesley. 'Kiawah Island,' she said firmly, 'was my worst nightmare.'

Europe lost, they lost the next one at The Belfrey as well and all too soon the third of the Gallachers' unenviable triple hailed into view – the Ryder Cup 1995 at Oak Hill Country Club, Rochester, New York. Going into the event, Bernard's record was nine Ryder Cups lost (two as captain, seven as a player) and one halved. 'I was preparing myself for the worst,' said Lesley. 'Because to lose would have been so awful from Bernard's point of view. You had to be prepared – just to be able to cope with it. I didn't like to think too much about winning. I didn't dare.'

Instead, in her widely admired role as Mother Hen, she thought about which sweets to pack, which CDs to bring, which videos to transport (*Fawlty Towers* and *Mr Bean*, among them) and what advice to dispense in the hair-raising days of run-up to the event. 'It was very, very tense. Very stressful. All those sort of adjectives. You've got the awful thought in the back of your mind. "Oh God, I hope we're not whitewashed." It's a torment really. Bernard and I discussed things openly. I knew instantly when something had upset him.'

And honourable and sensitive man that he was, there were plenty of things to upset him. His selection policy had been roundly criticised as being too woodenly attached to the European rankings, with not enough leeway for inspired 'captain's picks'. Ian Woosnam, a former US Masters winner, was affronted by Gallacher's initial rejection of him only to be delighted by an 11th-hour reprieve when José Maria Olazabal's injured toe precluded the Spaniard's inclusion. Tony Jacklin, the former Ryder Cup captain, made inflammatory, or at least insensitive, remarks about a link between Gallacher's captaincy and rudderless ships.

And then there was the Faldo divorce. *The Sun* in the spirit of true mischief if not patriotism chose the Monday the team were departing for America to announce: 'Faldo £10 million Divorce Shocker.'

'It was unforgivable, I've got to say,' said Lesley. 'I do think the tabloids ruin an awful lot of lives. They'd been sitting on that story a long time and then they chose their moment. And I will never forgive them for doing that. Never forgive. I think it was wicked.'

Even as the papers were being opened over breakfast, Gill Faldo, the second and soon-to-be ex-wife of Nick Faldo, was being driven the short distance from home in Wentworth to the Heathrow hotel where the whole team was meeting. Her husband was in America, where he was now a player on the US tour, and, it would transpire, a very close friend of a 20-year-old female college golfer, Brenna Cepelak.

Photographers on assignment began to muster in the hotel lobby. Mother Hen Gallacher was not having that. 'I stood out on the A4 to watch for her, to hand over her tickets and tell her to go straight to terminal four. I just didn't want Gill to come into the hotel where all the press were waiting for her. So I stood in the road from about 7.35 in the morning to 8.15. If anybody had seen me, known me, they would have said: "My God, what is she up to?" It was a very bad start.'

However, Gill Faldo was successfully intercepted and Concorde was ready to take off a few hours later with the team, wives, girlfriends, assorted children, nannies and caddies on board. 'I sat next to Gill on the plane,' said Lesley. 'She needed someone there on her side. Well, everybody was on her side really. But she needed to feel she had support. The women were all very good. We are a great lot. But for Gill it was a nightmare really. The press made it like that for her. *He* did, of course, but the press made it worse.'

And so with this wretched sub-plot playing away in the background, the 31st Ryder Cup literally and metaphorically took off.

At the other end of the journey, the European team was given a tremendous welcome by the Americans, who, if not smug, were wholly confident of victory. The tension was palpable and mounting. Johnny Walker's sponsorship was going to be indispensible.

It is a peculiar quirk of the Ryder Cup that in no other internationally renowned event are the wives of the protagonists so paraded and exposed. Some undoubtedly enjoy the rare shaft of limelight, to others it is pure, unadulterated torture. 'It's ridiculous. I hate it. I absolutely hate it. I think it's stupid,' said Lesley Gallacher. 'Wives at the Wembley Cup final – do they all line up and walk out? I don't know where it all hails from. But it's just part of the deal and you've got to do it. I remember – oh, gosh – 20 years ago, when the Ryder Cup was at Muirfield. I was a teenager and I had to go and collect a gift up in front of the whole American team. Well, I was ill. I was beside myself. I was wearing a cocktail dress and all you could see was my skin coming out in red blotches. Edward Heath, the Prime Minister, was there. It was my worst nightmare.'

At last, however, back in the present, the formalities were over and the game proper began. The cameras appropriately followed the action – Faldo and Montgomerie, in salmon pink, losing . . . David Gilford, in a state of grace, winning . . . Torrance and Rocca, soulmates, grinning – but their various traumas were scarcely greater than those of their wives who followed their husbands around the course.

'Oh dear, we were a bit hyper, I think,' said Lesley. 'You're nervous and you're nervous for everybody not just your spouse. One of the wives was offended by a remark made. It was nothing important, but the pressure is such that week that little remarks can get blown out of proportion. There's always lots of little unknown quantities that come into play. Little niggles. Big niggles, really.

'I remember donkey's years ago, Bernard was playing with Jack Nicklaus in a Ryder Cup. I was walking round with his wife, Barbara, and this guy in the crowd made a derogatory remark about Bernard. "This little squirt will never hole that putt," something like that. Barbara Nicklaus really laid into this man. "Do you realise you've just insulted our guests?" she said. She was really embarrassed. But, of course, it happens all the time.'

Insults were the least of the connubial problems. Suzanne Torrance had a relatively new baby to feed every few hours, Per-Ulrik Johansson's girlfriend became very upset by the order of play on the final Sunday and Gill Faldo was enduring a twilight existence with tremendous fortitude. 'She was great that week,' said Lesley. 'Terrific. Very strong. She had her moments, but, you know, it brought us together. Certainly the wives, because we were all very protective towards her. Very caring. Considerate.'

That, in essence, is the role of a Ryder Cup wife. To support, to succour, and endure the odd bit of gyp from their lifetime partner who's just fluffed a putt on the tenth. Colin Montgomerie was agitated when journalists reported him throwing a bottle of water at his heavily pregnant wife, Eimear, who was belting down the fairway behind him. 'That's the most horrific piece of journalism I've seen in a long, long time,' he said. 'It was hot, it was humid, so I said: "Look, for goodness sake, calm down. I'll get some water." So I got her some water but later I found out that's been construed as me barking at my wife, shouting at her. I think it's appalling.'

The spouses of soldiers in battle are usually left at home to knit the balaclavas. At Oak Hill, the partners were in armour themselves. Not to mention distress.

When Gallacher told Johansson he would like him, a rookie, out last on singles day, the Swede became instantly apprehensive and his girlfriend immediately upset. 'I could see what was happening,' said Lesley, fully trained in the art of bomb disposal after 20 years' experience. 'I said to her: "Look, if Per-Ulrik wins he's a hero, if he loses it's Bernard's fault. That's it really. There's no point in getting upset." And it was actually all right, in the end.'

Jane James, Mark James's wife, also demonstrated an emotional tendency. 'Sometimes you want to thump her but her heart's in the right place. She is tough. Sometimes I'd say: "Maybe we should all wear the same things." And she'd say: "Oh, I'm not wearing it." All this sort of carry on. She will tend to go her own way. I'm quite a strong person too but on these occasions, I think: "Oh, sod it. I'm not here to dictate. I'm just here to make things harmonious."'

'We're there to placate the men, keep them unstressed as much as possible in the domestic situation. We can't do much about the golf.'

So Mrs Ballesteros watched in awful fascination as her husband hit three fairways in three days. Mrs Woosnam had to suffer the angst once-removed as the Welshman doubled over as though in pain on the 18th green, hands over his eyes, as he missed the putt that would have beaten Fred Couples. And overshadowing all was the terrible plight of the out-going Mrs Faldo.

Four years ago at Kiawah, the pain had been of a different order. There, it was the gung-ho aggression of the American team, captained by Dick Stockton, that had precipitated a hostile and tense collision. Corey Pavin had worn a Desert Storm hat and the official T-shirts on sale all read: 'The Ryder Cup belongs in the USA.' Lesley Gallacher was outraged. 'I said: "How can you sell them? There's about 5,000 Europeans over here!" The guy was embarrassed. He said that's what he was sent. So the American PGA [Professional Golf Association] really didn't behave very well that week. The Americans were out to get us.

'I must say, at Kiawah, Corey was the first one to come in and say "condolences", but we didn't quite appreciate it at the time. He'd been a bit of an idiot that week. But he came to see us this time as well as the evening was drawing to a close. He said: "I'm delighted" . . . and all that. And he said: "At Kiawah, I didn't really know what it was all about." When he'd gone away Bernard said: "If that wasn't an apology, I don't know what was."'

Finally, old grievances forgotten, it came to this. Curtis Strange, the American, chipped seven feet short and missed at the 18th. Faldo had a four-foot putt that would save the Ryder Cup. He stepped up, petrified ('Everything but my putter was shaking') and knocked it in. Seve Ballesteros burst into tears.

'It felt fantastic, wonderful,' said Lesley, who was there, accompanying Gill every step of the way. 'But Gill had said to me beforehand, "What do I do if he wins? Do I go up? Do I cuddle him?" I said: "Go for it, Gill, you've got to be there. Just as if nothing's wrong." She didn't know what to do. And if you see the pictures of it, I'm there with my arm round – pushing her into him. But he sort of didn't want to know. I didn't realise that at the time, but a lot of people afterwards said: "Oh, he didn't want to give her a cuddle."'

In fact afterwards, a Nick Faldo almost moved to tears by the enormity of his win could speak only of his embrace with Seve Ballesteros whose face was awash as they fell into one another's arms. 'The best moment of my career was Seve,' said Faldo. 'For him to show the emotion he showed me, I'm very touched by that.'

A few minutes later, an exultant Irishman, Philip Walton, won the hole and match that sealed victory for the Europeans. 'Maybe the Americans know me now,' said Walton, who had been hailed as a total unknown all week. 'Tell 'em I'm related to all those Waltons on that TV show.'

Lesley Gallacher cannot remember whom she hugged first in those initial ecstatic moments when the Cup was won. 'Either Seve or a caddy, I think,' she said. But she does remember giving an impromptu interview to BBC Radio Five. Asked to describe her feelings, all she could think to say was: 'Actually, it's like having a baby. Such an amazing relief.'

PRIDE AND PREJUDICE

You women want equality, but you'll never get it because women are inferior to men in all sorts of ways – physically, intellectually and morally. There are exceptions, but on the whole women are inferior to men.
Seve Ballesteros, El Pais, 1980

There's this cartoon by Bill Stott depicting a man in pyjamas kneeling beside his bed, hands locked together in prayer. 'Dear God,' he is saying. 'Thank you for encouraging my wife to take up golf. Please don't ever let her get better than me . . .'

Something happens to men in golf clubs. Perfectly amiable, tolerant, family-loving men gather round the bar in the 19th hole and develop a pathological horror of women. 'If my husband sees a woman on the course at his golf club,' said Janice, a hospital secretary, 'he shouts: "Look out! Vermin about!"'

I know about this attitude. My father, one of the sweetest-natured individuals alive, used to let me caddy for him on a Sunday morning round North Middlesex Golf Club. I regarded this as a fabulous privilege, observed course etiquette closely, spoke when spoken to (usually about the Arsenal) and was suitably rewarded at the end by a glass of bitter lemon passed out of the window of the bar to the terrace below.

I could not be admitted to the bar because of my age. But then, enlightenment and feminism dawning, I realised I also could not be admitted because I was a girl. 'Why not, Dad?' I asked. Because, he explained patiently, it was an immutable law of nature. I dyed my hair pink by way of rebellion and had to caddy in a hat thereafter. But these small gestures of defiance have rarely dented male pride in their lair. It was an immutable law of nature then, and to a large extent, still is.

Laura Davies, the greatest woman golfer ever to swing a driver, cannot play on a Saturday or Sunday morning at either of her local clubs. 'I'm attached to two clubs, West Byfleet and Sutton Green, and both of them have restrictions on ladies playing at weekends. I think all clubs are like that, because they assume women don't work. Only in golf clubs; the rest of the Western world knows that women work and deserve to play at weekends as well as the men. I think it's a men's competition on a Saturday morning – absolutely no way would I get near the golf course. I don't think it will ever change.'

This is curious, to say the least. It is not as though men are unused to the sight of a woman with a putter in her hand (although, of course, she might be unblocking the drains at the time). Mary Queen of Scots was swishing a small white ball about in the 16th century, and scandalised society in the process. But not because she refused to let a foursome of male estate agents play through. Her husband, Darnley, had been murdered only a few days before. If this had been a man, his friends would have remarked upon the stoic common sense of a swift 18 holes; in a woman, it was rank betrayal.

For some sociological, historical and quite possibly hysterical reason, golf clubs are the last bastions of the retreating chauvinist. Even America, land of the free and Helen Gurley Brown, has its ancient and unbreakable customs.

'When I was nine in 1954 . . . I asked my father, a lawyer and a former member of Congress, why are all the people at Burning Tree Club men?' recalled Constance Casey in the *Washington Post* in 1992. 'My father explained that no women, no girls could ever go to Burning Tree because the men there were naked. Naked all the time. For weeks I tried to picture cabinet officers and senators striding down the fairways. Did golfbags chafe the senatorial things? How careful did Ike have to be when teeing off?'

Burning Tree, so the American journalist Marcia Chambers discovered in her book *The Unplayable Lie*, was a male golfer's idyll, in Bethesda, Maryland, a resort which had never permitted a woman on the premises as a member or even a guest. The female of the species was barred utterly except at Christmas when, as Chambers describes it, they were permitted to 'lay down their money at the pro shop for gifts for their men'.

It speaks volumes for the commitment of American presidents to the principle of female emancipation that Eisenhower, Nixon, Ford and Dan Quayle have all happily processed down its fairways. Or maybe not 'happily' exactly in Gerald Ford's case, the former American president who once said: 'I know I'm getting better at golf because I'm hitting fewer spectators.' It is also significant that when a change in the law decreed that Burning Tree must open itself up to women or face a retroactive tax bill of $1.2 million, the membership voted to pay the tax.

But even these sweet events do not quite prepare you for the 'Showdown at Cedar Brook', a confrontation on the links at a Long Island golf and tennis club which would eventually lead to the first ever criminal trial over tee-times in America.

To my knowledge, in Britain, it has never yet come to this. In 1988 Lee Lowell, a woman, was given permission to tee off early one weekend morning. Unfortunately, she met Roland Forman, the chairman of the men's golf commitee, on the tee. He began, so the subsequent court case heard, yelling obscenities at her. She removed herself to another tee. Forman and two accompanying men gave chase in their golf carts. Other male golfers appeared, like Indians over the horizon in a John Ford western. Eight to ten men stood in front of her. One unzipped his fly and urinated on the ground before her. Forman threw a golf ball at her. She did, however, make her escape, went to the loo and cried.

Then she dried her eyes and prosecuted. The judge in the trial declared of Forman: 'His actions on the golf course in pursuing a lone woman, speaking harshly to her, and bringing the enforcement of golf etiquette to the level of personal intimidation speak for themselves.' Forman was, however, acquitted. His actions did not reach the level of a crime in the eyes of the law. The dangerously narrowed eyes of womankind might tell you something different . . .

There is this other cartoon: a woman has just holed out from a bunker and she is saying, sand wedge in hand, to her grim-faced spouse: 'I was standing too close to the ball, my grip was all wrong, I wasn't keeping my head down, and what else . . . ?'

Golfing men treat golfing women as some sort of sub-species. They call them 'ladies' for a start. 'Why don't they call them women?' said Liz Kahn, woman golfer, journalist and campaigner against prejudice in the British golfing establishment. 'One man once said to me, "We don't want you in the men's bar because we can sweat and swear and talk about women." So I said: "Why can't you do that with us around? We're no longer in the last century. You haven't got to protect us."'

But beleaguered golfing man remains unconvinced. There is a classic moment in the infamous documentary *The Club* produced by Cicada Films for Channel Four Television in 1994. A male member of Northwood Golf Club in Middlesex is heard to opine: 'I fail to understand how women could turn up at nine o'clock in the morning and play golf. My wife couldn't. She's got to get the breakfast. Clear up the breakfast. How they're over here at nine o'clock in the morning puzzles me.'

And he meant it.

This attitude may go some way to explaining why Liz Kahn has found herself being treated like some hand-grenade with its pin removed by the masonic brotherhood of golfers. 'I've been thrown out of more places than most women have ever walked in,' she said.

She has claimed a hat-trick at the Royal and Ancient Golf Club of St Andrews, founded in 1754. For those who do not find the mere words 'Royal and Ancient' sending a shiver of veneration up and down the spine, it should be noted that this noble club is accepted worldwide as the supreme and ultimate authority on golf. Established by the Society of St Andrews Golfers, it represents the sport's spiritual home. Honorary membership of the R & A is a prize beyond measure. His Royal Highness the Duke of Edinburgh is one, as is his Royal Highness the Duke of Kent. Jack Nicklaus, Arnold Palmer and Gene Sarazan have also been granted this rarified status. One of the latest inductees was George Herbert Walker Bush, then President of the United States.

It would be fair to say that Liz Kahn doesn't have a chance of joining them. Despite playing off six in her prime, she has always found gaining entry through the portals of the great R & A a matter of deep and recurring difficulty. She made her first bold play during the British Open Championship in 1970. 'All the male journalists were having a drink in the bar there, so, as I was a working journalist too, I walked in to join them. This chap on the door said: "Sorry, Madam, you can't come in here."

'"Well, I'm a journalist. All my colleagues are in here," I said.

'"No. Ladies are not allowed in here," he said.

'"Well, how extraordinary," I said.

'"No, madam. Not even the Queen," he said.

'Quite frankly, in those days, I didn't know a lot. I thought, well, I'd better go out then. So I went out.

'The next time I tried to go in was a few years later. I was just standing inside the door because I wanted to talk to Gary Player. Keith Mackenzie was then secretary of the R & A, and he was a huge booming man. When he saw me, he roared at me to go out. I said: "Well, my journalist's badge says I can come in." He said: "Only wives of players can come in here."

'While all this was going on, a British professional I knew well had been standing nearby, watching with utter astonishment. He said: "If she was living in sin with a player – would that be all right?" As it happened, I wasn't, but it was a wonderful question. I laughed but Keith Mackenzie nearly bodily evicted me this time. He roared again and I had to go out.

'The last time I got evicted was 1990, when the Open was there again. This time I phoned up the deputy secretary before I went to find out the situation with working women journalists in the locker-room. He said that they would be allowed in.

'So I got through the front door, made my way downstairs and suddenly the locker-room attendant leapt up at me.

'"What are you doing here," he demanded.

'"I've come to interview someone," I said.

'"You can't come down here!"

'"Well, the R & A said I could."

'And, d'you know, the locker-room attendant bodily evicted me. He came at me from behind, steered me up the stairs by my elbows and straight out of the building. I was a bit shaken by this. I was nearly in tears really.

'Fortunately, I knew where I could find the club secretary, Michael Bonallack. I waited until he had finished his meeting because I didn't want to embarrass him in front of everybody and then I went up to him and said: "Michael, I've just been bodily evicted from the locker-room and yet I understand I'm allowed to go in."

He looked at me and his eyebrows went up and down when I said "bodily evicted". And he said: "No, you're not allowed in."

'I said: "But Michael, I was told I could, and I'm working."

'"But," he said, "this is St Andrews."

'"But," I said, "this is the Open Championship."

'Anyway, after two years of dialogue between us, I finally achieved equality in the locker-room for women at St Andrews during the Open Championship.'

Meeting Liz Kahn is like coming face-to-face with the nearest thing we have found to a golfing suffragette. 'What do you mean nearest?' she said. 'I'm the *only* thing we've got like a suffragette.

'To tell you the truth, I had no idea when I started what this would be like. I was there for Tony Jacklin's Open victory in 1969. Oh God, that's nearly 30 years. And I was bashed all the time. It was hell, quite frankly, and it still can be.

'The Press Golfing Society, which is for members of the press who play golf, wouldn't let me in for seven years. They said they didn't play at clubs where I could play. I said: "Where is that?" They sort of harumphed and couldn't come up with any. Eventually they said they didn't give women's prizes. I think I said: "What do you give? Balls?" I don't think that went down very well.

'But I must say, in fairness, that I belong now. I was the first woman member and ten years later I was their first women's captain.'

So things are looking up. The fair sex even exacted a full and terrible revenge on my poor father during one of his regular fourballs at the Imperial Golf Club in Hythe. His drive down the sixth was a marvel and his second shot of a length so majestic that it cleared the bunker-from-hell and sat up on a bank near the sea-front promenade, exactly in line with the pin.

Suddenly, a sight assaulted his eyes that almost deprived him of his senses. A person – worse, a woman – was stooping down towards his precious white Top-Flite and, horror, enclosing it in her dainty fist. Then she looked in his direction and waved. 'Hi there!' she trilled in an American accent. 'Is this yours?'

'Madam,' croaked the victim faintly, when his powers of speech had been partially restored, 'just put it back on the course, would you?'

She did. She threw it straight in the bunker.

It was reviving snifters all round that morning in the clubhouse. Sometimes a chap isn't safe, not even on a golf course.

LAURA DAVIES

I don't know what she weighs but, as my dear departed grandfather would say, she'd crush some grass.
                              Michael Parkinson on Laura Davies, 1994

Think of Britain's top golfers of all time. Nick Faldo: perfectionist but susceptible to making rude remarks and American blondes half his age. Tony Jacklin: the son of a Scunthorpe train driver who won the British and the US Open but his time at the top was only fleeting. Henry Cotton: a three-time British Open champion but construed as a rebel by the snobby golf establishment. Who else? Colin Montgomerie: brilliant but apt to kick sand in the face of a bunker. Sam Torrance: adorable but never won a major. Ian Woosnam: a Masters winner but dangerously fond of a lager.

Then think of Laura Davies. She is, and without much argument, the greatest woman player there is. You can phone her at home. She goes shopping with her mum. She plays football with her mates on a full-sized football pitch in her garden. She is pleasant, funny, unspoiled and blessed with the instinctive talent to hit a golf ball down a fairway that many men spend hours praying for.

She is a superstar minus a single superstar pretension. If she were a man she'd be in Pepsi commercials by now, the ultimate accolade western society can bestow (previously granted to the likes of Michael Jackson and Andre Agassi). If she had a 20-inch waist and looked like Claudia Schiffer, she'd earn ten times in endorsements the amount she does in prize money. But Laura Davies is herself: broad-shouldered, big-beamed and nearly six feet tall. So she is rather left to her own devices.

In 1996 she won the LPGA in America, one of the four majors on the women's circuit . . . 'And,' as she said, 'on the front cover of *Golf Weekly*, which is the big golf magazine over here, there was this postage-stamp-sized picture of me.

'If Nick Faldo wins the men's PGA, which is the equivalent, you know, he'd be on the front page, the back page and the middle pages. That's what disappoints me. I must admit when I saw that little picture – and the write-up was maybe half a page – I thought it was basically bloody disgraceful.

'All they moan about is how we haven't got a tennis player, haven't got this, that and the other, and yet they've got a golfer who's just won a major championship and they've got this postage-stamp-sized picture of me on the front cover. I thought that was a little bit wrong.

'Next time they want to do an article on me and they ring up, I'll say: "Well, are you that bothered? You didn't seem to be when I won my major."'

If this sounds somewhat crabbed, it is an utter misrepresentation of Davies's nature, which is invariably sunnier than the beachfront in Baywatch. She says what she thinks but her over-riding philosophy is to get out there and have some fun. Before discovering golf was her natural bent, she worked as a petrol pump attendant ('what a laugh we had'), as a supermarket checkout girl ('I had a hell of a time at Sainsbury's') and behind the window of the local bookies ('Now that really was great fun').

Her home in Surrey, she explains, is 'basically a sports facility. We've got a football pitch, a tennis court, indoor sports and one day we're building an extension that's going to have loads more games.'

She once missed the cut at a tournament in Phoenix because she had injured her wrist playing cricket in the hotel carpark. 'I went for a big, sweeping hook, fell over the kerb and landed on my wrist. It was a shame really because I was actually playing very well, but there you go.'

She loves spending money. 'I'm trying to find a Ferrari at the moment. A second-hand, red one but I can't track down the particular model I want. It's absolutely frustrating because any time I can spend money, I'll do it. I've bought lots and lots of cars. Anywhere between 15 to 20. My favourite one's the one I've got now, a BMW 850CSi. If I wasn't so greedy I'd stick with it because it's a fabulous car, but I've always had this thing about a Ferrari.

'And I do love clothes shopping. If I get a favourite thing I'll buy two or three of it and the last one never gets worn because I get bored with it by then. Obviously, I'm not really a fashion symbol' – she laughs – 'but I really like nice clothes and I always try to look as smart as I can.

'And I like to gamble, yeah! But I don't go silly. A pretty standard bet for me is one that costs £272 because you pick three horses and you have them in doubles or trebles. I might have a couple of those on a

Saturday afternoon. There's nothing better than watching a thoroughbred horse race on a Saturday afternoon if you've got a few quid on it.' She seldom bets on golf but she once won £9,500 when José Maria Olazabal won the '94 Masters at 16–1. 'Basically, I don't do it for the money. I do it for the entertainment,' she said.

'I love golf. I love winning. But at the end of the day it's just a game. That's probably why I go well, because it isn't life and death to me. There's always a game of tennis, a kickaround with a football, or a shopping spree with my mum.'

She is single and lives with her mother, Rita Allen, and her stepfather in her house-cum-leisure dome in Surrey. She travels 35 weeks of the year on the professional golf circuit. Fame has barely impinged on her at all. 'I don't like it and I don't dislike it. If people are interested in you, it means you're going well.'

But, in truth, she has always been painfully shy – 'oh my God, reading out loud at school was a misery' – and the demands of thank-you speeches have always caused far more dread in her heart than a low trajectory three-iron under the branches, over the burn, between the bunkers and around the contours of the green for a tap-in birdie. 'If I'm on the golf course and I've got a club in my hand, then the bigger the gallery the better. Because that's what I can do. I'm good at that. But hand me a microphone and I'm a vegetable. It genuinely ruins the immediate satisfaction of a round.'

The people she knows well describe her as 'a riot' and an element of mischief is detectable in her interviews. A man from the *Mail on Sunday* once prevailed on her to describe her homecoming from the US Women's Open with a hundred thousand dollars in her pocket. 'What's the first thing you say?' asked her interrogator.

'Hello,' said Laura.

'The second thing, then?' said he.

'Mum,' said Laura.

'The third?'

'What's in the post?'

'Fourth?'

'How's the dog?'

He gave up then.

Davies is not a great one for agonising over anything, and that includes her golf swing. 'Her preparation is a joke,' said leading American Nancy Lopez. 'I'll be grinding it out on the practice ground for hours. Then up strolls Laura, launches a few drives into the next county, loosens her shoulders with a couple of five-irons, then half a dozen swishes with the putter. And that's it. She's off again. The most strenuous bit is the walk to the first tee.' Davies has never had a guru and no publisher will ever make a fortune with her golf manual. Her advice runs to one simple sentence. 'Just hit the bloody ball,' she says.

She is, then, that most unusual of sporting luminaries, a doyenne without pretension, ego or a thousand lurid tabloid headlines to her name. You wonder how she has avoided the gossip columns? 'I don't do anything worth gossiping about,' she said. 'There you go, it's one of the sacrifices a top-class sportsman makes.'

Not always. Faldo did not become a notable celibate for the sake of his art around the green. Neither did Steffi Graf, romancing a Formula Three racing driver. Nor Chris Evert, for that matter, the Miss America who dated Adam Faith, Burt Reynolds, Jimmy Connors, John Lloyd, one of the Kennedys and present husband, Andy Mill, but not necessarily in that order.

Evert, nevertheless, had a pertinent comment to make about Davies's relative anonymity in the world of sport. 'It's insulting the way society demands that women athletes conform to some advertising man's image of what constitutes pretty. It's obvious society still has much to do when a supermodel like Elle MacPherson can get on to the cover of *Sports Illustrated* four times, yet the best woman golfer in the world has never been on it once.'

This – almost incredibly – is true. MacPherson has indeed been so honoured and not because she once led the New South Wales synchronised swimming foursome to second place in the Australian National Championships. No, her prominence, as it were, on the glossy pages of *SI* owes far more to her fortuitous shape, which Steve Martin once described as 'the kind of chassis which could inspire cardiac arrest in a yeti'. Not to mention my husband, who once interviewed the supermodel – a circumstance that required the sudden purchase of a rowing machine which now sits, utterly forlorn and forgotten, in our hall.

'If every synchronised swimmer looked like Elle MacPherson, football would be doomed,' he wrote following his meeting with 'The Body'. 'The turf at Wembley would be dug up to make way for an Olympic-sized pool, supporters would discard their once-beloved Stenhousemuir away strips and don sequinned swimsuits in the colours of Tottenham Hotstuff, Blackburn Belles or Brechin Breaststrokers. For the few ageing diehards who still cared, brief highlights of the FA Cup final would be shown on BBC2 immediately following the Open University.'

It's pathetic really.

But Davies, typically, bears not a batsqueak of a grudge. 'It doesn't worry me,' she said. 'I'm sure a lot of blokes like looking at Elle MacPherson on the cover of *Sports Illustrated*. It's nothing against her. Good luck to her I say. I've never been on the cover. Not even close. But it doesn't bother me. But if I *was* on it, I'd be the first one to buy it. I love things like that.'

However, leafing through the famous *SI* swimsuit issues (inducing cardiac arrests in yetis everywhere and boosting Time Inc's advertising revenue by many millions) one can detect a common thread – and not just the one holding the bikinis together. Sport and sex have become curiously intertwined. Otherwise how can you explain the sight of Elle biting seductively on her finger wearing a cossie only half attached to her person. 'Elle's IsaLomas suit ($52) should give her an unusual tan,' says the caption disingenuously. That clump you hear is the sound of falling yeti.

In this prevailing climate the likes of Laura Davies will always be diminished because no matter how sparkling and skilful, decent and genuine, she falls foul of the first law of sports marketing, that she should look like a nymphette and to hell with the nine iron.

'Well, there's not much I can do about my size, is there?' she said patiently. 'I've said it before, I'd like to look like Elle, but I don't. If I did I probably wouldn't be winning major championships. It's just the way I am. I've always played sport and because of that I've got pretty strong shoulders and a pretty strong frame really.'

Laura is not a girlie. Neither is she resentful. But when she clobbers the ball 360 yards down a fairway, chips on to the green with the audacity of a Ballesteros, wins 43 tournaments in 11 years as a pro, treats the press like old friends and herself to a Ferrari Testarossa (if only she could find it), you feel she deserves better of the Great British sporting public.

But at least she doesn't let it slow her down. Not behind the wheel anyway. She's not a fast driver, they tell you in the locker-room, merely a low flier. 'I did 168 on the German autobahn,' she admitted. 'But the car is built to go really fast. I mean, you wouldn't try that in a Skoda, would you? Obviously if you have a blow-out at that speed, you're dead whatever you're driving. But I always give the tyres a good kick before I set off. Just to make sure.'

CADDIES AND OTHER FOLLOWERS

Girls, of course, excel as caddies in Japan. Sam Snead had to be deterred from leaving his clubs behind and bringing his caddie home in the bag in their place.

　　　　　　　　　　　　　　　　　　　Henry Longhurst, 1978

Geisha girls not being readily available in western culture ('Make your own bloody tea!' springs to mind as a suitably liberated rejoinder) men have been forced to make other arrangements. But if they were really smart they would go out and get themselves a female caddie.

Only in this rare and tender occupation does the gentle spirit of devotion and service live on.

'Stand still please,' booms the voice of Fanny Sunesson, Nick Faldo's caddie since February 1990. She is addressing the understandably timorous spectators at the World Matchplay Championships. 'No cameras please!' 'Stand back on the left. We don't want to see any of you.'

It is the same everywhere they go, the dynamic golfing duo. He, the winner of the Masters 1996. She, doyenne of female professional golf caddies (indeed, the *only* female professional golf caddie), whose working life is dedicated to the peace and prosperity of her employer.

Two days before a major tournament Sunesson is out on the course, measuring. With a surveyor's wheel she notes the yardage of every hole with a pencil in an old exercise book. She draws maps of each hole. She compares notes with last year's. An ordinance survey cartographer could scarcely demonstrate more attention to detail than the former Swedish golfer who surrendered her sport to become a caddie of world renown.

Despite her necessary closeness to her employer, not the smallest suggestion of impropriety has ever been laid at her locker. Indeed, Faldo's second wife Gill, before their divorce due to an entirely different matter, seemed serenely happy that her difficult husband should enjoy the company of one so attuned to his moods. 'She knows how to handle him,' she said. 'She can calm him down when necessary. Sometimes his shoulders will drop when things go wrong, but she will jolt him back on course, keep him going.'

But Sunesson's role goes way beyond cheerleading. She devotes herself to the sustained perfection of his clubs, shoes and gloves as well as the Faldo game. She carries his 40lb golf bag around every course, to the lasting detriment of her back. (One specialist advised a six-month rest which did not elicit the required result. She merely hefted her burden on to her other shoulder.) She learns the precise distance to the hole from any part of the course, offers advice on the line of putts and can be occasionally required to hold Faldo's leg on the practice course to correct his sway. She can spend up to 12 hours a day in his company, playing, practising, discussing the finer points and, for that, Faldo is profoundly grateful.

'We have a great understanding,' he said. 'She knows me and my moods and can control them. I know I can be difficult at times, when things aren't going right, but Fanny has such a positive attitude.'

She also earns, rumour has it, around £250,000 a year and has her own clothing contract, which makes her one of the highest-paid women in golf. She is certainly one of the most astute. Had she remained in discus throwing, her favourite childhood sport, or clay pigeon shooting, her spare-time hobby, or even in golf (she played off five at her peak), she was unlikely to have reached the level of fame and riches she can now command.

On the other hand, one – perhaps all – of Lee Trevino's wives reached similar heights of wealth and notoriety, and didn't even have to 'Brasso' his sand wedge. 'I have to win this tournament,' said a hard-pressed Trevino at the US Open in 1974. 'My wife bought $50,000 worth of furniture last week. And you should see the house she built around it.' This is a situation with which many male golfers seem to sympathise. 'I'm not winning,' said Rex Caldwell, dejectedly. 'But I think my ex-wife is the twelfth leading money winner on tour.'

The trouble with female supporters, especially those in the spouse department, is that they have tended to become a touch disillusioned by the failure of their husbands to come home for years.

There was bad news for Trevino in 1983: 'It was a complete surprise to me, but, on the other hand, it didn't surprise me at all,' he said of his divorce from his first wife, Claudia. 'That'll happen when you haven't been home in 18 years.' And then there was the good news. 'Same name, that way I won't forget it,' he said of his second wife, Claudia.

'And I don't have to change the towels. I got a $1.4 million home with my initials all over it, so I might as well live with someone whose name begins with a C.'

As Walter Hagen once said: 'Call every woman "Sugar" and you can't go wrong.'

Trish 'Sugar' Johnson, one of Britain's finest golfers and the leading European money winner in 1990, may have misunderstood the concept of 'supporters on tour'. She is supposed to have one, not be one. But the daughter of a one-time Arsenal junior player, she fell in love with the lads at Highbury as a child and is now in the grip of a life-long passion. Not many other pro golfers have three season tickets for the North Bank. It can make playing golf a bit awkward.

'I suppose the best one really was Copenhagen,' she said, when prompted to recollect her most madcap dash from a golf tournament. 'I was out in the States in the middle of a four-week run and Arsenal were in Denmark for the 1994 Cup-Winners Cup final. I was on my way to Nashville when I thought, "This is ridiculous." We hadn't been to a European final for God knows how many years. So I thought, "Right. I reckon I can fly back from Atlanta, fly out to Copenhagen, watch the match, get back to London and fly to Nashville in time for the tournament to begin on the Friday." Unfortunately, after the final, it didn't quite work out like that.' Arsenal won. One-nil. Smith scored. 'Everyone was just annihilated after the match, to say the least. So I missed that tournament.

'The first Arsenal game I ever saw was against West Bromwich Albion at the Hawthorns. Well, we were living in Devon at the time. There was about seven of us. About 1982. Petrovic was playing. He scored an absolute corker just before half-time. Free kick.

'I've always supported them but only in the last four to five years have I been in the position, financially, to see them whenever I wanted to. I always lived in remote parts of the bloody country before that. But in the last four years, if it's been possible not to miss a game, I haven't missed it. This season's been the best actually because there's a guy who's a caddy, he used to caddy for Laura actually, and he's an Arsenal fan as well, so this winter we've been everywhere together.

'The older I get, the more I love it. I absolutely love it. It takes up a huge amount of time, but I'll tell you what's interesting. I've just bought a new computer, a laptop, and you can get into this thing just like the Internet. Last week I was in Washington and I discovered the most amazing thing – I could get right into the Arsenal Team Talk. It was just incredible. Every bit of gossip. Every single game this season there was a report on. So it's glorious. Now I'll never be away from them even when I'm away.'

One feels obliged to point out that she may have her priorities backwards. That sports celebrities are required to embrace hero worship rather than emit their own elsewhere. 'Yes, well,' she said. 'I find golf supporters very strange. Last week we were at the US Open and there were ten or twelve of us eating in this bar when a woman came up and said: "I've just driven 15 hours from Michigan to watch you lot play tomorrow." And we looked at her and thought: "What a nutcase!"

'I'm not keen on the travelling myself. Can't stand that and the fact that it's very difficult to have a relationship is not the best either. You can't be involved with someone and then say: "I'm off for six months. See you in October." I know it works the other way round. A woman will sit there and wait for the man but you find very few men willing to do the same.

'Helen Alfredsson has managed with Leo, but then Leo's a professional sportsman. He understands. Whereas if you went out with someone who didn't, they'd think: "What a strange person. Plays golf half the year and watches football the next."

'I did go out with a fella from the States for about five years. It ended about three years ago. He was a caddie – he still caddies – and I more or less thought we were going to get married and everything but it just didn't happen. And after about five years of doing the same things it got a bit stale really. So, you know, that was a long-term relationship and afterwards, even though I sort of broke up with him, it was quite a strange feeling for a long time. We're both fine now. Get on better probably.

'That's something – I suppose you could call it a sacrifice. But when you win a tournament, especially in America, you know you've beaten absolutely everybody. You're the best in the world that week. I've won ten tournaments so far, eight in Europe, two in America. Las Vegas and Atlanta.

'Las Vegas was a very strange feeling because I came from nowhere to win comfortably. I shot a 67 in a hurricane. I had a three-foot putt to win and four putts in hand but I was shaking like a leaf and the feeling in my stomach was dreadful. I thought I was going to faint. When it went in – well, there *is* no better feeling. *There Is No Better Feeling.*

'I would have loved to experience scoring a goal. The other day I was watching Arsenal's video of the season because I hadn't seen the Bolton game. And when I watched Bergkamp score that goal – I just go cold, I get goosebumps. Scoring that type of goal to me is like making the miracle shot. I think scoring a goal must be a fabulous feeling. I can see why Charlie George said it's better than sex.'

Arsenal and all things related are never far from her thoughts. 'I've met some of the players, very briefly. Only a few weeks ago I played in Paul Merson's testimonial golf day somewhere in North London. I met Dixon. Talked to him for quite a bit. Met "Merse" for a second. Stevie Bould was lovely, gorgeous, a real charmer. And I think he, sort of, knew me because he said things like, "Where are you playing next?" The only one I thought was a total and utter prat was the one that managed to get pissed out of his head in the middle of the afternoon. But there's no accounting for some people. As far as I'm concerned he's just a non-entity.'

Unlike some people she could mention. 'When I heard Dennis Bergkamp signed for Arsenal at the start of last season, I thought, "That can't be right. A player like him, signing for a club like us." But it's the best season I've ever known. The one reason I've been to every game is that Bergkamp's playing. Simple as that. We've still got the Jensens of this world and crap like that but I've never seen a player like Bergkamp. Liam Brady's been the closest thing but I even think Bergkamp's better. His touch, his skill, everything. I don't care how much he cost. Keep hold of him and build the team around him. It could be glorious.'

Not caring how much things cost is an endearing trait of Johnson's. 'I'm skint at the moment,' she said happily. 'I've got nothing but that's because when I've got money, I spend it. I bought this lovely Jaguar XJS once. Racing green. But it ended up being useless. It had fantastic speed but it was big for a sports car and it didn't have power steering. It was just one of those stupid things you do. I'd obviously won a bit of money the week before and thought, "OK. I quite like that. I'll have it."

'And I must admit I was in New York once for a tournament and I went for a walk down Fifth Avenue. All I wanted was a couple of gold bangles. About an hour later I walked out of a shop with a diamond bracelet and a diamond necklace. But – it was reduced from $15,000 to $6,500 so I figured I got a good deal.'

As in life. 'I've got three elder brothers and we were brought up by the sea in north Devon. It was brilliant. We lived near a golf course, the Royal North Devon, and they let me join the ladies' section when I was a junior. They even let me play in the men's medals when I got down to a five handicap. For a club with "Royal" in its title, that was fantastic.

'To be honest, if I had a chance to change anything in my life, I wouldn't change a thing. Nothing could be any better. I travel the world. I do something I'm very good at. I earn a lot of money. And I thoroughly enjoy it.'

Plus . . . 'I met Paul Merson's brother-in-law the other day. He's a very keen golfer. Plays at Ealing. Anyway, he said he'll take me up to watch Paul train sometimes. So I'm quite looking forward to the Arsenal's pre-season training. But I won't push it. I know what it's like when people come up – I've seen it done to my friends and it happens now and again to me – and it alienates people. I don't like to push in. At the end of the day, they're my heroes.'

PLAYERS

The LPGA needs a player that looks like Farrah Fawcett and plays like Jack Nicklaus. Instead, they've got players who look like Jack Nicklaus and play like Farrah Fawcett.
                    Anon, quoted in *Golf Digest*, 1981

Suddenly, lesbianism became an issue in women's golf. Perhaps it always had been at some unspoken level, but when the American golfer Muffin Spencer-Devlin chose to announce that she was gay at a tournament in 1996, the rumours materialized into solid fact.

Appropriately, Spencer-Devlin dressed in chainmail to be photographed by *Sports Illustrated*, her lifetime preoccupation with all things Camelot lending a suitably heroic lustre to her stand. 'Coming out is like an incredibly huge weight being lifted from my shoulders,' she said. 'No more living in the shadows. No more lies.'

She was not the biggest name in golf at the time. With three LPGA (Ladies Professional Golf Association) wins in 18 years to her credit, she is hardly the Laura Davies of Laguna Beach, her home town. But with this defiant act, she became a significant figure. Before her statement, generously and unsensationally reported in the States, she had been seen as a slightly eccentric figure more likely to make the news for her latest skydive or bungee jump or, indeed, short stay in a psychiatric hospital. She had been plagued by manic depression for most of her life, with the result that she could spend $30,000 on a two-week shopping spree in Europe or be taken off to New York's Bellevue hospital in a straitjacket following a disturbance in the lobby of the Waldorf Astoria.

Corporate America was watching all this. All those corporate dollars waiting to pounce on some clean-limbed, image-conscious sport like American football (drug problems); baseball (on strike occasionally); ice hockey (punch-ups galore); or the one-man show basketball has become. Women's golf was always going to struggle against this august line-up; the conservative, male establishment largely saw to that.

'Let's face facts,' said Ben Wright, a British commentator with CBS in an interview with the *New Journal* in America, 'Lesbians in sport hurt women's golf. It's paraded. There's a defiance in them in the past decade.' For this not-necessarily sensitive airing of his views he was laundered out of women's golf broadcasting, but the words hung in the air demanding rebuttal from the female professionals themselves.

Dottie Pepper, née Mochrie, a fearsome competitor, took up the challenge with the remark that the tour was merely a microcosm of society. 'We have breast cancer out here, divorce, the lot. We're just normal people.' Nancy Lopez enquired: 'Why doesn't Wright talk about the men on Tour who fool around on their wives?'

Nevertheless, as Spencer-Devlin received a 'Woman of Courage' award for her revelations during a tournament at Palm Springs, a tour player, a young mother, was heard to ask sorrowfully: 'Whatever kind of message is this we're sending out?' It would be naïve to assume she did not have a point. Middle America, reared on Doris Day and Angela Lansbury (and even Madonna likes guys even if she doesn't want to marry one), was being asked to disregard its prejudice. Prejudices, in fact. Not only have women invaded the golf course, some of them are smoking cigars.

But women's golf was beside itself with tolerance and understanding. 'I applaud Muffin,' said LPGA president and tour veteran, Vicki Fergon. 'I'm not saying every player will be thrilled about it, but we're a family and we respect each other.'

'I know there are still individuals who have problems with diversity,' said LPGA commissioner, politically and correctly. 'But we've come so far as a society that I don't see this as a topic that moves people.'

Spencer-Devlin, meanwhile, was moved to take 70 pills a day to curb her mood-swings but certainly presented a joyous face to the press as she contemplated an exchange of vows with her companion, Lynda Roth, a musician and composer, with whom she has lived since 1994.

'Muffin is dramatic, she's warm, she's funny, and she's a truly gifted athlete who has had to contend with great travails in life,' said commissioner Ritts, still pedalling. 'If someone tags her as gay and never experiences the rich colours of her life – well, it's a lost opportunity for them.'

Just why it should matter so profoundly with whom a person sleeps when they are only required to hit a golf ball pin-high has never been fully explained. Perhaps it is merely the curse of celebrity, demanding 'who, what and when' of any poor soul's sex life once they have featured on a TV highlights package. More pertinently, there might be a vestige of bigotry in the thoughtwaves that link female golfers with moustached spinsters with a passion for bunker practice and one another.

In which case, Jan Stephenson's (1983 US Open champion) modelling for *Playboy* and Nancy Lopez's (three times US LPGA champion) production of children must have blown more than a few mental fuses in their time. The term 'professional female golfer' covers a multitude of characters. For instance, Helen Alfredsson is a Swede but there her resemblance with Stefan Edberg ends. Her career in Swedish High School was marked by regular all-night parties and consumption of the seriously misnamed 'Long Island iced tea' (a combination of several potent liquors). 'I like them because they don't waste much time,' said the 1990 British Women's Open Champion.

While Edberg – forever whiter than his tennis whites – took up with fellow-player Mats Wilander's former girlfriend and claimed that the day he married her was the happiest of his life, Alfredsson became romantically involved with a former Mexican World Cup footballer, 13 years her senior, who was going through a divorce. 'I saw this guy with tight pants on, shirt open to here, and all these gold chains,' said Alfredsson, obviously not still in the first flush of infatuation. 'I said to myself, "You got to be crazy," but then I thought, "Well, why not?" We had a great time.' For this intense enjoyment, she paid. By now attending the US International University in San Diego on a golf scholarship, she was a member of the college team. Except when she was suspended. This happened with disarming regularity. Once for reading textbooks during golf practice and finally, forever, for dating Leo Cuellar, who was the school's men's soccer coach at the time.

She is invariably described in print as 'the willowy red-head' which cannot be objected to on sexist grounds by those of us who have described Edberg as 'the lissom-limbed blond' since his appearance on the tennis tour in 1983. Certainly, Alfredsson is unperturbed, posing for photos on the jet-black Harley Davidson she bought in 1995 before she had acquired a licence to ride it. She talks freely of the schoolgirl phase in which she indulged as a runaway model in Paris. 'I hated it. It was a meat market,' she said. She developed anorexia, lost two stones in weight and her hair began to fall out. But she came back from the brink.

As a child she had always possessed a combative streak. 'I liked to arm-wrestle the boys,' she said. 'And I always beat them.' (This would explain the likes of Edberg's docile nature.) So she departed Paris, went to America, met Cuellar and embarked on the Women's Professional Golf European Tour. Her boyfriend joined her as her caddie during the summers. Finances being tight, they slept in their car at night on the road and dined on prosciutto and cheese. It was worth it. She was voted WPGET Rookie of the Year in 1989 and did not miss a cut in six years.

In 1994, and now on the lucrative American tour, she shot an opening round 63 in the US Open at Indianwood Golf and Country Club. Eight under par. It broke the women's one-round Open record by two strokes. More significantly, it equalled the men's record held by Johnny Miller, Jack Nicklaus and Tom Weiskopf.

A good deal of mental revision was required in the wake of this performance. The men who said things like . . .

'One thing about caddying for these dames, it keeps you out of the hot sun.' (Joe Bean, *A Caddy's Diary*, 1992)

'Aware of their long life expectancy, they play slowly, hunt for a ball for 20 minutes and permutate their scores the way they figure out who has to pay for what after lunch.' (Rex Lardner on women golfers, 1960.)

'She said, "Oh, I'm so excited! I've never been on a par five in two before. If I sink this putt, it'll be my first eagle! I'll kill myself!" Her husband said, "It's a gimme."' (Buddy Hacket, *The Truth About Golf and Other Lies*, 1968)

. . . suddenly discovered their ammunition was running rather low.

It even transpires that some women golfers, far from being dizzy broads apt to sunbathe in the sand traps, have a competitive ire that makes Colin Montgomerie look like a poodle. Like the American, Dottie Mochrie, of whom it was once said: 'She's got a competitive drive most people can't even understand.' Whooping at her good shots, scowling at the bad ones, she has been known to conduct herself on a fairway rather like a battletrooper storming the beach at Normandy.

This is not the British way, it must be said. Lisa Dermott of Royal Liverpool Golf Club who made her Curtis Cup debut in 1996, may have been a one-woman storm in her time, but usually in a wine bar. 'I'm quite outgoing,' she admitted, from a hotel in Killarney where she performed the neat trick of conforming to a Cup team management's no-alcohol policy whilst also celebrating a friend's birthday party.

She took to golf at a young age when her grandfather cut down a four wood and encouraged her to whack balls all over the garden. By the age of ten she was good enough to play the ladies section of St Melud Golf Club, which proudly boasted a nine-hole course 'up the side of a mountain' in Prestatyn, near Llandudno. 'It was really, really small and quite tricky,' she said.

The 'quite tricky' might also apply to herself. For instance, it came to the attention of the staff at Prestatyn High School that one of their pupils was suffering various illnesses with alarming regularity on Thursdays. 'I see you were unwell last week,' a teacher might idly remark. Lisa would reply non-committally. 'I also see you did quite well in your monthly medal,' the teacher would continue.

'Ah . . .' said Lisa.

'But I was great really,' she says of her schooldays. 'I got seven GCSEs in the end. When I was there I worked.'

The dedication to golf, if not to academia, has brought her many rewards including the Welsh Women's championship for the second year in succession in 1996 when she beat the eight-times champion Vicki Thomas four and three in the final. But her success has in no way precluded an appreciation of normal life and frivolity as so often happens to the more battery-driven drones of the sporting world. It is entirely to her credit that she met her boyfriend in a club near Altrincham when he came over and asked a table of 20 women whether anyone would like a drink. 'Yeah,' she announced. 'I'll have a pint.'

Tennis

WIMBLEDON 1996

New Yorkers love it when you spill your guts out there. Spill your guts at Wimbledon and they make you stop and clean it up.
                                                            Jimmy Connors

Like the spartan rooms in a bachelor pad, Wimbledon needed a woman's touch. We'd seen the booming serves, the earth tremor volleys, the bludgeoning of baselines, the grimness of business. Now the men's singles final was about to begin and more of the same was threatened, especially from Richard Krajicek, an Ajax supporter from Rotterdam, who had beaten the reigning three-times champion, Pete Sampras, in the quarter-finals and served aces at 131 mph.

Then Melissa Johnson, bless her, intervened. All the world loves a waitress and never more so than when she's stripped down to the tiniest of pinnies and streaking across the grass of the Centre Court towards the Royal Box. Showing 'her netty bits', as *The Sun* explained carefully to its readers.

Amongst those delighted by her appearance were the two men's finalists themselves and the laughing Duke of Kent who might have found himself kneed in the heraldic crest had his wife not been the darling, ever amiable, Duchess.

The sense of anticlimax upon her departure was palpable. Krajicek won, it rained a bit and the only frisson of excitement was probably occurring in the tiny policeroom (one desk and a notebook) manned by PC Steve Wyatt in the bowels of the stadium. An arrested streaker was their most momentous event of a terribly dull week in which 'theft of purse' and a 'common assault' between a ticket tout and a security guard ('He pushed me' – 'No, I didn't. *He* pushed *me*!') were the only highlights.

However, the losing finalist, MaliVai Washington of the United States, bidding to become only the second black man to win Wimbledon following Arther Ashe in 1975, conducted himself with such grace in defeat, he was a redeeming feature of a generally lustreless tournament. As he took the acclaim of the crowd before leaving the court to the new Champion, he lifted his white shirt in gentle mockery of the streaker who had gone before. The crowd went wild. Not for nothing was Mr Washington voted into the Top 50 of America's Most Beautiful People, 1994.

All in all, it was a curious year. The seeds were scattered to the four winds (and rain) with barely a Pimms being drunk in the champagne bar. Or a champagne being drunk in the Pimms tent. For many people, it must be said, arrive at Wimbledon with the twin intents of seeing Andre Agassi in the flesh and hearing a barman utter the words: 'Are you being served?'

If so, Agassi was a disappointment. His flesh might have been willing, but his mind was elsewhere as he slumped to a first round defeat against a 25-year-old American qualifier, ranked 278 places below him, before heading to the airport where he declined to talk or sign autographs. 'Shame the tournament's over,' said an Aussie journalist on day two.

In a sense he was right. No Agassi, no fireworks, is one reasonable interpretation of modern tennis and had it not been for the rise and rise of the Briton – don't scoff – Tim Henman, who picked his way confidently through a gaping draw to become the Story of the Tournament this could have been one of the least gripping Fortnights of all time.

What happened to everyone? First, it rained and rained and rained until the court coverers and their sheets of tarpaulin became more recognisable personalities than the players (not difficult). Then Monica Seles, seeded two, went out to a blonde Slovakian football follower, Katarina Studenikova who had her boyfriend and a stuffed tiger with her in London for luck.

The Seles exit was followed swiftly in the men's event by Stefan Edberg (to Marc Rosset), Marc Rosset (to Patrick Rafter), Boris Becker (to 'popped' wrist), Michael Stich (to Krajicek) . . . and so it went on and on until there were two. Thus, the men's final was contested between two unseeded players for the first time in Wimbledon's history.

The women's event, naturally, was more decorous. Fondly, the women talk about 'depth'. In which case they must mean their ability to read Danielle Steel's romantic novels in more than one language. There is no depth in women's tennis, admirably revealed by the fact that Steffi Graf, playing with the handicap of a snivelling cold and cough, whacked her way through to the final, where she was joined with strict predictability by Arantxa Sanchez Vicario, having dropped just one set all Fortnight long against Kimiko Date of Japan.

Indeed, Graf's toughest challenge was in responding to an accusation by Martina Navratilova, the nine-times Wimbledon champion now restricting herself at the age of 39 to mixed doubles, that the German was exaggerating the nature of a leg injury. 'Steffi Graf could run the quarter mile at the Olympics,' said Navratilova. 'If you read the papers you'd think she belongs in the hospital, but if you look at her she's running like a gazelle.'

Graf was miffed. 'I saw Martina and she said she was sorry for the way it had come out. She should know better than to say those things. She's lucky she doesn't have to live with these things.'

There were other things Graf had to live with. Her father was in Mannheim Prison on tax avoidance charges and one entire bath in 'The Upper Ladies' dressing-room had been *filled* with long-stem red roses from an admirer. A foolish gesture when you think about the state of her sinuses, not to mention the state of her boyfriend, the Formula Three racing driver, Michael Bartels. However, she remains open to offers apparently. 'Marry me, Steffi,' cried a voice on the Centre Court. 'How much money have you got?' she retorted. He shut up after that. Not enough to get her dad out of jail, seemed to be the gist.

Meanwhile, the very existence of such a thing as 'The Upper Ladies' dressing-room caused some pause for thought. So British, so élitist, so redolent of class structure that Ivan Lendl once observed: 'Wimbledon is different. You have to wear those ties and badges, and you have to drop everything at four o'clock sharp so that you can have your cup of tea. And if you don't have a cup of tea at four they send you a letter to return your tie.'

The Radio Five commentator, Barbara Potter, an extraordinary exception to the rule in her playing days, being the granddaughter of a Pulitzer Prize winner and a student of history, psychology and European cuisine, has seen both upper and lower dressing-rooms ('But I can't get within barking distance of the men's,' she said with some disappointment).

'The "Lower" is big, blond and banal. Suitable for large numbers with showers, not baths, and long benches, not cubby holes. The "Upper" used to be reserved for God knows what aristocracy. Now, at least, it's a meritocracy with the highest-ranked players being allowed to use it. It's very cushioned, there's lots of dressing tables, several baths. It's more plush, more quiet and more deadly – in terms of intent.'

In terms of her demeanour, Mary Pierce would have preferred to skip the Upper echelon altogether and get changed in the Royal Box. 'She behaves like she's the Queen on the court, but that title belongs to Martina,' said Clare Taylor, a straight-talking Briton who was kept waiting on court by the fashionably late French-Canadian at the start of their match.

This disdainful performance did little to quell her popularity in certain quarters (male) which centres almost entirely round a dress. In Paris she had worn a clinging black halter-neck which the makers *Nike* called 'the Cross Back' and the male journalists would have called 'heaven' had they not lost their powers of speech. It was made, said *Nike*, from a functional material called Dri-fit that Arsenal are using for their shirts. The real point, however, is that it was not made from very *much* of it.

Graf had noticed. 'There's no way I could wear that dress,' she said. 'My shoulders are too big and I'd be scared to bend down.' Imagine, then, the outcry when Madame Pierce arrived at Wimbledon dressed for ward duty in a much more staid white nurse's outfit instead. At first, grown men wept but then, as Jon Henderson of the *Observer* noted, they came round to her way of thinking. 'The inference that male spectators would be less distracted by this more formal attire,' he said, 'showed a complete lack of understanding of what a crisp, white uniform that unbuttons down the front can do to a chap.' Anyway, Pierce went out in quarter-finals which just goes to show there is only so far that looks can take you.

And speaking of 'far' horizons, Mary Jo Fernandez, a normally sweet and Christian girl, was not best pleased by the distance she had to keep walking to and from the rain-interrupted play on Court 13. She had a point. At the Italian Open Lamborghini golf carts ferry the players to their courts. Some people say these players are spoiled, but I can't think why.

So where else did excitement reside? The year before, we'd had Jeff Tarrango's explusion, his wife slapping an umpire, Murphy Jensen disappearing (and claiming kidnap by aliens) and temperatures roaring into the 100s (admittedly with the help of a tabloid man's cigarette lighter under the thermometer). It was still hot, though. Shirli-Ann Siddall collapsed during her first doubles match. 'What about that then?' said the *Sun* man. 'Shirli-Ann Sizzle!'

Part of the sense of let-down certainly involved the scaling down of the Rotters' operation. As any number of former Champions could tell you, the Rotters are the great tabloid news-gatherers who down the years have reported such 'facts' as Seles missing Wimbledon because she was pregnant, Becker being served with a 'bonking ban' and Maria Bueno being engaged to – as Chief Rotter, John Jackson of the *Mirror* put it – 'a bloke who turned out to be a German pouf'.

Yet nothing, but nothing, surpasses the event in 1981 when McEnroe came into the interview room for the traditional post-match press grilling. Journalists being journalists . . . what happened next has been variously reported but since a video captured the outcome for posterity the basic facts are not in doubt.

Jackson, or perhaps it was James Whitaker, now the famed and eminent Royal Reporter, asked McEnroe if it was true his girlfriend, Stacey, had returned to America. McEnroe was outraged, so was a radio reporter from New York who demanded of Nigel Clarke of the *Mirror*: 'Is this a press conference or a circus?' A heated exchange occurred during which Clarke was affronted by the repeated use of a certain word he considered objectionable. He invited the American to step outside but then matters became pressing. He punched the radio man in the stomach and then – as a sort of follow-up volley – 'clumped 'im' behind the ear.

The resulting brawl involving at least nine individuals rolling around on the floor, with desks and chairs and notebooks flying, led the lunchtime news on television. Clarke's young daughter was waiting for Playschool. 'Mum!' she shouted. 'Mum! Someone's hitting Daddy on television.'

After the event, both *Daily Mirror* men were hauled before the Wimbledon Commitee (a far more daunting array of military characters than usually comprises a war cabinet) and asked to explain themselves. Clarke described the American's provocation. 'I was totally exonerated,' he said. 'They told me: "Quite right, old boy. But try not to behave like a yahoo in future."'

Wimbledon '96 was nothing like this. The players behaved, even the press behaved (up to a point). The closest thing we came to a Wild Thing was Stephen Bierley of the *Guardian* staying in the same London hotel as King Crimson, Iggy Pop and 'someone from Take That'. Bierley was not to know. He's a birdwatcher.

Even the St John's Ambulance were woefully underemployed, there being no heatwave nor Agassi-mania to contend with. Their principal calls to arms involved women with blisters in unsuitable shoes and swift help in the administration of a morning-after pill.

The most controversial decision of the Fortnight did not involve the players but the umpires – and it was a bitter pill that one of them had to swallow. There were five gold badge holders (badges again!) from whom to select the umpire for the men's final. Only one had never done the final before, making the choice, one would have thought, a formality. However, someone noticed that Jane Harvey was a woman. And so they gave the job to one of the others, more acceptable to the men's tennis tour by virtue of the fact he was born male.

But, as the Rolling Stones (*not* staying at Bierley's hotel) once said: it's all over now. Steffi Graf won again, coming closer to Margaret Court's record of 24 Grand Slam singles titles and to Navratilova's incredible nine Wimbledon tiaras. Richard Krajicek became the first Dutchman to win a Grand Slam. Yet neither Champion will go down as the star of the Fortnight.

That honour belonged to one man and one man alone, who rocked them in the aisles and under the rain-soaked blankets with a performance on the Centre Court of truly unforgettable proportions.

Cliff Richard, a rose in his buttonhole, a badge (naturally) on his lapel, a microphone in his hand, defied the rain and the earnest prayers of the musical to stage a one-man sing-along from the stands. 'Congratulations', 'All Shook Up' and the fantastically incongruous 'Summer Holiday' were belted out among others for the rich entertainment of the crowd. He was backed by his Supremes, in this case Pam Shriver, Gigi Fernandez, Ros Nideffer and Martina Navratilova, and there is no doubt about it, *some people were smiling*.

The bachelor boy and the streaker: a vintage set from Wimbledon '96.

LAZY FAT PIGS

When I go to the beauty parlour, I always use the emergency entrance. Sometimes I just go for an estimate.
                                                    Phyllis Diller

It was the reigning Wimbledon champion, Richard Krajicek, who once declared that female tennis players were a bunch of 'lazy fat pigs'. In this humble opinion, he was joined by many male tennis players who have expressed similar sentiments down the years. 'Crap!' said Pat Cash. 'Overweight,' said John Lloyd. Krajicek's words caused a sensation. 'The women in the locker-room were appalled and disgusted,' said the American tennis commentator, Mary Carillo. 'The men in the locker-room gave him high-fives for two weeks.'

It was the middle Saturday of Wimbledon 1992 and Steffi Graf had been embroiled in a difficult match with Mariaan de Swardt of South Africa which she eventually won 5–7, 6–0, 7–5. Perhaps Krajicek caught a glimpse of play. De Swarte had been raised on a Johannesburg farm by parents shockingly unaware of genetic engineering. She was big.

'You know my whole theory about Big Babe tennis,' said Carillo, explaining the phenomenon. 'If women are tall and strong they can play professional tennis at a very high level without being fast or fit. Because they're just *big babes*. They hit the ball really hard, really flat, and I mean, look at them. Mary Pierce is a big babe. Lindsay Davenport is a big babe. And Mariaane de Swardt would certainly fall into the big babe category. The lovely thing about it is that the women go along with it. They call themselves big babes now.'

Indeed de Swardt, an intelligent, thoughtful woman, admits: 'I will never be as slim as Steffi Graf. But I have other talents. It used to upset me, but now I just figure these people have nothing else to talk about. There's so much bad in the world, I find it hard to believe that people would choose to focus on negative things. But I admit it really bugged me in the beginning.'

The thing is, it never let up. At Wimbledon 1995, Paul Hayward of the *Daily Telegraph* risked considerable wrath by writing: 'Speculation on the subject of players' bodies takes us into a minefield of sexual politics. But the evidence of the eye is clear and need not be obscured by the fear of saying something unpalatable. Many would argue that the likes of Davenport, De Swardt and [Judith] Wiesner, to name just three, are demonstrably above their optimum fighting weights.'

It was a courageous and well-constructed point, somewhat at odds with the headline on the piece (written by somebody else): 'Overweight, Overpaid and Over Here For Dinner.'

'I got a considerable amount of flak,' said Hayward ruefully. 'The CEO of the Women's tour came looking for me, some of my female colleagues were not impressed and even some of the male writers had a go in print. I was very unhappy about the headline, to say the least.'

It was a case of the messenger being riddled with bullet holes but the real problem for women's tennis is that it is a swirling mass – not of fat-bottomed girls – but of contradictions. On one hand it wishes its proponents to be judged purely on athletic ability, ruthlessly expunging distracting fripperies like lipstick and lingerie and lavish femininity. In that case, they ought to be fit.

On the other hand, these are women and wish to be seen as such. Pam Shriver once burst into tears before walking on a court because she didn't like her shoes. Men can find this bemusing. 'When you're dealing with a woman, it's never one plus one equals two,' said Shriver's former coach Don Candy. 'It's always one plus one equals four and three-eighths. They're emotionally far out. Right before a match they always want to know how they look.'

The tyranny of looks. It can lead to all manner of public relations disasters like the official WTA (curves and cleavage) calendar. Or 17-year-old Monica Seles turning up at a tournament in Philadelphia wearing a pink suede coat with a pink fur lining. 'What kind of animal has pink fur?' yelled a fan. 'Thank you,' replied the wearer, walking on.

Gabriela Sabatini was a classic in her day. The winner of one solitary Grand Slam singles title, the US Open in 1990, she basically made a career and a $20 million fortune from smouldering. Not just smouldering, to be fair. All aspects of her sublime and sultry, pool-eyed, lissom-limbed, heart-stopping, libido-lifting beauty were under consideration since she first appeared, a budding belle, at Wimbledon aged 15.

The adjectives, incidentally, are used advisedly, having all been applied at some time or another to her delectable, dark-eyed . . . etc.

person. Even the rigorous news journalist, John Feinstein, formerly of the *Washington Post*, was told to stop 'panting in print' by his exasperated editor one year at Wimbledon.

You could argue his line was a gross misrepresentation of Sabatini as an athlete, a demeaning examination of her bodily, not her tennis, form. The difficulty lies in the extent to which she colluded with her image. Her looks were her vehicle to a fortune, and being of sound mind, she – or her agents – exploited them. The manufacturers of cars, drinks, clothes, watches flocked to associate themselves with her name. In 1989, 'Gabriela Sabatini – the perfume' was launched. It has since been joined by Magnetic and Cascaya and all three were in the top ten in Germany.

'Also I have a doll that is me. It is wearing the same outfit that I wear on the court and it has my racket and it comes in two sizes. The big one costs $2,500.' It was always contended that Sabatini's brain cells rarely collided with one another in the wide-open spaces of her mind, but who's stupid with gimmicks like that on the market?

But even as we speak, Sabatini is disappearing from view like Botticelli's Venus shrinking back into her shell. She wants to give up tennis and be a mamma by the time she's 30 and no doubt a disorderly queue of would-be's has already formed in Buenos Aires. In the meantime, her mantle as the unofficial tour 'looker' has been passed on to Mary Pierce, and what a very small mantle it is, revealing no end of legs and no shortage of bust.

Is it sexually impolitic to mention this? Pierce didn't think so, informing an audience once: 'I'm not ashamed of my body. I like to walk naked around my house and garden.' Besides ensuring she has a rush of offers to be her gardener, this also diffused the myth that tennis players must be strangely sexless creatures whose highest form of pleasure involves a backhand clipping the baseline.

Then again, the *New York Times* once stripped all mention of what Martina Navratilova and Zina Garrison were wearing at the 1990 Wimbledon final in a piece by their leading columnist, George Vescey. The editors believed it was sexist and insensitive to discuss women's clothes. Andre Agassi's clothes, body hair and baldness, by contrast, were fair game. Just like a number of the women, he wears earrings, paints his nails and (when he had hair) used mousse. Aged 17, he turned up for an Italian TV interview with a powdered nose and lipgloss. If equality is about treating the sexes in the same way, it seems hardly right that the media should examine every nuance of the Agassi-look and then contrive to look the other way when women appear.

It is surely right that women do not wish to be treated as sex objects, surely wrong that genuine human responses to them are rigidly expunged. That, anyway, is far from the wishes of the players themselves who have far greater humour and perspective on the subject than the stormtroopers of political correctness who mount guard over them.

'OK, some girls have broad-beamed bottoms,' said Pam Shriver with perfect equanimity. 'We all had a crack up a couple of years ago at Wimbledon when the fancy-pant bloomers were in vogue. You know, the knickers with the colours all over them. Well, Katrina Adams was pictured with her skirt way up and all you could see was these colourful bloomers. Katrina, you know, has a sizeable fancy-pant bottom and we all just cracked up. We had the picture pasted on the wall above the television in the locker-room so everyone would see it. We had some fun with that.

'We're not ashamed. I can show you some men's butts that are rather large as well.' You note, this being ornamental, gentle, fragrant womanhood speaking, she doesn't call them 'neanderthal fat pigs' in her analysis.

'The insulting just has to stop. It just does,' she went on. 'We should look at each other – the men and women's game – and say: "Hey, we're together at the Grand Slams trying to make tennis come across positively and not be nit-picking at one another."

'Something is said every year at Wimbledon – with Cash, with Krajicek, with Lendl – and you just shake your head. I saw Richard [Krajicek] the other day and we actually had quite a nice conversation. [About Thomas Muster and Fergie actually.] But every time I see him, I must admit I think about his comment and his insensitivity. Meanwhile, it's quite funny to think about all his injuries, because whichever way you look at it, they're a pointer to a lack of condition.

'But I don't think the "lazy fat pig" line warrants confronting. It was really such an immature thing to say. I don't think four years later, he would say such a thing. Hopefully, the older the guys get, the more they start to understand. They start to have girlfriends and they realise; hey, men and women are *not* the same, any way you cut it. And maybe some of them start to respect the fact that though we don't have the same build and the same muscles and can't serve the ball as hard, we are still training just as hard and going through the same job as the men.

'And we can be just as entertaining as the men, you bet. Towards the end of Grand Slam tournaments, the entertainment value of the women's game is incredible. You've only got to think of the French

Open final [Graf beats Sanchez Vicario in three sets], the 1995 US Open final [Graf beats Seles in three], the 1995 Wimbledon final [Graf beats Sanchez Vicario in three] to see that.

'We should feel very proud, not defensive. One thing I can't stand is – even at this stage – feeling defensive. Like at the Australian Open this year until that Sanchez Vicario–Chanda Rubin match that finished 16–14 in the final set, I was kinda like feeling defensive. Ahhh, we'd had equality of prize money, we'd lost it and I was wondering when the women would start playing great matches to prove they deserved it again.

'And finally, the good matches started to come and come and come, and I was like "Yesss!"'

This was Pam at her proselytising best and a party line followed with considerable verve by many on the women's tour. 'My attitude to equal prize money is really very simple,' said Anne Person Worcester, the tour CEO. 'The magic of a Grand Slam is that men and women are playing side by side. Men and women contribute equally to the entertainment value and therefore they should be paid equally.'

There was an element of gall in this argument which I pointed out. Men play more sets. 'We would be willing to play a five-set final,' she replied.

Men would still play more sets, not that they're necessarily of sufficiently shimmering quality to empty the Pimms tent, far from it, but at least there is an element of suspense in the men's game.

'The number one ranking went back and forth five or six times in 1995 between Steffi Graf and Arantxa Sanchez Vicario,' she countered, neglecting to mention that Graf had suffered a back injury and her father had been jailed for tax dodging. At Wimbledon 1996 Graf had won her first match 6–4, 6–1, her second match 7–5, 6–3, her third match 6–1, 6–2, her fourth match 6–1, 6–4 . . . the drama was not exactly riveting.

This is far from denigrating the women's game as an inferior spectacle. The women's singles final at Wimbledon in 1995 was indeed a spellbinding contest between Graf and Sanchez Vicario as both players ransacked every last drop of ingenuity and stealth to produce rallies of which men could only dream. It was, by far, the finest match of the tournament, a golden moment, but in all too many cases the preceding matches had been dross.

'A lot of guys at the Grand Slams think there's so few women that can actually win the mother . . .' said Carillo. 'I mean, Graf is obviously an extraordinary athlete. A real racehorse. And then these guys see a lot of the big babes and say, "You've gotta be kidding me! Why don't you just hand the winners' cheque to Graf now?"'

And the moral of this story? Don't judge a player by her looks but by her actions. And don't let the star-struck sponsors run the show. In 1991, in heaven knows what distracted desire to reward Monica Seles for her loyalty to their product, Perrier decided to present her with 'a special rock crystal golden necklace' acceptable to the feminine (as an ornament) and feminists (as an investment) alike.

'Diamonds stand for innocence. Gold stands for purity and success. Congratulations Monica,' said the master of ceremonies. Seles smiled, waved, accepted the gift and went. Goran Ivanisevic was there. 'This is really stupid,' he said.

MOTHER LOVE

O Mother, mother!
What have you done. Behold, the heavens do open,
The gods look down, and this unnatural scene
They laugh at.
                              Shakespeare, *Coriolanus*, 1608

Tennis dads have suffered a gruesome press but any tennis parent can be dangerous. Any mother that's willing to let her prepubescent daughter pound hundreds of thousands of tennis balls with a coach thrice her age, and sometimes a sexual predator in whites, at the expense of education, exploration, maturation and fun, is in serious danger of having a prodigy on her hands. And then she's in trouble.

A brief rollcall should suffice.

(1) The Underarm Serve (Yourself) – as applicable to Jennifer Capriati, who turned professional three weeks short of her 14th birthday, chewed sugarless gum almost incessantly, insisted on painting her bedroom black, got spots to the horror of her sponsors Oil of Ulay, got bored to the horror of women's tennis and was caught shoplifting in a jewellery store.

To this she later added an arrest in a Miami drugs bust and shortly before her withdrawal from Wimbledon 1996 the news wafted to these shores that another police report had been filed when she lashed out with her fists at her current boyfriend after finding him with his arm around a 23-year-old waitress.

(2) The Forehand Smash – as applied by Jim Pierce to his daughter, Mary, on a sufficient number of occasions for him to be ultimately restrained from attending her matches as coach, father or anything else. 'Mary spat on me. I tried to slap her,' he said in one explanation of his actions. 'But I caught the corner of her glasses and knocked them off.'

His real name, it transpired, was Bobby Glenn Pearce and he had changed it not for aesthetic reasons like Jeremy Bates whose real first name is Michael but because Bobby Glenn had convictions for forgery, armed robbery and receiving stolen property. He also had schizophrenic and paranoid tendencies, which, whilst some people would claim these to be common in tennis, were rather more dangerously pronounced than most.

Mary, upon his removal, won the Australian Open.

(3) The Backhand Lob – as perfected by Peter Graf, who missed Graf's seventh Wimbledon victory due to his incarceration in Mannheim jail on tax dodging charges. The lob was fine but the disguise was wanting.

A former boxer and used car salesman, he had many of the virtues required to raise a daughter of such athletic might that no-one could live with her on the tennis court. In the process, however, he might have alienated some members of his family who not only objected to his arrest but also to the paternity suit filed by a 22-year-old German model who claimed Peter Graf was the father of her child. This proved not to be the case but Steffi Graf lost to Seles in the French Open final in the immediate aftermath. 'I will never stop hating the press after this,' she said. No-one doubts she carried on loving her father.

There were more. Lots more. All these dads living their life through their offspring and, more to the point, giving up their day jobs and living off their offspring's earnings. Karolj Seles (who was also obliged to be subsidised by his daughter when they moved to America from the Hungarian enclave Novi Sad in soon-to-erupt Yugoslavia) was appalled.

'Girls all too young. Monica, Jennifer, Steffi. They start too early. There should be rule. It's hard, this life. Somebody always there, always saying, "Sign this! Do this! Wear this! Meet my friend!" And press, one day they say good. Next day, bad. One day, she's nice person. Next day, not nice. I tell Monica, don't read, don't listen. A young girl can't take it. You can't live like that.'

Under pressure, women's tennis *did* make a rule. No more 13-year-olds. And almost no more 14-year-olds, except, for fear of a lawsuit, a couple of girls who were already under the wire. Thus Martina Hingis (named after the one but no longer only Martina) appeared and soon became the youngest ever winner of a Wimbledon title when she won the women's doubles with Helena Sukova in 1996.

For a while there, people thought the grand unveiling of Anna Kournikova might also take place in the summer of '96. But to the relief of many who have circled in her orbit, dodging the meteors and firestorms, the moment was postponed to a later occasion.

Kournikova is Russian. 'She's a phenomenon,' said Cino Marchese, who signed her to an agent's contract on behalf of International Management Group when she was 11. 'She's a freak,' said Gene Scott, a tennis entrepreneur, who had witnessed her discovery at a preliminary exhibition for the Kremlin Cup in Moscow. 'Anna was clearly the player with the best potential,' said Scott. 'But she was a mini monster even then. She was very cute but almost freakish in how spoiled she was.'

Interestingly, Kournikova has a mother. Biologically, she would have possessed a father too but it was the mother, a young blonde woman called Olla, who sat alongside all her junior matches at the Grand Slam events. This caused her American coach, Nick Bollettieri, some alarm. So much so that he was eventually moved to ban the woman from his practice courts.

'When I saw Anna at the French Open and then at Wimbledon, looking constantly at her mother and getting a warning for coaching, when I saw her not smiling, when I saw her not developing her game – I said: "Nick, are you going to let this happen to perhaps the most gifted youngster you've ever had?"' The answer then was no. But Scott had seen enough to wonder whether the little tsarina with the dancing earrings, rope of blonde hair and 90 mph serve would ever make it on the women's tour.

'I think it's already over,' he said. 'I don't know whether Nick's got the courage to take the drastic action that Bjorn Borg's father did when he locked all his racquets away for six months. Borg never threw a racquet again.'

It had not gone unnoticed that the wooing process of the agents in the case of Kournikova had involved taking her to swish Manhattan restaurants and keeping her out until midnight. I saw her once at Smith & Wollensky's, famous for its vast steaks and Bloody Marys, where she caused a small stir by falling off her chair – whether from tiredness or exuberance was not clear.

In any case, it made the words of an IMG submission to the Age Eligibility debate all the more profound. 'If she [the young girl] is surrounded by people telling her she is the next great star,' wrote one enlightened soul, 'we cannot continue to be surprised when she develops an arrogant, bossy, defiant, or know-it-all nature.' Was that a cry from the heart?

It went on to say: 'Likewise, if a girl at that age constantly receives signals that she is a good girl when she wins and bad girl when she loses, we are creating a child whose entire self image revolves around winning. For a time, this can be highly motivating, but in the end, it is almost always completely debilitating. We're talking about kids trying to please mommy and daddy on a dramatically magnified scale because their problems are being played out not just at home but also in front of live audiences, in newspapers and on television around the world.'

That never stopped Jimmy Connors wanting to please his 'mom'. Perhaps the feistiest man ever to wield a racquet, certainly the greatest crowd pleaser New Yorkers have ever seen with the possible exception of Babe Ruth and Madonna, Connors stopped speaking to *Sports Illustrated* for nigh-on ten years when Frank Deford wrote a piece in 1978: 'Raised By Women To Conquer Men.'

'Connors hated how close Frank got to it. To the dynamics of it all,' said Mary Carillo, the sage of the TV commentary box in America (who, incidentally, became a professional tennis player out of college to pay a $200 bar bill).

Essentially, Deford contended that the unswerving love and devotion lavished on Connors by his mother, Gloria, and the grandma he called 'Two Mom' was the basis of his ability to cut a power-hitting, double-fisted swathe through men's tennis in 1974. He won three of the four Grand Slam events that year and beat a helpless Ken Rosewall in two of the finals (US and Wimbledon) for the loss of only *eight* games. The score in New York almost defied belief: 6–1, 6–0, 6–1. People were seriously wondering whether *anyone* could live with the 22-year-old phenomenon.

Someone, of course, was living with him. His mom. 'His mother is the only person he trusts,' a knowledgeable citizen of East St Louis, where Connors grew up, told Deford for his story. 'They're not really comfortable with anybody else. They have such overpowering loyalty to each other that they're incapable of any lasting outside relationships. Their own relationship is spooky. I swear, it's always been like there was a tube going from her veins into his.'

Wimbledon was treated to first-hand experience of this in 1972 when the teenager made his debut. It was Jimmy's first trip abroad and Gloria Connors was reprimanded by the umpire for over-zealous coaching of her son from the sidelines. She was instantly lampooned in the tabloids as the kind of pushy American mum who had foresworn apple pie for ambition.

They adopted the Millwall mentality – no-one likes us, we don't care – and became closer still. 'You know, he was so much like his grandmother especially,' said Gloria. 'We were a team. We were three peas in a pod.'

As a result, Connor's father, Jim, who died of cancer in 1977, was somewhat withdrawn from the fray. He learned of Jimmy's engagement to Chris Evert on the radio. When he won Wimbledon in 1974, Jimmy could not find the time to take his father's congratulatory call.

'Two Mom' had told Gloria: 'Don't bring anyone else into the picture. You made him, Glo. Don't ever hand him over to anybody.' And her daughter took her at her word. 'I played him every day – every good day – of the year, every year. And we played hard. We taught him to be a tiger. "Get those tiger juices flowing!" I would call out, and I told him to try and knock the ball down my throat, and he learned to do this because he found out that if I had the chance, I would knock it down his. Yes, sir. And then I would say, "You see, Jimbo, you see what even your own mother will do to you on a tennis court?"'

Connors was 16 when he first beat his mother at tennis. 'Gee, mom, that hurt. I didn't mean to do that,' he told her apologetically at the net. But Gloria was ecstatic. 'No, no Jimmy,' she said. 'Don't you know, this is one of the happiest days of my life?'

Five years later he won everything in sight. Curiously, though, the reign of the tiger didn't last. Arthur Ashe beat him in the 1975 Wimbledon final, a classic and gently brutal deconstruction, after which some believed Connors was never the same again. Even the unqualified love of his mother couldn't restore the magic. He still had the eye of the tiger, but the forehand of a kitten was pretty useless against the gathering mastery of John McEnroe and Bjorn Borg.

He grew up in the end. Aged anyway. He married a *Playboy* model, became a father and ascended to icon-status in New York where his passion and propaganda, his obscenity and scatology, his undaunted arrogance and unquenchable aggression were a mirror to Manhattan soul. The mob loved him. Aged 39 he reached the semi-finals of the US Open and perhaps that was one of the other happiest days of Gloria's life.

Footnote: Tremendous news for Britain. Not only did Tim Henman, the 6ft 1in right-hander from Oxford, reach the quarter-finals of Wimbledon in 1996, he also possessed a mother who played at county level and was a member of the All England Club. Furthermore, his great-grandmother was a tennis pioneer, one of the first women to switch to an over-arm serve. It is enough to give Britain genuine hope, for now we know what the love of a good mother can do. Tiger Tim?

THE WOMEN'S MOVEMENT

If a woman wants to get in the headlines, she should have quintuplets.

Bobby Riggs, tennis player, 1973

It's as though lesbianism in tennis no longer exists. 'Nobody's asked me about it in a long, long time,' said Anne Person Worcester, the chief executive officer of the Women's Tennis Association over lunch one day at Wimbledon. I believe her. The lesbians of today are very distant cousins from the ones who went almost heroically before.

First Billie Jean King, then Martina Navratilova, both pre-eminent superstars on the women's tour in their prime, came out as gay. In King's case, she had no choice. Rona Barrett, the then Hollywood ace gossip columnist, had just announced on *Good Morning America*, ABC's breakfast television show, that Billie Jean had been involved in a lesbian relationship with her former secretary, Marilyn Barnett. Even so, she need not have called a press conference, which she did (while her lawyers pulled their expensively cut hair out). Nor submitted to a Barbara Walters interview, which she did (lawyers ditto).

Navratilova, presumably, could have maintained a silence about her liaisons with Sandra Haynie, Rita Mae Brown, Nancy Lieberman and Judy Nelson, who would serve her with a sensationally reported palimony claim, but chose, with considerable courage and to substantial financial loss, to be open about her life.

Person Worcester acknowledged the debt. 'I think by having some high-profile women who were very honest about their sexuality, when they didn't have to be . . . it took the whispering out of things.

'Now our players present themselves as élite athletes first and foremost and the way they choose to conduct their personal life, so long as it is honourable, is their own business.'

I asked her if she didn't fear for the privacy of at least one Wimbledon finalist who was in a relationship with a fellow player. 'Not really,' she said. 'I'm not afraid of what the tabloids might do. They make stories up. They wrote that Monica Seles withdrew from Wimbledon in 1991 because she was pregnant. There's so many absurd things said that I could easily spend my whole life just trying to correct the rumours.

'I'd never ask one of our players to lie, and deny that they were a lesbian. It's completely their personal choice. But I've never, never, not once, heard a sponsor mention it. If they're focused on personal issues, maybe they should get out of sport sponsorship.'

Navratilova had a different experience. Being a lesbian cost her, in terms of respect, affection, admiration, money. She talked about it once in relation to the revelations that Magic Johnson, the American basketball star of almost mythic proportions, had tested positive for the HIV virus. 'If it happened to a heterosexual woman who had been with a hundred or two hundred men, they'd call her a whore and a slut and the corporations would drop her like a lead balloon. And she'd never get a job in her life. It's a very big-time double standard.'

This was fair comment from a woman of indisputable eminence in her sport who watched as Seles was paid thousands for having her hair cut, Jennifer Capriati was sponsored by Oil of Ulay before she was old enough to have spots and Gabriela Sabatini brought out everything from her own perfume to a smouldering-eyed doll. Navratilova didn't have 'one damn endorsement outside of racquet and shoes'.

Fact: conservative, corporate America was uncomfortable with gay women. Fact: little Chrissie Evert and her growing band of men (Jimmy Connors, Adam Faith, Burt Reynolds, Jack Kennedy . . .) was construed as pure as a snowflake compared to her long-time rival. And truly horrendous fact (as uncovered by the author Michael Mewshaw in his book *Ladies of the Court*): some parents, according to one USTA official, could tolerate the thought of sexual harrassment of their daughter by a male coach because they were 'paranoid' about the possibility of a lesbian experience.

'It is . . . people living in the Dark Ages,' said Martina. 'I mean, what do they think, that gay women attack every young girl that they see? That is the problem with the whole stigma of gay people, that all they think about is sex – which is not at all the case, just like heterosexuals don't just think about sex the whole time.'

Except, possibly, footballers, she might have added.

'We are all the same, and the labels that are put on and images that people have of gays attacking people in elevators and doing this kind of crazy stuff, it just amazes me.'

The supreme irony of it all is that these two women, so reviled in some quarters for the side-issue of their sexuality, were the very same people that helped liberate women's tennis from its whalebone corset of amateurism and brought it full-blooded professional status.

Billie Jean, the fireman's daughter, earned 39 Grand Slam titles in singles, doubles and mixed doubles. She was an activist, all right, but her energy extended way beyond the boundaries of the tennis court and still does. 'There's so much magic on that stage,' she said of Wimbledon in 1991 when in the vibrant throes of coaching Tim Mayotte and Navratilova. 'I tell Tim and Martina that this is their stage and these are their moments. They should wake up every morning like they've been shot from a cannon.'

That was a wonderful self-portrait. She was fired with an enthusiasm that came very close to self-destruction at times. She came to Wimbledon at 17 and won the doubles, unseeded, very much the little cannonball of her own description. Billie Jean Moffitt, the bustling teenage tomboy, bristling with ambition in her Edna Everage glasses. She won her first singles title in 1966, receiving a £50 gift voucher for tennis wear in the process, but not then, not ever, the acclaim of the crowd.

She was too intense, too ruthless for the Wimbledon audience, who loved above all the Christine Truman style of play which involved modesty, hearty effort and cardigans. And too homosexual? But nobody knew then and especially not when she married Larry King and so became Billie Jean King of legend.

By 1975 she had won six Wimbledon singles titles and Elton John had written *Philadelphia Freedom* for her, leading to her acknowledgement of the title Mother Freedom. And in that role she was to slay – if not the dragon – then a particularly fine pig.

Her Battle of the Sexes victory over Bobby Riggs was claimed to be one of the significant milestones of the sport, proving beyond contention that women had a prominent role to play in major league sport. In truth it was a made-for-TV special which drew the largest goggle-eyed audience in tennis history. It might have made new men out of chauvinists. Knowing chauvinists, I somehow doubt it.

It was 1973 and Margaret Court, the Australian tennis star, had just lost, out-psyched and out-manoeuvred, to the 55-year-old Riggs. 'I went bananas,' said King. 'I was about to board a plane in Honolulu when I heard Bobby had won 6–2, 6–1. I walked down the aisle of the plane with lockjaw because I knew I would have to play him. All of the implications of the match flashed through my mind: it would be for the women's movement and all of the inequities women felt so deeply.'

A veteran of Grand Slam hyper-tension, she nevertheless threw up in the locker-room before the so-called Pigs v Libs confrontation. Then she was carried on an Egyptian litter into the Houston Astrodome where 30,472 people were agog in wait. 'This was what I had always wanted: arenas, sequins and night-time tennis. I was wearing a white dress with blue trim and rhinestones, a blue sweatband and bright blue tennis shoes. Bobby gave me an enormous caramel sucker in a gesture of goodwill. I gave him a pig wearing a pink bow.' King won 6–4, 6–3, 6–3 and a point was proved. 'Before that,' she said, 'women were chokers and spastics who couldn't take pressure. Except, of course, in childbirth.'

They thought as much about Navratilova at first, a woman to whom crying came more easily than it did to Paul Gascoigne. When she defected from what was then Czechoslovakia to America in 1975, she proceeded to cut a swathe of acquisition across the country. Doughnuts, jewellery, cars. At one point her garage contained a Toyota Supra, a Pontiac J, a BMW 733, a silver Mercedes, a Porsche 928, a 1975 Rolls Royce Silver Cloud and a white Rolls Royce Corniche convertible. One of them had the registration plate: 'X-CZECH'.

Not surprisingly, she suffered a decline on the tennis court. In 1976 cameras zoomed in on the sight of the ex-Czech, sobbing and distraught, having lost to one Janet Newberry, a name of little consequence except in sugared fruit circles, in the first round of the US Open. 'She had that dramatic Slav temperament that requires the stimulus of a crisis,' said the late, great tennis guru Teddy Tinling. 'She goes from arrogance to panic with nothing in between.'

She began life, like Chris Evert, as a brunette in tennis whites but although they shared a passion for blonde rinses down the years, there the comparison ended. Evert had a youth filled with Florida sunshine, her dad's smart coaching and, for a while there, Jimmy Connors. Young Martina Subertova lived in more spartan surroundings and in more disturbing times in a town near Prague. She was nine when her father, Kamil, committed suicide and 11 when the Russian tanks rolled across the border.

Tennis was both a distraction and an escape. By 16 she was possessed of a fine forehand, a terrible two-fisted backhand and a new name, Navratilova, after her stepfather. In that guise, she launched her formidable career, beating Christine Truman in her debut at Wimbledon in 1973. Seventeen years later she plucked a few strands of grass from the Centre Court to remind her of the day she made history. By beating Zina Garrison 6–4, 6–1 in the final she won her ninth

Wimbledon and broke the long-standing record of Helen Wills Moody.

Just as significantly, she had broken through the reserve, and in some cases overt antipathy, of the great British crowd who had been apt to view her as a grasping, butch ex-Communist defector. She once criticised Wimbledon for awarding the women less prize money than men. 'It was as if I'd insulted God,' she said. She would hear voices in the crowd shouting: 'Come on Chrissie, I want a real woman to win.'

Perhaps these sad souls were never won over, and certainly not by the sheer persistence of her brilliance. In 1984 between 15 January and 6 December she won 74 matches in succession. In the doubles she and Pam Shriver remained undefeated for more than two years. But statistics could never win hearts. In the end, it was the slow and perhaps grudging realisation that here was one of the greatest athletes the world had ever produced, and, moreover, one who had overcome the curse of her brittle temperament. Gazza never did that.

Moreover, she talked. About the ozone layer, the whales and the state of women's tennis. She cracked jokes in self-taught English and donated fortunes to charity. Her private life might be a multi-faceted disaster area at times but she had honesty and courage to declare herself gay when she might have been better served by denial. And she was funny with it.

'Martina, are you still a lesbian?' inquired a male sportswriter.

'Are you still the alternative?' she replied.

In the 1990s, the lesbians on the tennis circuit are a more metaphorically supine brigade. Perhaps there are no more fights to be fought when a fourth-round loser at Wimbledon takes home almost £30,000.

This almost certainly says less about lesbianism than it does about the more passive and homogenous nature of the players wielding racquets today. Locked in their own little world of practise, play, eat, sleep, practise, many of the young players know little and care less about what has gone before.

'What saddens me about some young players,' said King, 'is not merely that they lack devotion to the history of the game, but that they have little curiosity about anything around them.'

An exception was, and remains, Pam Shriver, who has no doubt where a debt of gratitude is owed. 'Martina helped to break down barriers because she was open about being gay. She talked about it, she answered questions about it and then people got to know her. They thought, "She's gay. Big deal," in the end.

'I think Martina will go down in history as a bridge builder and barrier breaker between the two sides, between lesbians and people who were, maybe, a little homophobic. They got to know her at Wimbledon. They saw her emotions and all she was going through. And, finally, they thought: "I quite like her."'

For her part, Navratilova pays a different homage. 'We wouldn't be where we are without Billie Jean King,' she said.

LOVE ALL

> *HER: You did mean those three little words you whispered to me in the cinema, didn't you?*
> *HIM: Course, I did . . . I had seen it.*
> Frank Muir and Denis Norden, *The Glums*

Love can be a terrible thing. To have that emotive word attached to your name at Wimbledon usually means you have just been soundly thrashed by Steffi Graf. Love, literally, means nothing in tennis.

Never let it be said, however, that the players have shown any sign down the years of resolving to keep their celebrity lives uncluttered by affairs of the heart. Birds do it, bees do it, Chris Evert was always doing it, and few of her racquet-wielding cohorts have failed to follow suit.

But a strange asymmetrical pattern emerges from the resulting maelstrom. Consider this. Jimmy Connors dated the actress Susan George and Miss World Marjorie Wallace before marrying a *Playboy* model. John McEnroe was joined in matrimony to film star Tatum O'Neal, had three children, split up and has just become a father for the fourth time with his girlfriend, the singer, Patty Smith.

Andre Agassi came to Wimbledon one year in the company of 'The Voice', Barbra Streisand. Now he's affianced to 'the Blue Lagoon', Brooke Shields. Boris Becker wed a singer, Barbara Feltus. Gary Muller (6ft 3in, blond, but never even made the top 20) married Richard Harris's ex-wife, the actress Ann Turkel. Bunny Austin made the *Movietone News* in 1931 when he married the actress, Phyllis Konstam who once came to Wimbledon with Gladys Cooper.

The litany could go on and on, which gives rise to one pressing question. How come the guys get to marry film stars and so forth, while the women get stuck with their coaches? Perhaps the Women's Tennis Association have been addressing the wrong equality issue all this time. Never mind the prize money, where are the 'Himbos'?

'Well,' said Anne Person Worcester, the women's tour CEO, never one to concede an advantage to the men, as we sat across a table at Wimbledon and considered this extraordinary imbalance, 'you have Steffi Graf with a racing car driver.' Not exactly Michael Schumacher, though, is he? We were talking Formula *Three*.

'You have Gaby [Sabatini] who goes on dates with Michael Bolton, the American singer, and Brady Anderson, who's a famous baseball player. She brought him to my engagement party a couple of years ago, he's second or third baseman for the Baltimore Orioles.

'Steffi goes to NBA games and has a nice friendship with Dave Robinson who's a basketball player. Um . . . Seal [singer] takes Mary Pierce to the MTV [music] awards and, I understand, has a crush on her. And I understand Hootie, the lead singer of Hootie & the Blowfish, has a crush on Monica.' *Hootie & the Blowfish*?

'You got to get with it!' said Person Worcester, quite reprovingly, I thought. 'It's a band from South Carolina and it's all the rage in the States right now. And Hootie, himself, has a crush on Monica, I hear. Young, good-looking black guy, African-American.

'But, you know, Gaby knows every celebrity in South America. We get a lot of celebrities to our LA tournament. They come out of the woodwork. They have friendships with a lot of the players. But our players have always found boyfriends out of the limelight. I don't know why. I've never really thought about it.

'Don't forget our players are younger than the guys. You know, Martina Hingis is 15 years old, she's not going to have a boyfriend.'

'Yeah, she's not going to go out with Brad Pitt, is she?' I said, trying desperately to reclaim a little street cred.

'She might want to. I know I do.' For the record, Person Worcester is happily married, has a little boy, Tommy Zachary Worcester, and was joking. I think.

The women on tour have to be careful. The combination of being young, female, lonely, famous and rich can act as a powerful aphrodisiac on men you would not necessarily want your mother to meet. 'Sometimes I had fans watching me out on court,' said the American Elise Burgin, who was tour jester for many years. 'Sometimes I had guys in raincoats.'

In their artificial, enclosed environment, it makes perfect sense for women to marry the men to whom they are naturally emotionally close. Manuela Maleeva married her coach, François Fragnière. As did Rosalyn Fairbank becoming Mrs R. Nideffer as far Wimbledon was concerned. Larissa Savchenko wed her coach to become Mrs L. Neiland.

As far as Barbara Potter (unmarried) can tell, this is supremely sensible. 'With men's polygamous instincts in full flow on the tennis tour, you can understand why they like to date a beautiful stream of actresses,' said the former American player whose wit is gainfully employed at Wimbledon every year for Radio Five. 'But women are looking for something more in a relationship. Someone who provides companionship. Someone who isn't just there for a night in bed. Someone who will be there the next morning.

'I don't think that realisation hits men until they're 30.' *Thirty.* I looked at her with utter incredulity.

'OK, 80,' she said. 'I was trying to give them the benefit of the doubt.'

You only had to peep round the tarpaulins of Wimbledon '96 to see she was absolutely right. First there was the publication of a survey in Austria which revealed the astonishing fact that 207,000 out of 3,000,000 Austrian women wanted to have Muster's child. And some weren't even fussy *how*. The traditional method or artificial insemination – either would suffice.

Apparently, Muster was prized even above Arnold Schwarzenegger for his tan, his fitness, and the hours he has devoted to teaching under-privileged children. His coach, somewhat mischievously, suggested Muster would be prepared to comply with the highest bidder. And the subject of this delicate matter, far from being embarrassed, appeared to be delighted. 'The Royal Family have already been on to me,' he said.

And, come to think of it, 'Thomas the Tank Engine', as he is known, had gazumped even the tennis-playing spouses of Hollywood wives. He had been seen with an ex-Windsor wife. His courtship, or perhaps just companionship, of the Duchess of Fergie had been of such enormous interest to the British newspapers since their meeting in Qatar in January 1996 that his 20-year-old student girlfriend, Mariella Theiner, felt obliged to become his ex.

Sadly for the Rotters of Wimbledon, they were never able to challenge him on the details of his relationship with the ex-Duchess. He pulled out of the tournament before it began, citing a strained thigh. Whether his immediate destination was San Lorenzo's with Fergie or an Austrian spermbank was never ascertained.

Then there was Richard Krajicek, unseeded but not unaccompanied. As the tournament progressed, so did the fame of his blonde, blue-eyed girlfriend in the VIP box who turned out to be – as befits one associated to a man ranked outside the top ten – a television presenter rather than a full-blown film star.

However, her moments in the limelight were suitably ornate and Daphne Decker was elevated from bit part to guest star as the tournament wore on. Undoubtedly, her highlight was the post-match interview she gave after Krajicek had been presented with the trophy and, before that, the sight of Missy Johnson streaking.

'If there had been ten topless women out there, Richard wouldn't have noticed. He's so focused on his tennis,' she said confidently, in vivid contrast to the evidence of the pictures which featured her beloved, eyes on stalks, with a huge grin across his face.

It does, perhaps, become clear why Person Worcester was given stern advice in her early days on the tennis tour: 'Don't date a player.' But the admonition carries little weight with the fans. There was a time when a tribe of women, the much-maligned groupie troupe, would follow the tennis circuit around the world. Cutbacks have been necessary in these more stringent economic times, and even the threesome known, rather ungraciously, throughout the tennis world as 'Top Dog, Deputy Dog and Dog's Dinner' failed to show at Wimbledon.

But romance bloomed anyway. Jane Tabor, the eminent umpire, arrived in her fairly new incarnation as Jane Harvey (Mrs). She had met her husband, intriguingly, whilst teaching him the finer points of umpiring on a British Tennis Umpires' Association course. Any vestige of concern people had about a teacher dating her pupil were eradicated by the news that they turned out to be neighbours in the west country.

Life, however, was by no means simplified by their union. 'I do about 30 weeks on the road I suppose. And Graham's not always there. I'm obviously travelling more than he is. He's a budding star. So it is difficult. Even if we're in England we still have to stay away from home. Sometimes I'd really like a routine life again because I've been doing this for 12 years.

'Before I married Graham, there had been the odd relationship but I think that's something I have to keep quiet about,' she said with an amiable laugh. 'Obviously, as an umpire you're not there to fraternise with the players, male or female. To go out with the male players – not a good idea.

'I don't know if I ever really had a favourite to watch. Although we've just done a little survey actually for our newsletter. Graham, my husband, and another guy were going round asking everybody who were the most fanciable male and female tennis players in the the past or present. I think Edberg's come out top for the men and Sabatini for the women. I always enjoyed watching Edberg *play* and he's such a nice guy. Always one of the greatest to officiate.'

I understood from this that Harvey had umpired many a men's match, even McEnroe in his heyday. It made no difference. The ATP Tour (male) were still not of a mind to make her the umpire of the men's singles final at Wimbledon '96.

She took this slight without a trace of rancour. 'There's a limit to what you can push for as a woman. I'm very content with what I've got now. The ATP use women to a certain extent at their challenger events and things, but they're not going to use them at the top level. I don't know why. They turn round and say you don't see female officials in soccer or baseball or American football, or whatever. So . . .

'I think men feel slightly intimidated, to be honest. They test you initially to see if you know what you're doing, but then they feel slightly intimidated by having a woman umpire. They can't release themselves as much as they could if they had a guy up there.

'But in general I think everyone is treated pretty fairly. When it comes to line officials, I think the women are better than the men anyway. It just is that there are so few women in comparison to men. As a woman you have to prove yourself twice over, that you're as good if not better than the men. They can make several mistakes and it's still OK. You can make one mistake and that will be held against you for a long time. Men can get away with it somehow.'

And so they do. Dating royalty, marrying Hollywood, squiring models *and* earning more prize money in the process. Only the rich pageant of Chris Evert's social life seemed to balance up the record slightly, and now she has been lost to retirement, motherhood and the ultimate 'Himbo', the swooningly handsome, ex-international downhill skier, Andy Mill.

And it was no good looking to the babe from Barcelona, Arantxa Sanchez Vicario, to lighten the darkness. Word was, she was seeing an *accountant*.

Other Sports

SNOOKER

I know I've got a reputation like George Best. I always tell them I'm a great potter. They know what I mean.
                                                            Alex Higgins

There is an element of The Chippendales about snooker. The lights dim, the hush intensifies, the anticipation mounts and, suddenly, a pink curtain is flung back with the panache of Mae West throwing off a stole. You expect a male stripper, at the very least, to emerge in all his oily glory. Instead a whey-faced, hair-gelled lad with a misspent youth hoves into view, snooker cue in sweaty hand and dressed as a maître d'.

We are seated, silent as a troupe of librarians, at the Crucible Theatre in Sheffield, where few dramas are as real and closely observed as the on-and-on-going Embassy World Championships. The winner will be announced next Monday fortnight (although it's always Stephen Hendry) but in the meantime the fraying of nerves becomes an almost audible drone. This could be torture to the protagonists. And, as a matter of fact, it is. 'I was so nervous going into the arena, I could just see myself falling down the stairs. They should get a bannister there for newcomers,' said Mick Price on his debut.

Snooker is a curious sport, an odd amalgam of purity and villainy. On one hand you've got bookies and biryanis and beta-blockers; on the other hand, the sort of blameless life led by the exemplary Steve Davis (until his trysts with a nightclub dancer were revealed across five pages of *The Sun*). In Sheffield, the two cultures merge under the unforgiving lights and relentless gaze of the cameras.

Alex Higgins, the bad boy of snooker, called the World Championships 'my passport to carnal pleasure'. But looking round the auditorium during a morning early-round match, all you can see is bespectacled grannies, carefully unwrapping packets of sandwiches from tupperware boxes on their laps. They follow every kiss, screwshot and pot with knowing intensity. But one doubts they would dress up as go-go dancers for the gratification of one of the players. More likely they want to take him home and feed him. They are filled with maternal sympathy for those poor, pale, pouch-eyed boys who all look in desperate need of a good lamb chop.

Riotous behaviour amongst the crowd at the World Championships, therefore, is limited to the squeaky polishing of glasses. But certain elements of the press find this an unbearable disappointment. Thus, Ian Doyle, Hendry's manager was entertained by the sight of a young and spectacular female journalist, unleashed by one of the tabloids on the 20-year-old player from Essex, Ronnie O'Sullivan. Ronnie Oh was in trouble at the time for assaulting the assistant press officer of the tournament and ridiculing an opponent by playing left handed.

'This female turned up at Sheffield just after the Ronnie fracas,' said Doyle. 'She was gorgeous. I hate to say this but she had the best pair of knockers I've seen in a long time. She had the figure of Venus de Milo and she got into his room eventually to do a story for the paper.

'You've just got to be so careful, it's frightful. When Stephen came out of his press conference on the Monday after winning his sixth World Title, one of the press guys said to me: "Listen! I can get you big money if we can have a picture of Stephen and his wife, Mandy, in bed with the trophy between them."

'I feel so sorry for Princess Di. I have met her fleetingly. She's prefectly entitled to have her own life. The carry-on is frightening, absolutely frightening. I mean, who the hell cares who she goes to bed with? The most important thing I can do with my players is just advise them. Fortunately, Stephen, bless him, has seen everything.

'He was doing a TV show down in London once and he went to a nightclub with some of the people. Now, he's not a nightclubbing type as a rule but he did go on this occasion. As usual people came up wanting autographs, and the next thing we know there's a paper on the phone saying, they've got this picture . . . it was a set-up. One of the girls who asked for an autograph was a hooker. It was a set-up. We had murder with them. We left it entirely in the hands of our lawyers and in the end the picture was never published.'

Women and snooker players have enjoyed a long but not necessarily equal alliance down the years. It was Tony Knowles who explained: 'I never buy them a drink. I never buy them a meal. I never dance with them. The only thing I offer them – apart from myself – is a lift home. And it works – every night of the week and sometimes several times a night.' The romantic beast.

It was Doyle who said of Mandy Tart, Hendry's long-time girlfriend:

'If this girl tries to come between Stephen and the title, then she'll have to go.' And go she did.

'Ian virtually suggested that I should give Mandy up,' said Hendry, between practice sessions shortly before the 1996 World Championships, remembering the sacrifices asked of him to achieve his eerily super-human status. 'Which I did for a year. At the time I hated him,' Hendry laughed hollowly. 'But, er, it worked out in the end. We still sneaked two or three meetings unbeknownst to Ian. She wasn't over the moon about it at all. But we're probably the stronger for it now. It was a big decision. I was only 17. I had the rest of my life to think about.' Hendry paused for thought for a moment. 'Probably,' he admitted, '95 per cent of boys would have told Ian to get stuffed.'

Which is a sentiment expressed by the odd snooker widow here and there to her bewitching but wayward spouse. 'If I found him with another woman there would be Mercedes sports car wheelmarks right up the front of his shirt,' said Avril Virgo. Jimmy White's long-suffering wife, Maureen, accused her husband of possessing 'scummy hangers-on' and, taking the hint, White moved out of the house. He remains, however, one of snooker's irrepressible characters.

'How am I?' he said, when he reappeared after surgery for testicular cancer. 'Sweet as a nut!' He can certainly do no wrong in the eyes of the grannies, which is probably as well for a man who was once accused of looting a handbag in Tooting (case dropped), connected with a ring of Thai vice girls and sentenced to 120 hours of community service for driving whilst four times over the legal alcohol limit. Even his pet, 'Splinter', was dog-napped. Things happen to Jimmy. Naughtiness is his virtue.

Perhaps that explains the appeal of the whole sport, particularly to women. Heaven knows, it's not the ripple in their muscles.

Jimmy White took himself to Paris for surgery on his bald patch. 'My bald patch was like that,' he said, cupping two hands around an imaginary cricket ball. 'Now it's like that.' An imaginary ping-pong ball was described. 'I'm going to have it done again an' all. This guy, he's brilliant. He invented this clip and they put it under your skull and it pulls your skin together. Honest, I swear to God. It's like a face lift from the top.'

Hendry, on the other hand, abandoned all hope of repair years ago. 'If I wasn't a snooker player, I don't think people would look at me twice,' said the greatest player of all time. 'I've had spots and everythin'. Girls wouldn't look at me twice if I wasn't who I was. It's been 100 per cent snooker. I've sacrificed everything, parties, girlfriends, for snooker.

Even at school I only had a couple of girlfriends. But it was just trivial really. I can't even remember if I kissed 'em.'

Davis said something remarkably similar. 'To be boring and ugly like I am is a boon in sport. If you are boring, you will do endless hours of practice and not think there's anything better you could be doing. When I look in the mirror I see a wreck. I'm just a weed. My chest is the same measurement as my waist.'

Sadly for Davis, chest measurements of a different kind came to be aired in public when a young woman allegedly acquired £30,000 from *The Sun* to relate in vivid detail a night in the company of Steve 'Suddenly-Very-Interesting' Davis. The story was a credit to Davis's fitness level but rather sullied his Persil-white reputation. Only a day or two before the story broke he was telling the man from the *Daily Telegraph*: 'I think I might have been there [the dance floor of Annabel's nightclub]. I dunno. I only seem to go up to London when I get drunk. And then I never know where I've been.' He does now.

But marital infidelity has never come between the pensioners and their players. White, Higgins, Davis, could not entirely expunge the grannies' goodwill no matter how generous the sportsmen's libido. Hence the continuing interest of sponsors and David Vine. When Hendry won the 1994 World Championships, so great was the pride of his sponsors that they bought him a racing green Bentley. 'I got to go to the factory and pick everythin' out. It was like furnishing a house. What kind of walnut would you like? What type of carpets do you want? But I only drove it once. I hated it. I felt such an idiot. It's in a museum now.'

When he won the 1995 World Championships, they gave him a Ferrari. That was more like it. 'It's fantastic,' he said. When Karen Corr won the Women's World Championship in 1995, they gave her a moped. 'I had a little trot round Delhi on it,' she said. 'But I never saw it again after that.'

India would seem a long way to go to test drive a Honda were it not for the fact she was already there. So low had women's snooker fallen in the esteem of British sponsors that the event was moved, lock, stock and tables, to the other side of the world where billiards is considered the number one sport. So Corr won her second World Championship in a dressed-up table tennis room in a Delhi leisure centre with a 50-strong crowd in attendance. Kinetico Honda (moped manufacturers) were one of the main sponsors; hence the wheels to augment her £5,000 winner's cheque.

Women have had an arduous time breaking into a sport which,

trailing clouds of fag-ash and beer-breath, has been seen as traditionally male. By males, that is. 'We feel snooker is a man's game,' said Charles Dandy, secretary of the Smethwick Working Men's Club, defending a ban on women spectators. 'We feel that if a man wants to give vent to his feelings, he should not have to look over his shoulder before he does so. This rule is to stop women hearing bad language.'

It did not, in fact, stop women hearing bad language. Their own, for instance, in rage against ancient prejudice. 'It's archaic. Those pompous little men are just living in the Dark Ages,' said Teresa Burnell, who was banned for a year, with her friend, from Otteshaw Social Club for playing snooker. 'Their attitude is truly pathetic.'

But prevalent, nevertheless. 'I've played exhibitions in clubs where there's a notice on the door which says: "No women allowed in the snooker room",' said Mandy Fisher, the woman who runs the World Ladies Billiards and Snooker Association. 'Some conservative clubs still see women as second-class citizens.'

One wonders what might have happened had Margaret Thatcher in her pomp turned up and insisted on contesting a frame with the lads (taking extra relish in pocketing the pink). The handbagging that would have greeted the embarrassed refusal might have changed the status of the women's sport forever. Instead, women's snooker is still a bit of a gimmick, a novelty, in the firmament of sport.

'It's something that really hurts,' said Fisher. 'It's sad. Reporters, men, have often said that women should wear mini skirts and low cut blouses, if they want to get noticed. That's just ridiculous. This isn't topless darts. We take it seriously.

'When I was expecting my second child, Matthew, five years ago, I qualified for the finals of the World Championships. It was a bit tight. I was scheduled to play my quarter-final on the day the baby was due. Anyway, the final eight were expected to attend a press conference in London a few days beforehand. I said to Barry Hearn, who was staging the event, "You don't need me. You've got the other seven. Can't you just say that I'm about to have a baby?" He said, "No, no, we want you down."

'Well, when I went down I was the focus of the whole thing, being so heavily pregnant. I went down in my slippers because he told me I was going to be hidden away amongst the other girls. Instead, I had to go to Hyde Park and have my picture taken with all the other girls pointing at my belly and Barry Hearn wearing a doctor's stethoscope.

'It was all so sad. It wasn't about snooker. It was about me. In the end, I had the baby three days early and I decided to play the quarter-final, which created even more publicity. We drove down, I breastfed Matthew in the toilets and then went to play my match while my husband held the baby in the audience. I lost. It was the day my milk came in. I'm not making excuses. I would probably have lost anyway. I wasn't a favourite to win or anything. I just wanted to show there's no reason why women can't compete, even when they've just had a baby.'

Life, however, has a habit of throwing up little compensations. If Corr feels under-rewarded, if Fisher felt like a freak show and if Alison Fisher, Britain's most famous female snooker player, fled to play the billiards circuit in America where the pickings were considerably richer, at least their inconspicuousness has advantages. No-one has burst into their hotel room at three o'clock in the morning, with a couple of half-dressed hookers and a flash-popping photographer. Ridiculous as it may sound, Stephen Hendry's manager, Ian Doyle, insisted that a tabloid newspaper used this very method to entrap his client in a steamy sex scandal that would spice up the snooker player's somewhat tediously sin-free image.

'We were staying in a London hotel and what happened, basically, is that the night porter took a bung to let the press in. About three o'clock in the morning there comes this knock on Stephen's door. Except it's not Stephen's door any more. We always swap his room around, just to be on the safe side. So my road manager, John Carroll, opens the door to be confronted by two ladies who certainly looked very much like hookers and a photographer between them. They fled pretty quickly, let me tell you. But it just gives you some indication of the lengths the papers will go to. These are the things that happen.'

'No, that's never happened to me,' said Corr, with uproarious laughter. 'Nobody knows me.' Except 50 people in Delhi, she might add.

POLO

Playing polo is like trying to play golf during an earthquake.
                                              Sylvester Stallone, actor, 1990

The chap in the Panama hat, Old Harrovian tie and blindingly striped blazer (Marks and Spencer) stood dreamily in the midst of a rural idyll, chomping on quails' eggs and black olives. Only birdsong, a zephyr breeze and the gentle *pfsssst* of a bottle of Veuve Clicquot being teased open disturbed the tranquility of the English country scene.

The noise, when it came, began as a low rumble with a curiously rhythmic pulse. Rabbits were startled, birds took to the air, even the Old Harrovian paused, alert, mid-canapé.

'Here they come,' he announced excitedly, eyes fixed to the horizon. And, sure enough, a cavalcade of giant transporters suddenly hove into view, one after another, in a seemingly endless stream, while overhead the blades of two black helicopters slashed through the air. We had gone from *Bambi* to *Apocalypse Now* with barely a beat in between.

This, believe it or not, was the prelude to a polo match. No-one – not the Queen at the FA Cup final nor Ruud Gullit in the Chelsea dressing-room – arrives with quite the fanfare and flourish of Mr Kerry Packer to the annual ritual of the Gold Cup at Cowdray Park. The helicopter spares him the stultifying traffic jams of West Sussex. He does, after all, live four minutes away by road.

Best known for his cricketing adventures, the Australian television tycoon became a devotee of the Sport of Kings relatively late in life but his passion is no pensioner's pastime. 'It's like a drug to him,' said the Old Harrovian. 'He's completely besotted,' said an immaculately clad PR for the event, making up smoked salmon bites in the back of a caravan.

This is a bit of luck for polo, which is an incredibly expensive sport. The juggernauts that had just shattered our peace were in fact the massive, modern horse transporters carrying 16 polo ponies at a time. Each lorry cost £70,000; each pony £40,000. They say Packer spends £500,000 on his polo in Britain every year, which may account for the deference in which he is held.

Once the province of the Hussar and Lancer and all those other cavalry officers to whom polo was an indispensible joy in the days and the land of the Raj, the game now survives thanks to the rapture of converts like Packer. In the 1990s, the leading characters are magnates, bankers, sheikhs, sultans and Kenny Jones, former drummer of The Who.

Yet the image of polo is indelible. A toff's pursuit, redolent of vintage champers, the creak of hamper and the clank of inherited titles on parade. So the pre-eminence of Packer's team, Ellerston White (named after his polo club situated on a 9,000-hectare cattle station in New South Wales), which won the Gold Cup at Cowdray Park in 1995, beating a Swiss banker's outfit, the Black Bears, was more than a sports event. It was the triumph of money over birth, and bloody-minded determination over circumstance, when you consider that six years previously Packer suffered a massive heart attack playing polo in Sydney.

According to legend, he lay without a heartbeat for 15 minutes and it was only the extraordinary coincidence of an ambulance passing the very gates at the time that allowed him to be revived at all. Now, conspicuous by their presence, two ambulances always wait alongside the polo field when he plays. One from the local hospital and one of Packer's own.

The Australian is no Jack Walker, content to pour millions into a sport while watching from the sidelines. He is there. On a horse. Charging from one end of the field to another, wielding a mallet in piratical fashion in his fist, on a pony that seems – to the naked eye – to sag rather more in the middle than the others pelting around. Mr Packer is 6ft 6in, weighs not far off 18 stone and was 59 in the summer of '96.

'I've got great admiration for the man,' said Terry Hanlon, the Des Lynam of polo commentary. 'It takes a lot of guts to get on a horse when you have a heart condition. But Kerry doesn't mess about. It's no secret he's had a by-pass operation, but when you're riding an eight-year-old horse, you've got eight-year-old legs.' And four of them, as well.

The earnest consideration of a good set of fetlocks is fundamental to the sport. Hence the importance of women. Jilly Cooper and others have made it abundantly clear that the feminine role is to stand on the sidelines in electric sexual thrall to some chap on a horse proudly bearing the name Carlos Gracias Nugent, or something of that ilk. Possibly some women do conform to this masculine idyll, but none of the ones I've ever met.

'In the beginning I just used to ride polo ponies, but I got rather bored,' said Lila Pearson, the Danish-born wife of Charles Pearson, son of the late third Viscount Cowdray of Cowdray Park, who helped introduce his spouse to polo and then rather wished he hadn't. He went to Russia once and by the time he came back Lila was playing chukkas. 'Charles wasn't very keen. He thinks girls bring polo into disrepute. There's a lot more women members now and he says it's all my fault. You can't keep them out.'

Clearly the decorous handmaiden bit, the Princess Di function of merely presenting the trophies (to her husband, Prince Charles, and to her lover, Captain Hewitt) has flown out of the stately home window. The aristocratic woman these days needs more than smelling salts to produce an acceptable rush of adrenalin, and polo is a better alternative than most. Indeed, Colonel Alec Harper, who served in India between the Wars, remembers being knocked off his horse three times by a woman.

'It's very exciting,' said Lila. 'I think it's a bit like motor racing – that's my other passion, cars – it's very fast. When you hit the ball cleanly and it really goes a long way, you get such a sense of satisfaction. It's that combination of playing a game and having a horse there at the same time. The control and rapport can be really wonderful.

'I do like aggression and I'm very competitive when I'm out there, although I never lose complete touch with the hilarity of it all. Some people take it terribly seriously. I do think women riders should take it seriously too but, at the end of the day, we've got so much to think about. It can be difficult to concentrate 100 per cent when you've got two children at home. It can be difficult trying to juggle.'

Carinthia, her daughter, was just one year old and little George unthought-of, when she played her first polo match in 1994, part of the Cowdray team to play Stowell Park at Cirencester. Such was her proficiency that her handicap was swiftly reduced from minus two to minus one and in 1995 she was preparing for her first full season with her own team, the *Jersey Lillies* when she discovered she was pregnant again.

'That finished everything. I'd got it all worked out. I was planning to get pregnant at the end of the season, sometime around July, but it happened in January instead. I thought at first, if I just ignore it, it will go away. Then I felt really guilty about having that thought at all.'

So husband Charles was granted a reprieve, but it was only a short-lived one. The mother of his two children forewent the 1995 season only to reactivate herself in 1996.

'I think probably Charles worries about me getting hurt and I must admit it's not a very feminine sport. You end up covered in bruises. I've broken my finger when a ball has hit me. I had a huge and very peculiar swelling on my elbow. I've had mammoth bruises where I've been hit. And I've nearly fallen off after a crash with another horse. Once I ended up, just for a split second, embracing my horse's neck.

'Charles has a typically English attitude to this. He thinks there's a place for women and a place for men, and the place for women is not on the polo field. On the other hand, I have to say he's very supportive now. Now that he's seen I'm not absolutely useless and I'm not going to make a complete fool of myself, he's been wonderfully supportive. His father was the same, which is amazing when you think that he was the man that recreated polo in this country, he was the father of English polo.'

With stupendous aptness, the alliance between Lila and Charles Pearson began on an English polo field. She – 'mad keen on horses' – attended her first polo match during a holiday from Denmark 'to watch the horses rather than the players. Charles and I were really just friends at first and I never would have thought I'd end up marrying him. He's very, very shy and for a long time I felt I didn't really know him. And it certainly wasn't the polo that attracted me. If anything, he's really much keener on flying his helicopters and his shooting. His helicopter and his grouse are his passions.'

When Charles overcame his reserve, the couple lived together for five years – 'that caused a bit of a stir,' said Lila – and then married in Chelsea Registry Office in 1992. Following his father's death in 1995, Charles inherited the 60,000-acre Dunecht Estate in Grampian, and his father's mantle as the guardian of polo. But so great are the financial demands of the sport, even he had to consider downgrading the Cowdray Park high-goal team for an enterprise of less staggeringly costly proportions. It must be quite a help, in that case, to have your wife riding for free when a ten-goal (the highest handicap) player like Carlos Gracida can command around £250,000 a season.

The other advantage for Cowdray is that women are liable to be less dangerously combustible on the field. 'Very, very rarely have I ever been pushed into making a comment during play because I'm quite aware that people shouting and swearing is not pleasant for the spectators. But you do get the odd moment. Sometimes Charles shouts at me and I shout back *but I don't swear.*'

The odd word out of place is nevertheless a feature of the game. 'Like polo ponies, the players can be of any size and are frequently well-bred,' noted the writer Rintoul Booth. 'Though you would not have guessed from the shocking language they use.'

The heat of the moment can be a tyrannical thing, overriding nobility of birth, breeding and mien in one mallet-swinging cavalry charge. Patricia Hipwood surrendered her job as fashion editor at *Harpers and Queens* and moved herself, her children, her nanny and her dog back to Britain shortly after emigrating to California, to marry the British polo player (and former Bristol Rovers football trialist) Julian Hipwood.

Interestingly, she guards polo's honour and denies any sexist leaning in the sport. 'No, no, I don't think I'm sidelined as a player's wife. But then perhaps I'm forgetting 18 years ago or something. But certainly as an *older* wife I don't think so at all. I think that probably there are some wives get over-enthusiastic a bit, which nobody likes terribly but I don't think there's any anti-women feeling at all.

'Julian's just sitting here, just let me ask him . . . he just said some wives are a bit of a menace because they get too mouthy, which is basically what I just said. Some wives do get a bit over-enthusiastic. But, I must say, if Julian has a fall I don't go racing on to the ground with my arms in the air, shrieking. But maybe one or two do.'

Speaking of which, Ruby Wax came to a match once. 'It was very, very sad,' said Brigadier Arthur Douglas-Nugent, the Cowdray Park polo manager. 'She came along and had a splendid day but all she wanted to talk about was how much money we had.'

Such vulgarity, and such a waste of precious time. For as the Brigadier kindly explained: 'Madam, you give up polo *only* when the money runs out.'

OCEAN RACING

A coarse sailor is one who in a crisis forgets nautical language and shouts, 'For God's sake turn left!'
Michael Green, writer

It might just be the most extraordinary football match ever played, even bearing in mind the existence of Partick Thistle. The pitch was the heaving deck of an ocean-racing yacht under full sail on the way to Cape Horn, the players were wearing about eight layers of thermal underwear and the penguins hadn't paid to watch. What's more, someone tampered with the ball which wasn't FIFA-issue either. In actual fact it was a blow-up globe.

'I used to sit in the toilet – it was the only place you could get any peace and quiet – and mark our latest position on it with a black pen,' said Tracy Edwards, the skipper of *Maiden*, the yacht that carried an all-women crew to a historic and celebrated completion of the Whitbread Round The World Yacht Race in 1990. 'Then we'd kick it around on deck. It was great because the ball was the only way we had of visualising how far we had actually gone.'

Maybe that wasn't such a good idea. When you are down to the icebergs in the Southern Ocean, the nearest yacht is 1,000 miles behind, the air temperature outside the hatch is minus 40 and dinner is brown powder with green lumps in it (again), the last thing you want to think about is how far you have gone – or more to the point, how far there is to go.

In the event, *Maiden's* race was an eight-and-a-half-month odyssey, an extraordinary amalgam of tragedy, triumph and, eventually, treachery when the voyage was over. 'Hell is here,' wrote Edwards in her captain's log (stardate, November 1989). But she was wrong. Hell would be what happened next.

Maiden was no gimmick, no febrile feminist's plot to overturn the male-dominated docksides of ocean racing. It was a challenge, an adventure and a natural progression for a sportswoman who had left home at 16 and found herself working in a bar in Pireus, Greece, when the owner of a boat came in looking for a new stewardess.

People laughed at first. 'Managing directors were rolling on the floor in mirth with tears running down their faces,' said Edwards of the reaction of the business community to her pleas for money. 'I think they had visions of a broken boat and a dozen dead women.' But Edwards, who barely swims and stands 5ft 2in in her deckshoes, was suffused with such inexplicable faith and stubborn valour that, in the end, Royal Jordanian Airlines underwrote the project. She regretted the dearth of British interest. Surely Virgin could see a valuable tie-up? 'No,' said Edwards. 'He said no. Anyway, nobody would fall for it.'

Certainly, *Maiden's* 12-woman crew that set sail from Portsmouth were as fully attached to husbands and boyfriends as any group of women have a right to be. 'I think everyone was surprised about how good-looking the girls on *Maiden* were. They were expecting some Russian, hulking shotputter types and when there weren't any, they said things like: "how fun, how pretty". I was called pint-sized and diminutive. I mean, "diminutive" – how rude!'

But a funny thing happened on the way to the Antarctic. The women became so bound together emotionally, so locked in their own mortal world that whenever the outside world intruded at stopovers, they experienced a wild and unreasoning resentment. 'It was weird. Something we'd never dreamed would happen,' said Edwards. 'Husbands and boyfriends would arrive on the boat and discover that trying to deal with 12 women who've just spent five weeks at sea together was mind-blowingly difficult. We'd fused together in such a tight little team. We used to get to the point that some innocent soul would set foot on board and we'd all be seething under our breath: "Get off our boat!" You'd been waiting all this bloody time to see them, and then when you did, you wanted them off again. It must have been really daunting for the men. In the end, they just used to peel the women off, like sheepdogs, and our team was split up for the duration of the stopover.

'In any case, stopovers are very distracting and very destructive to a team. You want to party desperately. You find yourself in a strange emotional state. You recognise that you're vulnerable. It's quite a dangerous time. You could make some silly mistake. But usually what happens is that everyone goes out and gets absolutely slaughtered and collapses. Relationships are very difficult and very stressful in races like that. You have to be the sort of person who can have a fling and leave it at that.'

And the sort of person, she might add, who is prepared to sleep in four layers of thermals, eat reconstituted lamb and peas every Monday for eight months, endure moments of blind terror when the boat goes over sideways and knows what to do in the event of: sperm whales, icebergs, hysteria, broken noses and somebody falling off. To those of us who regard scraping frost off the car windscreen as the height of an Arctic adventure, the idea of circumnavigating the globe in anything without a ballroom and a quoits deck is pure, unadulterated folly. Edwards, zealot, dynamo and a ballet dancer's daughter, was of a different stamp altogether. At the age of 27, she made *Maiden* happen.

'When it was all over, I suddenly realised I'd spent eight years of my life doing two Whitbreads. All of my twenties were gone. I needed time to recoup, get away. Then I got kicked in the back by a horse.' And that was the least of her agonies.

As part of her inauguration to Britain's hall of sporting fame, Edwards received an MBE, a swift divorce, a door-stepping newspaper and the near-mortal blow of a best friend turned traitor. 'I was dead for a while. There's no other way to describe it. I was dead.' An old school friend found her cowering behind drawn curtains in her marital home and literally dragged her back to her old home town in Wales.

'I thought I'd never speak to a stranger again as long as I lived. They hurt me so much. Oh, it was only one newspaper but it felt like the world. Six months after the race, this paper approached Nancy [Hill, *Maiden*'s sail trimmer] and said: "Tracy's earning millions. Don't you think it's a bit unfair?" They took her out to lunch, stuck a tape recorder under her nose and the green-eyed monster did the rest. We counted 46 inaccuracies in the article they wrote and 16 outright, nasty and damaging lies. I've never forgiven her really. *Maiden* was too special to have that happen.

'They said I'd made a fortune. We didn't make a penny. We owed money. I'd sold my house in 1988 to pay for *Maiden* in the first place. The crew got £8,000 tax-free each after the race. I didn't get it. I had to sell the boat to give it to them. That's what annoys me most about the whole frigging thing. The lies.'

By the time the creative writing class had finished, the captain had been re-characterised as 'Little Adolf' and the crew were being recast as a bunch of spiteful and mutinous rivals whose various black eyes at each port of call were now being re-examined in a different, more sinister, light.

'But it wasn't like that,' said Edwards. '*Maiden* was the only crew, apart from one, that didn't change all the way round. Of the 23 boats,

21 sacked people, changed people, put people on and off. At the end of the race we all lived together on shore for a month, almost as if we couldn't bear to be parted. Various husbands and boyfriends arrived and had to drag the women off, practically kicking and screaming. They were all at my wedding. Nancy was my bloody bridesmaid, for God's sake.'

In the end, the offending tabloid retracted the article and paid substantial damages which Edwards donated to charity. She had survived, she remarried and she rejoiced when the newspaper that had come close to ruining her life went out of business. 'There is a God,' she said exultantly.

Then she met Will Carling, the relatively unknown captain (pre-Di) of the England rugby team. 'We met at a reception at 10 Downing Street before he was famous. We found ourselves standing in the corner of the room with the swimmer Adrian Moorhouse. We were the least famous people in the room.' Gazza was the hero at the time, kissing Mrs Thatcher for the benefit of the cameras.

A few weeks later she was offered a role in Carling's company that lectures businesses on the value of team spirit and motivation. And, they might add, overcoming the pain of public humiliation.

'Will's very hurt by all the things that have happened,' Edwards said in oblique reference to his liaison, however profound or otherwise, with the Princess of Wales. 'He knows he's made mistakes but he's willing to face up to them. He's very dignified. I think he's misjudged by an awful lot of people. They think he's arrogant because he has this huge amount of self-confidence. It's such a shame in Britain – if you're successful and motivated and have self-belief, you're seen as arrogant, if you're not, you're seen as a failure.'

The backgrounds of Carling and Edwards could not be more disparate. He, the product of a close family and a public school; she, a schoolgirl smoker behind the bike sheds whose father died when she was ten. Her mother has multiple sclerosis and her stepfather . . . 'Well, we don't talk about my stepfather. That's why I left home when I was 16.'

Eventually, she was coaxed back to life by her new career and old friends and the thought occurred to her that she might like to go sailing again. Round the world perhaps. Non-stop this time. With another all-women crew in defiance of convention and the elements. She decided to take part in the Jules Verne Trophy, an open challenge to sail around the world in less than 80 days. While she was about it, she would try to break the record of 74 days and 22 hours set by Robin Knox-Johnston and Peter Blake.

But first there was Chris, her new husband, to consider. 'I thought I was going to shock him. But he wasn't at all surprised. He knew. He knows me.' They were married in Swansea on 4 November 1994; dangerously near Fireworks Night people who know her marital history well might say, but their concern is happily unnecessary. 'I feel much more comfortable with my second marriage than I did with my first. I knew what I was doing was wrong when I married Simon but neither of us could stop it. It was like a snowball running downhill.'

And so, in a catamaran bought from the New Zealand Apple and Pear Marketing Board, Edwards prepared for the second great all-women adventure of her sailing career. *Maiden* was gone but the quest of the *Lady Endeavour* was born.

'When I went sailing on her for the first time, it was absolutely wild,' she said, in the sort of tone that women normally reserve for Sean Bean. 'I'd seen her loads of times. I knew I wanted her. But when she went out ... she's so powerful. She crouches on the water. She looks like this sort of predator, waiting to go sailing. The closer you get, the bigger she becomes. She's the size of a tennis court. Her mast is 102 feet high. She's absolutely the most impressive boat I've ever seen in my life.'

Her enthusiasm is tangible. 'It's the challenge, putting yourself to the test, surviving each day, pushing back the boundaries. I'll never experience again that feeling we had in *Maiden* of coming into Australia when we'd won that leg. It was indescribable. It was the ultimate. If someone had lit a touchpaper we'd have all just gone up.' She draws a visual 'kaboom' in the air.

That moment made it all worthwhile. The cold: 'You don't think you can get that cold. It's not possible. Everything wants to shut down – your body, your brain. You get out of bed and there's a hatch open over there and it's minus 40 outside. A couple of the girls got frostbite on their cheeks.' The injuries: 'Sally [Creaser, safety officer, ironically enough] was coming out of a hatch when we broached – oh, I shouldn't laugh – and she catapulted head first into the winch. Smashed her nose and ended up with two black eyes.' The dangers: 'Claire [Russell, the doctor] fell off. Luckily, she had her harness on but I've never seen anyone look so surprised. We called her the "Flying Doctor" after that.' The terror: 'The times you experience terror are when you broach in the Southern Ocean and nobody has seen it coming. The deathroll. The boat goes over. The mast is in the water. The adrenalin rush is unbelievable. Afterwards you have this hysteria. Everyone laughs really loudly ... because you've lived through it.' The celibacy: 'We had a calendar at Christmas with nude men all over it and we had a good laugh at that. But I don't think women are affected by it in the same way as men.' Death: 'You don't want to confront the fact you might die. You push it to the back of your mind and forget about it. Seven people went over the side in that Whitbread race. One died. It was almost overwhelming. We didn't know him, but so many of us stood and looked at the water and tried to imagine what it would be like to go over the side in that place. It almost made us sick with terror.'

Put like that, the pleasures of ocean racing seem somewhat diminished by its pains. But Edwards has flown with the albatross, run with the dolphin and witnessed sunsets that ignite the night sky like an explosion. 'If I could paint you what I've seen, you would say that I lied,' she said, the ultimate reproach to the rest of us who prefer our spirit of adventure in bottles clearly marked 'brandy'.

A Question of Sport

A QUESTION OF SPORT

I believe that sex is a beautiful thing between two people. Between FIVE, it's fantastic...
                                                    Woody Allen, 1972

OK, thanks girls. I have just spent six months of my life and 70,000 words in the urgent bid to prove that women have a higher, deeper, purer appreciation of sport than man has ever acknowledged, only to discover the wilder sexual fantasies of Amanda M. Bateman of Bradford.

Required to list her all-time top ten male ball players, she began with Darrall Shelford, rugby league. 'Bronzed Kiwi god,' she explained. 'When he scores a try he floats over the line. I want to see him do the Hakka naked.'

And so high-mindedness died.

Nevertheless the response to the most wide-ranging survey ever of female attitudes to male ball players (well, the only one actually) produced a result that might surprise those who suspect our interest fails to rise above the elasticated waistband on Will Carling's shorts.

Our hero, by a considerable margin, proved to be a man rarely mistaken for a male model, not exactly basking in the first flush of youth and no stranger to brashness, controversy or being roundly condemned by his own long-suffering wife. Step forward I.T. Botham.

'Great entertainer. Puts bums on seats, even in the pantomime season.' (Wendy Watson, Derbyshire)

'A winner through and through. Even on *A Question of Sport* hates being beaten. A very soft side to Boff too – charity work isn't all for effect.' (Lucinda Green, six times Badminton winner and Olympic silver medalist.)

'The greatest all-rounder in the world. Turns a game around with either bat or ball.' (Jo Jordan, but not the Leeds and Scotland centre-forward.)

'Has a twinkle in his eye.' (The combined forces of the Women's

Sport Foundation.)

'For not conforming under pressure.' (Tracy Edwards, who would admire that sort of thing.)

'Rebel, non-conformist, lets his ability do his talking. Doesn't give a toss. Just wants to win. 100 per cent to everything.' (Clare Taylor, ditto.)

And so the tributes continued. His passion, his talent, his commitment, his charity work were admired. 'A match-winner.' 'A crowd pleaser.' No-one mentioned sex (unless the latter remark was more sweepingly intended). This was a triumph for womankind, I foolishly imagined. Then it got worse.

'Jamie Redknapp, football,' nominated the irrepressible Ms Bateman. 'Tidy bloke. The things he does with a ball make you want to run up and down your stairs twice.'

'Vinnie Jones, football,' volunteered Kerry Ledwidge of Huddersfield. 'Thug with sensitivity. The thinking woman's "bit of rough".'

'Robin Smith, cricket,' Jo Jordan again. 'Brilliant player of fast bowling (not so good with spin). Gorgeous man. Real fighter. Gave me a kiss!'

'Bishen Bedi, cricket,' suggested Jackie Carlile of the Wakefield Women's Cricket Club. 'Fine collection of turbans.'

'John Kirwan, rugby union,' said Alison Burrell from New Zealand with a passionate regard for her compatriot. 'Excellent player. Loyal to the game. Not to mention the fact he was my Dad's butcher's son.'

'Colin Montgomerie, golf,' was Fiona Grant's number five. 'My dad called him a miserable toad, so I paid attention and found him amusing to watch, the old sour puss.'

'Allan Clarke, football,' Isobel Williams, Radio Five Live. 'The man with more style than Yves St Laurent. Fallen from grace a bit but still a legend. Held his sleeves. Skinny.'

'Paul Mariner, football,' Tracy Moore of Stratton, Dorset. 'When I was eight years old, he was playing for Ipswich and I was under the impression he was also "Woody" from the Bay City Rollers, so I thought he was the best.'

'David Platt, football', Janet Tedstone of Bradford's contribution. 'Unbelievable forehead.'

In the circumstances, it may be best that we cut short that particular line of enquiry and go straight to the results.
1. Ian Botham.
2. Will Carling

3. Eric Cantona
4. Gary Lineker
5. George Best
6. Nick Faldo
7. Glen Hoddle
8. Rob Andrew
9. Steve Davis
10. John McEnroe
    Kevin Keegan
    Jimmy White
    Andre Agassi
    Jamie Redknapp

I'm saying nothing, except to express incredulity that intelligent women can ignore the obvious merits of Charlie George, one of the greatest players never to have scored for England. For the record, he sits majestically at the prow of my own top ten, thereby demonstrating that some women are hopelessly led by pure sentimentality, emotion and bias (not unlike every male Scottish football fan I have ever met):

1. Charlie George: the scorer of Arsenal's double-winning goal. Possessor of a striking perm, two-footed brilliance and a surprisingly fine heading ability (notwithstanding the curls). A whippet-lean wizard with anachronistically thunderous thighs. I could go on . . .
2. George Best: icon. ('A legend in his own stupor,' said Kerry Ledwidge, placing him at No. 9 on her list.)
3. Jimmy White: wheyfaced and wayward. ('The sort of person you want to mother,' said Lesley Taylor, naming him as her No. 10.)
4. Bunny Austin: a gentleman and a player from a bygone tennis era whose fierce honesty and gentle humour has never dimmed.
5. Alan Knott: wicket-keeper and aerobics performer ahead of his time.
6. John McEnroe: divinely talented paranoid.
7. Ruud Gullit: style.
8. Liam Brady: guile.
9. Brian Moore: bile.
10. Sean Bean: does anyone need an excuse?

Do not, however, be misled by the odd hint of Arsenal mania discernible here. There are many knowledgeable women at work in the field of sport whose choices are as informed, clear-eyed and unbiased as those of any male pundit. Perhaps more so. Women, after all, don't loathe David Ginola on principle.

The Top Ten Male Ball Players by Frances Edmonds:
1. Bobby Charlton: an all-time great, not only for his wonderful pile-drivers but because he transcended football to become an inter-national sporting ambassador.
2. George Best: Oh Georgie, where did it all go wrong?
3. Denis Law: 'The king' of Old Trafford in the Busby era. (OK, so I'm a Man Utd fan.)
4. Imran Khan: great all-round cricketer who realises that there *is* a life after cricket. (How many sad acts don't?!)
5. Dennis Lillee: don't tell anyone that Australia's most ferocious fast bowler used to carry my daughter's bundles of Pampers from Sainsbury's for me!
6. Clive Lloyd: the greatest West Indian captain and one of their finest batsmen. An admirable role model and inspirational man.
7. John McEnroe: for heaven's sake, at least he was never *boring*.
8. Fred Perry: can you imagine if this country had a three times Wimbledon champion nowadays? The man would be a billionaire and venerated, not shunned (as Fred was) by the LTA.
9. Magic Johnson: because he truly is.
10. Barry John: his qualities in rugby were like those of George Best in football – instinctive, untutored, transcendent. A genius.

Lucinda Green's Top Ten:
1. Rory Underwood, rugby union, winger: a pilot who flies high in all ways. Most capped winger.
2. Eric Cantona, football: Hot-blooded Frenchman who has real bite and class – and kick to the jaw line.
3. Andre Agassi, tennis: Seriously individual character. Wild side to his super-concentrated game. Bit small to be as sexy as some feel.
4. Ilie Nastase, tennis: Huge humour. Never forget him diving under the side-line tarpaulin at Wimbledon when disagreeing with a line call. Hot-blooded, charismatic, seriously attractive.
5. Ian Botham: See above.
6. Bill Beaumont, rugby union: Nature's gentleman. A gentle, kind, unbrazen guy. Antithesis, in outward personality, of Botham. Very sharp and funny but never unkindly so.
7. John McEnroe, tennis: Everyboy loved to hate him as he played the spoilt brat and exceptional tennis. Not pretty in my eyes.
8. Jonathan Davies, rugby union: So funny, so quick and so tiny. I always thought rugby players were huge.
9. Johnny Kidd, polo: Immaculate conception to look at. Tall, elegant, real Golden Boy. Showjumped internationally too, but still led a jet-set life.
10. Emlyn Hughes, football: Still fit, gorgeous, friendly and so funny even though he is long since retired. His transition into the world of business without losing his love of sport and life is a great inspiration.

Rachel Heyhoe Flint's Top Ten:
1. Seve Ballesteros, golf: Silky swing, stalking walk, saw him privately burst into tears after losing in Ryder Cup match at the Belfry, 1989.
2. Gary Sobers, cricket: Greatest all-rounder, three types of bowler in one body. Electric batting. Tiger in the field.
3. Brian Lara, cricket: Amazing eye for ball. Power play when in full flight.
4. Viv Richards, cricket: Sheer arrogance while batting. Scorned orthodoxy in order to crash ball all over field.
5. Ernie Els, golf: Cool, casual and a swing that tells you never to hurry your own.
6. Brian Laudrup, football: A ferret on wheels, sniffs out any goalscoring opportunity when others would have failed.
7. Peter Schmeichel, football: Giant of all goalkeepers. Would never pick a fight with him. Electric reactions.
8. Sachin Tendulkar, cricket: Great wristy magician. Sees ball so early. Fabulous placement of shots.
9. Michael Holding, cricket: I swear his approach to the wicket was on wheels. Elastic delivery. Violently venomous.
10. Bruce Grobbelaar, football: I had to 'bung' him in for his sheer eccentricity. A character who mocked the seriousness of sport.

The Top Ten, according to Tracy Edwards:
1. Ieuan Evans, Wales rugby captain: For being the only man who makes me care whether an egg-shaped ball is smashed on the the ground between two posts.
2. George Best: For being George Best.
3. Ian Botham: See above.
4. Gareth Edwards, rugby: A true sportsman with the nicest smile. One of the all-time greats.
5. Will Carling, rugby: For having the most watchable thighs on a rugby pitch and because I want that drink he owes me.
6. Steve Davis, snooker: For not trying to be something he's not, even under great pressure and jokes.
7. Ian Woosnam, golf: Even after earning all that money he has never forgotten who he is or where he comes from.
8. Bobby Moore, football: Will he be the only Brit to hoist that Cup?
9. John Barnes, football: for being one of the most gorgeous men to kick a ball.
10. Jonathan Davies, rugby: For coming home to Wales.

Other nominations included:
Eric Cantona: 'Nearly as good as Jimmy Johnstone. Charismatic crowd controller.'
Nick Faldo: 'Cool, confident – Fanny always on hand to help. Collecting ex-wives.'

Gordon Banks: 'Came over as a kind person.'
Henri Leconte: 'Service with a smile.'
John Jeffries: 'Distinctive hair, always able to see him on the pitch.'
Daley Thompson: 'Nominated for his little known amazing football ability, that he is a god, has a hamburger-head hairdo, a dodgy moustache and still sends a little shiver down my spine.'
Jimmy White: 'Admire his battle against hair loss.'
Paul Ince: 'Nice eyes.'
Rory Underwood: 'Got a nice mum.'
Tony Underwood: 'See above.'
Kenny Dalglish: 'Integrity, talent, modesty and incomprehensibility in one package.'

And finally . . .
Vijay Amritraj: 'I don't think he's the one I mean but there was one sexy Pakistani player in the 1960s.'

Well, not quite finally. Long after the deadline for a response to the questionnaire was past I received the following missive from the Wild Woman of Borneo herself, otherwise Gail Gyi of the West's Women's Rugby Club.

'Hi Sue,' she wrote. 'Yes, I'm still alive and kicking.' And she enclosed her deeply-considered Top Ten.
1. Kenny Logan, rugby: Young, fast, gorgeous.
2. Ally McCoist, football: Youngish, fast, gorgeous.
3. Eric Cantona, football: Young, fast gorgeous.
4. Ryan Giggs, football: Young, fast, gorgeous.
5. Jamie Redknapp, football: Young, fast gorgeous.
6. Sam Torrance, golf: A man for all seasons who has had incredible highs and lows.
7. Tim Rodber, rugby: The next captain of the Five Nations Champions, 1996–97, England.
8. Gavin Hastings, rugby: An example of Scottish manhood beyond compare. An inspiration.
9. Ellery Hanley, rugby league: Inspirational character. Paved the way for rugby league's superstars in the 1990s.
10. Geoffrey Boycott, cricket: Stubborn, persistent, blunt, ex-England cricketer. Above all a true Yorkshireman who never says die.

There was a postscript. 'Derek is now my ex, so I doubt you'll get any info from him. He says he needs space. Yeah – outer space. Ha ha. Love, Gail.'

SELECT BIBLIOGRAPHY

Another Bloody Tour, Frances Edmonds, Kingswood Press, 1986
Belles of the Ball, David J. Williamson, R & D Associates, Devon, 1991
The Courts of Babylon, Peter Bodo, Simon and Schuster Inc., 1995
Cricket and Rugby for Mums, A. Sue Porter, Souvenir Press, 1995
Hard Courts, John Feinstein, Villard Books, 1991
In a League of their Own, Gail J. Newsham, Pride of Place Publishing, 1994
Ladies of the Court, Michael Mewshaw, Little, Brown and Company, 1993
Laws of Association Football, The FA, Pan Books, 1995
A Mixed Double, Bunny Austin and Phyllis Konstam, Chatto and Windus, 1969
More Cricket Extras, David Rayvern Allen, Guinness Publishing, 1992
Running for Clocks and Dessert Spoons, Ian Clayton, Yorkshire Art Circus, 1988
The Unplayable Lie, Marcia Chambers, NYT Special Services Inc., 1995
Will Carling, the Authorized Biography, David Norrie, Headline, 1993

INDEX OF NAMES

Accrington Stanley FC, 125
Ackford, Paul, 65, 69, 86, 87–8
Ackford, Suzie, 65–6, 86–8
Adams, Katrina, 172
Agassi, Andre, 164, 171, 186, 215, 216
Alfredsson, Helen, 153, 158–9
Allen, Jan, 121
Allen, Rita, 147
Allen, Woody, 213
American football, 156
Amiss, Dennis, 121, 128
Amritraj, Vijay, 218
Anderson, Brady, 187
Andrew, Rob, 215
Andrew, Sara, 86
Anne, the Princess Royal, 63, 76
Anne, Queen, 22
Arlott, John, 123
Arsenal FC, 15, 32, 35–7, 38–40, 44, 45, 152, 153–4
Arsenal Ladies football team, 49
Ashby, Bob, 94
Ashe, Arthur, 163, 179
Atherton, Michael, 100, 120, 124
Atkinson, Dalian, 54
Atkinson, Ron, 54
Austin, Bunny, 186, 215

Ballesteros, Seve, 136, 137, 139, 217
Baltimore Orioles baseball team, 187
Bampton, Debbie, 53
Banks, Gordon, 218
Barbados, Miss, 110, 116
Barnes, John, 15, 17, 218
Barnes, Suzy, 15–19
Barnett, Geoff, 38
Barnett, Marilyn, 180
Barrett, Rona, 180
Bartels, Michael, 165
baseball, 156
basketball, 156
Bateman, Amanda M., 213, 214

Bates, Ken 43–4
Bates, Pam, 44
Bean, Joe, 159
Bean, Sean, 58–9, 215
Beaumont, Bill, 217
Becker, Boris, 164, 167, 186
Bedi, Bishen, 123, 214
Bedser, Alec, 113, 129
Bergara, Danny, 46
Bergkamp, Dennis, 154
Bernard, Jeffrey, 54
Best, George, 215, 216, 219
Biddle, Frances, 103–4
Bidwell, Marie, 99, 103
Bierley, Stephen, 167
Bird, Dickie, 100–2, 104
Birtles, Gary, 27
Black, Cilla, 83
Black Bears polo team, 200
Blair, Olivia, 44–7
Blake, Peter, 207
Boca Juniors, 24
Bollettieri, Nick, 177
Bolton, Michael, 187
Bonallack, Michael, 143
Boniek, Zbigniew, 9, 41–2
Booth, Rintoul, 203
Borg, Bjorn, 177, 179
Botham, Becky, 115
Botham, Ian, 109, 110, 113, 114–18, 123–4, 127, 213, 215, 217, 218
Botham, Kathy, 10, 113, 114–18
Botham, Liam, 115, 117
Botham, Sarah, 115.
Bould, Stevie, 154
Boycott, Geoffrey, 121, 219
Bradford Bulls women's rugby league team, 91
Bradford Northern rugby league team, 92, 93–4
Brady, Liam, 44, 154, 215
Brear, Mrs Alice, 91, 96
Brearley, Mike, 99
Bremner, Billy, 31, 32
British Lions rugby team, 72
Broadhurst, Joanna, 50

Brontë, Charlotte, 8
Brown, Helen Gurley, 140
Brown, Rita Mae, 180
Bueno, Maria, 167
Burgin, Elise, 187
'Burkey' 16, 17, 18
Burnell, Teresa, 197
Burnet, Alasdair, 78
Burnet, Heather, 80
Burning Tree golf club, 140–1
Burrell, Alison, 214
Busby Babes, 26
Busby, Ian 'Buzz', 78
Busby, Sir Matt, 25, 26,27,
Bush, George, 142
Byrne, Patrick, 104

Calcavecchia, Mark, 133
Calcavecchia, Sheryl, 133
Caldwell, Rex, 151
Candy, Don, 170
Cantona, Eric, 17, 21, 215, 216, 217, 218
Capriati, Jennifer, 175, 181
Carillo, Mary, 169, 178
Carlile, Jackie, 214
Carling, Bill, 77
Carling, Julia, 74, 76, 86
Carling, Will, 71, 74–5, 75–7, 86–7, 207, 215, 218
Carroll, John, 198
Casey, Constance, 140
Cash, Pat, 169
Cedarbrook golf club, 141
Cepelak, Brenna, 134
Chambers, Marcia, 140
Chappell, Greg, 124
Chappell, Ian, 115
Charles, Prince of Wales, 75, 77
Charlton, Bobby, 48, 216
Clarke, Allan, 32, 214
Clarke, Nigel, 167
Clough, Brian, 25, 26, 27, 30
Coates, Ralph, 28
Connors, Gloria, 178–9
Connors, Jim, 178–9

INDEX ☆ 221

Connors, Jimmy, 148, 163, 178–9, 181, 186
Cooper, Andy, 78, 79
Cooper, Gary, 94
Cooper, Jilly, 200
Corr, Karen, 196, 198
Cotton, Henry, 145
Court, Margaret, 168, 182
Cowdray, Colin, 121
Creaser, Sally, 208
cricket, 99–132
Croydon football team 15, 18
Cuellar, Leo, 153, 158
Czechoslovakia football team, 27

Dalglish, Kenny, 219
Dandy, Charles, 197
Darnley, Lord, 140
Date, Kimiko, 165
Davenport, Lindsay, 169–70
Davies, Jonathan, 217, 218
Davies, Laura, 10, 139–40, 145–9
Davis, Steve, 193, 196, 215, 218
de Swardt, Mariaan, 169–70
Decker, Daphne, 189
Deford, Frank, 178
Derby County FC, 27, 39, 40
Dermott, Lisa, 159–60
Diana, Princess of Wales, 74–5, 75–7, 86, 207
Dick Kerr Ladies football team, 23, 48–9, 53
Diller, Phyllis, 169
DiMaggio, Joe, 74
Dixon, 154
Doncaster Belles football team, 10, 15, 50
Douglas-Nugent, Brigadier Arthur, 203
Doyle, Ian, 194–5, 198
Driver, Clem, 125
Dubai football club, 33–4
Duncan, Jenny, 33
Duncan, Johnny, 33
Duncan, Tommy, 33
Dunlop, Roddy, 67
Dwyer, Suzannah, 43–4

East, Ray, 129
East Midlands women's football league, 29
Edberg, Stefan, 158, 164, 189
Edinburgh, Duke of, 105, 14
Edinburgh Wanderers rugby club, 71
Edmonds, Frances, 28, 110–11, 112–13, 123, 130, 216

Edmonds, Phil, 111, 129
Edward II, King, 22
Edward, Prince, 76
Edwards, Gareth, 218
Edwards, Tracy, 204–9, 214, 218
Elizabeth II, Queen, 77
Ellerston White polo team, 200
Ellis, Vicky 'Sicky', 78
Els, Ernie, 217
Emburey, John 113, 130
Emburey, Susie, 113, 116, 129
England men's cricket team, 75, 109, 112, 113
England men's football team, 25, 27, 43, 75
England men's rugby team, 66–7
England women's cricket team, 25, 50, 119, 120–21
England women's football team, 25, 50, 51, 52–3
Espeseth, Gro, 52
Evans, Ieuan, 218
Evans, Mike, 40
Evert, Chris, 148, 179, 181, 183, 186
Everton FC, 39

FA (Football Association), 22–3, 49, 52, 55
FIFA, 52
Fairclough, Sir John, 40
Faith, Adam, 148, 181
Faldo, Gill, 134, 136, 137, 150–1
Faldo, Nick, 134, 135, 137, 145, 148, 150–1, 215, 218
Featherstone Rovers rugby league team, 92, 93, 94
Featherstone Ladies rugby league team, 91, 96
Feltus, Barbara, 186
Fergon, Vicki, 157
Ferguson, Alex, 25, 26, 27, 29, 30
Ferguson, Darren, 27
Fernandez, Gigi, 168
Fernandez, Mary Joe, 166
'Fez',16, 18
Fisher, Alison, 198
Fisher, Mandy, 197–8
Fisher, Matthew, 197–8
Flint, Rachel Heyhoe, 10, 103, 119–21, 128–9, 217
football, 15–98
Ford, Gerald, 140
Forman, Roland, 141
Fragnière, François, 187

Gallacher, Bernard, 133, 134, 135, 136
Gallacher, Lesley, 133–4, 136, 137–8
Garrison, Zina, 171, 183
Gascoigne, Paul, 56, 74, 207
Gatting, Mike, 109, 123
Gatting, Mrs, 112
George, Bob, 39
George, Charlie, 24, 28, 35–40, 154, 215
George, Susan (née Farge), 35
George, Susan (actress), 187
Germany women's football team, 52
Giggs, Ryan, 218
Gilford, David, 135
Ginola, David, 50, 56, 215
Glanville, Brian, 48
golf, 133–62
Gooch, Graham, 100, 129
Gower, David, 104
Grace, W.G., 129
Gracida, Carlos, 202
Graf, Peter, 176
Graf, Steffi, 10, 148, 164–5, 166, 168, 169, 173, 176, 187
Grant, Fiona, 214
Gray, Eddie, 31, 32
Grayson, Paul, 66
Green, Lucinda, 213, 216–7
Green, Michael, 204
Grobbelaar, Bruce, 217
Gullit, Ruud, 48, 215
Gyi, Gail, 81, 82–4, 219

Hackett, Buddy, 159
Hagen, Walter, 152
Halford, Alison, 56
Hampshire cricket club, 117
Handley, Jodie, 18
Hanley, Ellery, 219
Hanlon, Terry, 200
Hanna, Herbert, 103
Harper, Colonel Alec, 201
Harvey, Graham, 189
Harvey, Jane (née Tabor), 168, 189
Hastings, Gavin, 219
Haynie, Sandra, 180
Hayward, Jack, 128
Hayward, Paul, 170
Hearn, Barry, 197
Hearts FC, 66
Heath, Edward, 135
Henderson, John, 166
Hendry, Stephen, 193, 194, 195–6, 198
Henman, Tim, 164, 179
Hetherington, Gary, 94–5

Hetherington, Kathryn, 94
Hewitt, Major, 75
Heycock, Michael, 102–3
Hibernian FC, 66
Higgins, Alex, 193
Hill, Karen, 86
Hill, Nancy, 206
Hingis, Martina, 176, 187
Hipwood, Julian, 203
Hipwood, Patricia, 203
Hoddle, Glenn, 215
Hogarth, Frank, 78
Holding, Michael, 217
Holloway county cricket club, 37
Holloway county football club, 37
Hong Kong football club, 25, 39
Hughes, Emlyn, 217
Hunter, Norman, 31
Hurst, Geoff, 57
Hurst, Judith, 57
Hutton, Sir Leonard (Len), 119, 121

ice hockey, 156
Illingworth, Ray, 109, 112
Illingworth, Shirley, 109
Imperial golf club, Hythe, 144
Ince, Paul, 218
Indianwood Golf and Country Club, 159
Ivanisevic, Goran, 174

Jacklin, Tony, 134, 143, 145
Jackson, John, 167
James, Jane, 136
Japanese women's football league, 53
Jeffries, John, 218
Jensen, Murphy, 166
Jephson, D.L.A., 99
Jersey Lillies women's polo team, 201
Johansson, Per-Ulrik, 136
John, Barry, 216
John, Elton, 182
Johnson, 'Magic', 181, 216
Johnson, Melissa, 163, 189
Johnson, Trish, 152–5
Johnston, Brian, 123, 128
Jones, Kenny, 200
Jones, Vinny, 214
Jordan, Jo, 213, 214
Juventus, 41

Kahn, Liz, 141, 142–4
Keane, Moss, 72
Keegan, Kevin, 46, 215

Kell, Alice, 23
Kelly, Graham, 16, 55
Kennedy, Jack, 148, 181
Kennedy, Ray, 38
Kent, Duchess of, 17, 163
Kent, Duke of, 142, 163
Khan, Imran, 216
Kidd, Johnny, 217
King, Andy, 56
King, Billie Jean, 180, 182–3
Kirwan, John, 214
Knott, Alan, 215
Knowles, Tony, 194
Knowsley (later Liverpool) women's football team, 15
Knox-Johnston, Robin, 207
Konstam, Phyllis, 186
Kournikova, Anna, 176–7
Kournikova, Olga, 177
Krajicek, Richard, 163, 164, 168, 169, 172, 188–9

LPGA (Ladies Professional Golf Associatio), 145, 156
Lamb, Allan, 109, 112, 123
Lamb, Lindsay, 'Mrs Lamby', 109, 111–12
Lara, Brian, 217
Lardner, Rex, 159
Latin, Penny, 81, 82
Laudrup, Brian, 217
Law, Denis, 216
Lawrence, Amy, 44–7
Lear, Megan, 121
Leconte, Henri, 218
Ledwidge, Kerry, 214, 215
Leeds United FC, 27, 31–3
Leicester City FC, 33
Lendl, Ivan, 165
Leonard, Jason, 66
Le Tissier, Matt, 56
Lever, John, 129
Lieberman, Nancy, 180
Lillee, Dennis, 124, 216
Limerick Bohemians rugby team, 72–3
Lineker, Gary, 22, 75, 215
Linighan, Andy, 45
Little, Tommy, 78, 79, 80
Littlejohn, Kim, 67
Liverpool Ladies football team (previously Knowsley) 15, 16–17, 49–50, 52
Liverpool FC, 15, 16–17, 36
Lloyd, Clive, 216
Lloyd, John, 148, 169
Logan, Kenny, 219
Lomu, Jonah, 70–1, 82, 88
London Broncos women's rugby league team, 91

Longhurst, Henry, 150
Lopez, Nancy, 147–8, 157, 158
Lord's, 99, 102, 104, 119, 127–30
Love, David, 133
Lowe, Mandy 'Flo', 50
Lowell, Lee, 141
Lumsden, Jan, 120
Lynch, Dick, 25
Lynch, Sean, 70

MCC (Marylebone Cricket Club), 99–100, 102–3, 106, 127–30
McBride, Willie John, 72
McCoist, Ally, 219
McEnroe, John, 167, 179, 186, 190, 215, 216, 217
McGee, Bert, 55
Mackenzie, Keith, 142, 143
MacLean, Evelyn, 63, 66
McLeod, Shiona, 81
McNab, Bob 'Nabbers', 38
MacPherson, Elle, 148
Maktoum brothers, 34
Maleeva, Manuela, 187
Manchester City FC, 36
Manchester United FC, 17, 25, 27, 29
Mansfield men's football club, 56
Maradona, Diego, 24
Marchese, Cino, 176–7
'Maria', 18
Mariner, Paul, 214
Martin, Steve, 148
Mary, Queen of Scots, 140
Mason, Tony, 104
Mayotte, Tim, 182
Mee, Bertie, 40
Merson, Paul, 155
Mewshaw, Michael, 181
Mill, Andy, 148, 190
Miller, Johnny, 159
Miller, Keith, 110
Millichip, Lady, 16
Millichip, Sir Bert, 16
Mills, Yvonne, 103
Millwall Lionesses football team, 49
Monroe, Marilyn, 74
Montgomerie, Colin, 133, 135, 136, 145, 159, 214
Montgomerie, Eimear, 136
Moody, Helen Wills, 184
Moore, Bobby, 57, 218
Moore, Brian, 69–70, 215
Moore, Penny, 66
Moore, Tina, 57–8
Moore, Tracy, 214

INDEX ☆ 223

Moorhouse, Adrian, 207
Muir, Frank, 186
Muller, Gary, 186
Muster, Thomas, 188

Namath, Joe, 70
Nastase, Ilie, 216–7
Navratilova, Martina, 165, 168, 171, 180, 181, 183–5
Nelson, Judy, 180
Nelson, Sammy, 38
New York Jets, 70
New York Yankees, 74
Newberry, Janet, 183
Nicholson, Bill, 21–2
Nicholson, Grace, 21–2
Nicklaus, Barbara, 135
Nicklaus, Jack, 135, 142, 159
Nideffer, Ros (née Fairbank), 168, 187
Nigeria women's football team, 52
Nixon, Richard, 140
Norden, Denis, 186
North Middlesex golf club, 139
Northwood golf club, 141
Norway women's football team, 52
Nottingham Forest Ladies football team, 29
Nottingham Forest FC, 25, 26, 27, 28, 29, 39, 44

O'Neal, Tatum, 186
O'Sullivan, Ronnie, 194
ocean racing, 204–212
Olazabal, José Maria, 134, 147
Oldroyd, Eleanor, 103
Olsen, Egil 'Drillo', 52
Orwell, George, 78
Otteshaw Social Club, 197
Oxley, David, 95

PGA (Professional Golf Association), American, 137
Packer, Kerry, 199–200
Palmer, Arnold, 142
Parker, Reg, 95
Parkinson, Michael, 145
Parr, Lily, 48, 53
Pavin, Corey, 137
Pearce, Liz, 28
Pearson, Carinthia, 201
Pearson, Charles, 201, 202
Pearson, Lila, 201–2
Pele, 32
Pepper, Dottie (née Mochrie), 157, 159
Perry, Fred, 216

Pierce, Jim (aka Bobby Glenn Pearce), 175–6
Pierce, Mary, 165–6, 169, 171, 175–6, 187
Platt, David, 214
Player, Gary, 142
Poland football team, 41–2
polo, 199–203
Popplewell, Sir Oliver, 128
Portsmouth FC, 25
Potter, Barbara, 165, 188
Powell, Hope, 17
Press Golfing Society, 143–4
Price, Mike, 193
Provan, Danny, 44
Pursey, Jimmy, 28

Quayle, Dan, 140
Queen's Park Rangers FC, 44
Question of Sport, 213–219

Radford, John 'Raddy', 36, 38
Rafter, Patrick, 164
Raith Rovers FC, 33
Ramsay, Sir Alf, 57
Rangers FC, 56
Rantzen, Vicky, 119
Rea, Chris, 128, 130
Reading FC, 25, 29
Real Madrid, 32, 40
Redford, Florrie, 23
Redhill women's rugby league team, 93
Redknapp, Jamie, 214, 215, 218
Redmond, Laurie, 86, 87
Redmond, Nigel, 86
Reeve, Dermot, 124, 126
Reeve, Monica, 125–6
Revie, Don, 31–4
Revie, Duncan, 32
Revie, Elsie, 31–4
Revie, Kim, 32
Reynolds, Burt, 148, 181
Rice, Tim, 128, 129
Richard, Cliff, 168
Richards, Dean, 66
Richards, Viv, 123, 124, 217
Richmond, Fiona, 22
Riggs, Bobby, 180, 182–3
Rioch, Bruce, 40
Ritts, Commissioner of LPGA, 157
Robertson, John, 27
Robinson, Dave, 187
Robson, Bobby, 43
Robson, Bryan 26
Rodber, Tim, 219
Rosewall, Ken, 178
Rosset, Marc, 164

Roth, Lynda, 157
Royal and Ancient Golf Club of St Andrews, 142–3
Royal Liverpool golf club, 159
Royal North Devon golf club, 154
Rubin, Chanda, 173
rugby, 63–98
Rugby Football Union, 76
Rugby League Council, 94
Russell, Claire, 208
Ryde, Louie, 15
Ryder Cup, 133–7

St Helens women's football team, 23, 48
St Melud golf club, Prestatyn, 159
Sabatini, Gabriela, 170–1, 181, 187, 189
Sampras, Pete, 163
Sarazan, Gene, 142
Saudi Arabia football team, 43
Savage, Ann, 81–2
Savchenko (Mrs Neiland), Larissa, 187
Schmeichel, Peter, 217
Scott, Gene, 177
Seles, Karolj, 176
Seles, Monica, 164, 166, 170, 173, 174, 176, 181
Shankly, Bill, 27, 31
Sharp, Pamela, 58
Sheffield Eagles women's rugby league team, 91
Sheffield United FC, 58–9
Sheffield Wednesday FC, 45, 55
Sheldon, Craig, 92, 93
Sheldon, Jackie, 92–4
Sheldon, Leanne, 92, 93
Shelford, Darrall, 213
Shields, Brooke, 186
Shriver, Pam, 168, 170, 172–3, 184–5
Shula, Don, 31
Shula, Dorothy, 31
Siddall, Shirli-Ann, 166
Smales, Tommy, 93
Smethwick Working Men's Club, 197
Smith, Patty, 186
Smith, Robin, 214
Snead, Sam, 150
snooker, 193–198
Snowball, Betty, 121
Sobers, Gary, 217
Society of St Andrews Golfers, 142
Southampton FC, 39

Spencer-Devlin, Muffin, 156, 157
Stallone, Sylvester, 199
Stapleton, Frank, 44
Stein, Jock, 31
Stephenson, Jan, 158
Stephenson, June, 121
Stich, Michael, 164
Stockport County FC, 46
Stockton, Dick, 137
Stoke City FC, 38
Storey, Peter, 38–9
Stott, Bill, 139
Strange, Curtis, 137
Streisand, Barbra, 186
Studenikova, Katarina, 164
Subbuteo, 28, 44
Subertov, Kamil, 183
Sudbury, Mark, 55
Sukova, Helena, 176
Sunesson, Fanny, 150–1
Super League, 91
Sutton Green golf club, 140
Swanton, Jim, 122, 123
Sydney football team, 39

Tarrango, Jeff, 166
Tart, Mandy, 194–5
Taylor, Bob, 110
Taylor, Clare (cricketer and football player), 15–16, 17–20, 50–1, 52, 214
Taylor, Clare (tennis player), 166
Taylor, Graham, 27
Taylor, Lesley, 215
'Taz', 15, 16, 19
Tedstone, Janet, 214
Tendulkar, Sachin, 217
Thatcher, Margaret, 197
Theiner, Mariella, 188
Thomas, Vicki, 160
Thompson, Daley, 218
Thompson, Sir Harold, 33
Thompson, Raelee, 120, 121
Tinling, Teddy, 183
Tolstoy, Leo, 41
'Tommo', 16, 18
Tommy (driver of Dick Kerr Ladies team), 48–9
Torrance, Sam, 135, 145, 219

Torrance, Suzanne, 135
Tottenham Hotspur FC, 21–2, 28–9, 47
Tranmere Rovers FC, 55
Tredrea, Sharon, 120
Trevino, Lee, 151
Truman, Christine, 182, 183
Tufnel, Phil, 105
Turkel, Ann, 186

Underwood, Annie, 88–90
Underwood, James Ashley, 88, 89
Underwood, Rory, 66, 70, 88–9, 216, 218
Underwood, Tony, 88–90, 218

Valley of Peace cricket club, NZ, 130
Venables, Terry, 46
Vescey, George, 171
Vicario, Arantxa Sanchez, 165, 173, 190
Vine, David, 196
Virgo, Avril, 195

Wade, Sharon (née Dooley), 86
Waddell, Herbert, 63
Waddell, Marjorie, 63, 68
Waddington, Tony, 57
Wainwright, Rob, 66
Wainwright, Romayne, 66–7
Wakefield Women's cricket club, 214
Walesa, Lech, 42
Walker, Jack, 200
Walker, Kaz 'Whacker', 50
Wallace, Colin, 78–9, 83
Wallace, Marjorie, 186
Walters, Barbara, 180
Walton, Philip, 137
Warwick Panthers women's rugby league team, 93
Warwickshire County Cricket team, 124, 126
Washington, MaliVai, 163–4
Watson, Wendy, 213
Wax, Ruby, 203
Webb, Josh, 28
Webb, Luke, 28

Webb, Neil, 25–9
Webb, Shelley, 25–30
Weiskopf, Tom, 159
West Bromwich Albion FC, 152
West Byfleet golf club, 140
West Ham FC, 47
West Hartlepool rugby club, 117
West, Mae, 74
West of Scotland men's rugby club, 79
West of Scotland women's rugby club, 'West's', 78–83
Wheatley, Arthur, 88
Wheatley, Harold, 88
Whitaker, James, 167
White, Jimmy, 195, 196, 215, 218
White, Maureen, 195
Wiesner, Judith, 170
Wilander, Mats, 158
Williams, Isobel, 214
Williams, Mrs, 91, 96
Willis, Bob, 117, 129
Wimbledon FC, 27
Wimbush, Wendy, 121–4, 130
Wodehouse, P.G., 63
Women's Rugby Football Union, 87
Women's Sports Foundation, 213
Woosnam, Ian, 134, 136, 218
Worcester, Anne Person, 173, 180–1, 186–7, 189–90
Worcester, Tommy Zachary, 187
World Ladies Billiards and Snooker Association, 197
Wright, Ben 157
Wright, Billy, 74
Wyatt, Marjorie, 100–2
Wyatt, PC Steve, 163

York, Duchess of, 'Fergie', 188
Yorkshire women's cricket club, 50
Yorkshire women's rugby league team, 93

Zico, 42